Teaching Writing in Middle and Secondary Schools

Theory, Research, and Practice

Margot Iris Soven
La Salle University

D1512120

Allyn and Bacon
Boston • London • Toronto • Sydney • Tokyo • Singapore

To my parents, Paul and Esther Korman

Senior Series Editor: Virginia Lanigan
Series Editorial Assistant: Bridget Keane
Marketing Managers: Brad Parkins and Ellen Mann Dolberg
Production Editor: Christopher H. Rawlings
Editorial-Production Service: Omegatype Typography, Inc.
Composition and Prepress Buyer: Linda Cox
Manufacturing Buyer: Suzanne Lareau
Cover Administrator: Jenny Hart
Electronic Composition: Omegatype Typography, Inc.

Copyright © 1999 by Allyn & Bacon
A Viacom Company
160 Gould Street
Needham Heights, MA 02494

Internet: www. abacon.com

Library of Congress Cataloging-in-Publication Data

Soven, Margot.
   Teaching writing in middle and secondary schools : theory,
research, and practice / Margot Iris Soven.
      p.   cm.
   Includes bibliographical references and index.
   ISBN 0-205-18897-4 (alk. paper)
    1. English language—Composition and exercises—Study and teaching
(Middle school)   2. English language—Composition and exercises—
Study and teaching (Secondary)   3. Education, Secondary—Activity
programs. I. Title.
LB1631.S6597   1999
  808'.042'0712–dc21
                                            98-35502
                                              CIP

Printed in the United States of America
10 9 8 7 6 5 4 3 2 1   03 02 01 00 99 98

Contents

Preface

I have taught methods courses and conducted workshops on the teaching of writing for almost twenty years, and I have taught writing for more than twenty-five years. It's hard to believe. But now it is time to take stock and to share my knowledge and experience with practicing teachers and students in teacher preparation programs, who are embarking on what I consider to be a great adventure—the teaching of writing.

Unlike the readers of this book, I had no one to "package" this information for me. Perhaps I was lucky. Each time I learned something new, I felt as if I had made a great discovery. Research in composition was a relatively new field when I returned to teaching freshman composition as an adjunct instructor at Drexel University in Philadelphia in the seventies. I soon realized how little I knew about teaching writing, despite my previous high school teaching experience. One day during the fall semester when I was feeling particularly inept, I headed for the Drexel library, took down a recent copy of *College English,* and started reading about the "composition revolution." While I had been at home, raising a family, a new field was busy being born. What's more, research in composition offered hope for improving the writing skills of not only the "best and brightest," who through trial and error had always learned to write, but of all students.

My career took a new turn. I returned to graduate study and became the first student at the University of Pennsylvania to receive a Ph.D. in research in composition.

In this book I have tried to convey the exhilaration I have felt as a teacher of writing as I introduce readers to this field, to the important theory and research developed during the last twenty years, and to the methods of teaching writing supported by this research. Much of this exhilaration is a response to the development of new theories of composing and the development of writing ability. Another source of excitement is the research conducted by classroom teachers at all levels, from elementary school through college. These teachers experiment daily with new teaching methods, refusing to be satisfied with the status quo. I gain much satisfaction from my own research on writing assignments and, most recently, on the use of the portfolio as an alternative to traditional assessment techniques.

But I still rely on my writing classes for my greatest sense of accomplishment. When students, who at the beginning of the semester say they do not like to write and they are terrible writers, end the semester no longer afraid to write and more confident in their writing ability, when they see that writing is not only a form of communication but, in addition, a means of exploring their own ideas, I am grateful that teaching writing is what I do.

Acknowledgments

I would like to thank the following reviewers for their comments and suggestions: Philip M. Anderson, Queen's College, New York; Michael Angelotti, University of Oklahoma; Marilyn E. Calabrese, St. Joseph's University; Jamie Myers, Pennsylvania State University; Eileen I. Oliver, Washington State University; Chris Thaiss, George Mason University; and Norman Weinstein.

M. S.

1

What English Teachers Need to Know about Writing

English teachers have their work cut out for them. The English curriculum requires instructors to teach all of the language arts: reading, speaking, listening, and writing. This is a formidable task. However, the English teacher's greatest challenge is teaching writing. In this brief introduction, I will explain why this is the case, and outline some of the skills and concepts English teachers need to do the job.

Let's start with attitude. Ask almost any high school student two questions: "Which is your most favorite subject in your English class? Which is your least favorite subject in your English class?" The answer is predictable. By the time most students enter high school, they are beginning to dislike writing. My own children loved to write in elementary school, where they often sallied forth on a school trip, clipboard in hand for taking notes to be transformed eventually into a report. They wrote short stories and poems, often illustrated, and, of course, the traditional Mother's Day and Father's Day cards. They wrote recipes for meals eaten during colonial days, compiled them into booklets, and then cooked the meals at home or at school. One of my sons wrote a book about the Pilgrims and dedicated it to his favorite uncle. They wrote proposals for new playground equipment addressed to the local school board and letters to children in other grades or pen pals abroad. Much of this writing was collaborative. Even book reports, usually dreaded in high school, were enjoyable to write.

Often their writing was not graded, and when it was, it was graded liberally, with form and presentation often taking a backseat to content. Writing was fun . . . they got to write for purposes that were meaningful to them without much fear of criticism. Their novice efforts were applauded. For example, in first grade, Ruthy wrote,

> If I were an insect, I would be a butterfly and I would fly in the sky. And I would get on people's hands and people would push me off.

Her teacher's comment: "Great!"

But, at some point in my children's education, probably during the sixth or seventh grade, writing instruction began to change, and writing was no longer fun. Grades suddenly became important but were often confusing. For example, my oldest son, Joshua, was assigned an essay entitled "Snow," with almost no instruction in how to write it, and he received a C grade with no comments on the paper. When he asked the instructor to explain the grade, the results were predictable. His teacher became quite defensive, perhaps because she was not sure why she had rated the paper as a C.

In contrast to their declining motivation to write, my children continued to enjoy the literature part of their English courses. The authors of *Freedom and Discipline in English,* a landmark study of the practices of teaching writing in the sixties—the findings of which still go unchallenged—help us to understand why. They say,

> *Since the teaching of literature takes its point of departure from the text itself, it is appropriate that the discussion of it should always begin with the text. In the teaching of composition, however, there is no text to begin from: the point of departure for it is properly the student about to compose a text. For him [her], and for the person to teach him [her] the difference is crucial. It is not just that analysis is different from synthesis, or that learning to see and to understand is different from learning how to show and to communicate. The difference goes deeper, to the very quick of the student's life, where like any writer, he exposes himself to public scrutiny, lays his mind bare for all to see. (College Entrance Examination Board 80)*

Maintaining Students' Positive Attitudes toward Writing

High school students will continue to enjoy writing if teachers continue to provide meaningful writing experiences without increasing their fear of evaluation. Students will be motivated to write if they have something worth writing about. In 1644, when John Milton was assigned to write an essay on education, he said that he thought it was a mistake to force young people to write before they had anything to say or a desire to say it (College Entrance Examination Board 80). High school teachers must create invitations to write that are as compelling as those invitations extended in the earlier grades.

In "Prose with Integrity: A Primary Objective," Donald Stewart says that the empty generalizations we receive in students' papers are often the result of students' uncertainty of the aims of writing and their lack of engagement in the subject matter (230). The issues young people care about are good starting points for writing assignments. This semester, a student in my writing class was intensely engaged in writing a research paper on the hypnotic effects of the computer. He wanted to heighten awareness of what he sees as a problem—peers who have become asocial as a result of the amount of time they spend on the Internet.

But the challenge of teaching writing hardly ends with the assigned task and the student's motivation to accomplish it. The authors of *Freedom and Discipline in English* say ". . . it is precisely when he does have something to say and the desire to say it that the student feels himself most open to attack, and most sensitive about what he has said" (81). Writing reveals not only the content the student has chosen to discuss (Will the teacher think that this is a good idea? Will the teacher think that I am smart or stupid?) but the student's ability to say it. Instructors must be aware of students' apprehension about being judged when evaluating their writing.

Another factor that affects students' attitudes toward writing is their increasing awareness of the disparity between speech and writing and the necessity of learning the conventions of written discourse. In the elementary grades much student writing is closely related to speech. Because writing about personal experience is often the most common kind of assignment in elementary school, students can comfortably use their daily language in their writing. It is perfectly acceptable to say, "I have lots of friends." At this point in their education, students have not yet been confronted with the difference between colloquial and formal language.

Only teachers with considerable knowledge about writing can teach the conventions of academic writing. Teachers must not only know the differences between speech and writing, but they must be able to describe these differences and the rationale for learning them. Furthermore, as most teachers know, writing for different purposes and audiences requires different styles of writing. Teachers must be able to clarify the characteristics of the business letter as opposed to the newspaper article, or of the academic essay, the most popular form of writing assigned in secondary schools. This process is further complicated by the increasing awareness of the slippery definitions of these categories. The authors of *Freedom and Discipline in English* comment on the changing emphasis in teaching composition from "correctness" to "appropriateness."

. . . an English teacher today, confronting a student's composition, may feel more alone, on his [her] own than did teachers 50 years ago. Certainly he [she] has never been more on his [her] own. . . . He [she] cannot justify his corrections by reference to rules alone, and often prove he [she] is right simply by reference to a dictionary. He [she] must fit himself [herself] to be more than a proofreader, to become something closer to an expert, a sympathetic editor. (College Entrance Examination Board 84)

How You Become an Effective Instructor of Writing

What kind of preparation and training can help writing teachers assign meaningful invitations to write, and teach students the writing skills they must learn in secondary school?

Most important, teachers of writing should be writers themselves. George Hillocks compares the writing teacher to the piano teacher. He says that "teachers of piano need not be great concert pianists, but we expect them to play with more than mediocre facility" (195). The same is true for teachers of writing. It is not necessary for writing teachers to write like Shakespeare or Hemingway, but they should know how to write letters, essays, reports, and even short stories and poems if they teach these genres. Writing should be a part of their lives. It should be something they do routinely and with confidence. Ideally, they should *like* to write. Minimally, they should be able to execute the writing they assign to their students. Without a personal knowledge of writing, they will never develop the empathy they need for working with novice writers.

As with the piano teacher, whom we expect to have an understanding of music composition theory, the teacher of writing should have a knowledge of the theories that explain the writing process and the characteristics of written prose. The last twenty-five years of research have contributed much information to both areas.

The writing process has been studied from a variety of perspectives. Some researchers have focused on describing the writing process as it applies to all kinds of writing (e.g., Flower and Hayes; Perl; Calkins; Graves), whereas others have studied the process of composing different kinds of writing (e.g., Hillocks; Kinneavy; Moffett). Theories about the process of composing have also been studied by examining the processes of novice writers versus professional writers (e.g., Flower and Hayes; Sommers).

Many studies, such as James Kinneavy's *A Theory of Discourse*, have helped us to describe the characteristics of different kinds of writing. Thanks to this research, when we ask students to write a persuasive essay, we are able to describe the organization and style of a typical argumentative essay in great detail. Descriptions of writing have not been limited to professional writing.

Analyses of student writing, for example, those by Odell and Bartholomae, have helped us understand the pattern of reasoning underlying common errors as well as the stages of the development of writing ability.

Teachers of writing must be familiar with new writing curricula and teaching techniques. Although experts still do not know what is the best curriculum and the most effective combination of techniques for teaching writing, much progress has been made and there is a lot for us to learn. Teachers of writing need to be well informed about the latest research on many issues, for example, what constitutes a successful writing assignment; how to best teach the prewriting, drafting, and revision process; how to teach students to write effective sentences; and how teachers can evaluate writing effectively and efficiently.

Teachers of writing need to learn about using writing as a tool for learning. The writing across the curriculum movement, which encourages attention to writing in all disciplines, is based on the growing body of research on writing as a mode of learning and on the principle that all teachers are teachers of writing. Responsibility for teaching writing must be shared by faculty in all disciplines, if students are to become competent writers. The teaching of literacy skills is no longer confined to the English department. It is everyone's job. A familiarity with writing across the curriculum pedagogy is essential for English teachers, who are frequently called upon to teach their colleagues in other disciplines how to assign and evaluate writing. Texts such as *Writing Across the Curriculum in Middle and High Schools,* by Rhoda Maxwell, and *Roots in the Sawdust: Write to Learn Across the Disciplines,* edited by Anne Gere, are just two of the many books available to high school teachers as resources for implementing a writing across the curriculum program.

What Do You Already Know about Writing?

Take heart. You already know a great deal about writing and the teaching of writing—what works and what does not work. If you are an undergraduate, you have been a student of writing and a writer for more than thirteen years. If you are a graduate student or a teacher, you have had even more writing instruction and have been a writer yourself for a considerably longer time. With a little bit of prodding you can probably remember how you learned to write; you can identify the people who had the greatest impact on your development as a writer, whether they were teachers, parents, siblings, or friends. Possibly, you can recall the things they did and said that were most helpful. Oddly enough, you may not need much prodding to remember those individuals who were less helpful to you as a developing writer, whose influence was either negative (maybe they placed too much emphasis on correctness) or nonexistent.

Perhaps you have faced problems with your writing that your instructors could not help you solve. For example, when asked about her previous writing instruction, one of my students said, "Yes, it was in the sixth grade that I started to procrastinate with papers. I now know that I put off writing my papers, and I would get tons of writer's block. The writer's block also gave me an excuse to put off writing papers more. Writing for me became a vicious cycle of procrastination and disappointment when I received a grade which could have been better if only I started earlier." She later remarked that she had to wait until her college writing course before she met up with an instructor who could help her "turn back the tide of procrastination."

You also know a lot about writing from your own writing experiences. You probably have written essays, reports, business letters, a diary, and perhaps short stories or poems as well. You know about the problems of getting started, drafting, and revising, and you may have developed methods for solving these problems.

All of this knowledge will help you teach writing. You can model teaching practices that were helpful and avoid teaching practices that were discouraging, and share both your failures and successes with your students.

How Can This Book Help You to Become an Effective Writing Instructor?

This textbook will help you integrate your previous knowledge about writing and about teaching writing with recent composition theory and research. It will invite you to question the information it provides based on your own experiences as a student and writer, and, if you already teach, as an experienced teacher of English. Conversely, it will urge you to question your previous assumptions about teaching writing from the perspective of the information it presents.

Chapter 1, What English Teachers Should Know about Writing, recommends that a teacher of writing be familiar with the recent advances in theory, research, and practice.

Chapter 2, New Goals for Writing Instruction, presents a brief history of research in composition. Theories and research explaining the writing process are summarized.

Chapter 3, Teaching the Writing Process, reviews teaching methods in the context of the research discussed in Chapter 1. Assignments at the end of the chapter encourage you to describe your own composing process and experiment with a variety of composing process strategies.

Chapter 4, Teaching about Sentences, introduces you to transformational grammar theory and the role it has played in the development of techniques such as sentence combining. These contemporary theories and techniques are contrasted with traditional sentence pedagogies. You will describe your own style of writing as well as experiment with a variety of sentence pedagogies, such as sentence modeling and sentence combining, as you review strategies for teaching sentence skills.

Chapter 5, Evaluating and Responding to Student Writing, describes alternative purposes for evaluating writing and methods of evaluation appropriate for each purpose. Research on responding to student writing is reviewed to help you evaluate the relative value of competing pedagogical practices such as student conferences and written comments. Sample papers are provided for you to experiment with evaluation and response techniques.

Chapter 6, Designing Writing Assignments, reviews the principles of assignment design. This chapter includes model assignments. End-of-chapter activities include opportunities for constructing your own assignments.

Chapter 7, Writing about Literature, focuses on the kind of writing most frequently assigned in secondary schools—essays about literature. This chapter also presents alternatives to the traditional analytical essay for writing about literature. Assignments at the end of the chapter encourage you to construct assignments about literature and write in response to them.

Chapter 8, Composition Curricula: Four Approaches, discusses issues related to composition curriculum design and provides samples of writing curricula from different school districts. You will design your own writing unit as you synthesize the material from previous chapters with the information in this one.

Chapter 9, Reflection, Research, and Teaching Writing, explains how to do classroom-based research to evaluate the effectiveness of your teaching. It includes sample journal entries by practicing teachers.

Chapter 10, Joining the Profession, demonstrates how you can participate in the professional dialogue on teaching writing. It explains the advantages of affiliating with the National Council of Teachers of English. Even beginning teachers can contribute to the profession through publications and presentations based on their teaching practices. This chapter also urges you to speak out on public issues related to the teaching of writing, such as tracking students and developing national and statewide assessment programs.

Conclusion

No book on teaching writing can be comprehensive. Robert Probst's memorandum for his course on Methods of Teaching English is an apt description of the purpose of this text:

> *It is intended to be a beginning, and as such, it will leave you with more questions than answers. In doing so, it accurately reflects the state of the profession*

which continues to investigate many basic unresolved problems. . . . Our goal will be to acquaint ourselves with the thinking in the profession, incomplete as it may be, so that our decisions in teaching English may be as firmly grounded as possible in reason, or, at least, in instinct re-examined. (Smagorinsky and Whiting 120)

If this text fulfills this purpose, then my effort to record some of my experiences, the accumulated wisdom of my fellow researchers, and the good ideas of the junior high and high school teachers who have contributed to this text will not be in vain.

Questions for Discussion and Writing

1. Which was your favorite subject in elementary school, middle school, and high school? Explain.

2. When you receive a writing assignment, do you expect to receive an A, a B, or a C? Explain.

3. Do you welcome the opportunity to take a writing course? Explain.

4. How do you feel about teaching writing? Explain.

5. Read "Prose with Integrity: A Primary Objective" by Donald Stewart (see References). Write a summary of the article.

References

Bartholomae, David. "The Study of Error." *College Composition and Communication* 31 Oct. 1980: 253–269.

Calkins, Lucy. *The Art of Teaching Writing.* Portsmouth, NH: Heinemann-Boynton/Cook, 1986.

Flower, Linda, and John Hayes. "Problem Solving Strategies and the Writing Process." 2nd. ed. *Rhetoric and Composition: A Sourcebook for Teachers and Writers.* Ed. Richard Graves. Upper Montclair, NJ: Boynton-Cook, 1984: 269–283.

———. "The Cognition of Discovery: Defining a Rhetorical Problem." *College Composition and Communication* 31 Feb. 1980: 21–32.

Freedom and Discipline in English: Report on the Commission of English. Princeton, NJ: College Entrance Examination Board, 1965.

Gere, Anne Ruggles. *Roots in the Sawdust: Writing to Learn Across the Disciplines.* Urbana, IL: NCTE, 1985.

Graves, Donald. *A Case Study Observing the Development of Primary Children's Composing, Spelling and Motor Behaviors during the Writing Process.* Durham, NH: University of New Hampshire, 1981.

Hillocks, George. *Research in Teaching Composition.* Urbana, IL: NCTE, 1986.

Kinneavy, James. *A Theory of Discourse.* Englewood Cliffs, NJ: Prentice-Hall, 1974.

Maxwell, Rhoda J. *Writing Across the Curriculum in Middle and High Schools.* Boston: Allyn and Bacon, 1996.

Moffett, James. *Teaching the Universe of Discourse.* Boston: Houghton Mifflin, 1968.

Odell, Lee. "Context-Specific Ways of Knowing and the Evaluation of Writing." *Writing, Teaching, and Learning in the Disciplines.* New York: MLA, 1992.

Perl, Sondra. "The Composing Process of Unskilled Writers." *Research in Teaching English* 13 Dec. 1979: 5–22.

Smagorinsky, Peter, and Melissa E. Whiting. *How English Teachers Get Taught: Methods of Teaching the Methods Class.* Urbana, IL: NCTE, 1995.

Sommers, Nancy. "Revision Strategies of Student Writers and Experienced Writers." *College Composition and Communication* 30 Feb. 1979: 378–388.

Stewart, Donald. "Prose with Integrity: A Primary Objective." *College Composition and Communication* 20 Oct. 1969: 229–231.

2

New Goals
for Writing Instruction

A Brief History

The word *composition* derives from the Latin *cum* (with, together) and *ponere* (to place). The materials to be put together in written composition are the details from personal sensory experience, from vicarious experience, and from reading, listening, and observing. Skilled writers must be skilled observers, skilled readers, and skilled thinkers. And skilled writers must be able to tailor their writing to specific purposes and audiences. In other words, composition is an extremely complex activity that requires many skills besides a knowledge of grammar. Yet, before the 1960s, the goal of most writing instruction was to teach "correctness." It was thought that the appropriate subject matter for a composition program was grammar and usage. When I was a student preparing to teach high school English in the sixties, learning how to teach writing consisted of reading two texts: *Teaching English Grammar* and *Teaching English Usage*, both by Robert Pooley (1946). During my first year of teaching in a Chicago high school, I tried to teach the rules of grammar and usage to my innocent charges—not very successfully, I admit—and that was the sum and substance of my writing program.

Between the time I graduated from college and the time I began my studies in graduate school, some fifteen years later, research in the teaching of writing had really taken off. Prompted by several new trends in English education, and a growing concern about "why Johnny can't write," methods of teaching writing were being transformed by research in teaching pedagogy, focused, for the most part, on the elementary and postsecondary levels. The new paradigm was to teach writing as a process and to emphasize *writing as a mode of discovery.*

Although educational reform is always gradual, several landmark events spurred interest in reforming the teaching of writing and, more generally, the teaching of English. The Dartmouth Conference, the new open admissions policy at the City University of New York, and the publication in England of *The Development of Writing Abilities (11–18)* by Britton, Burgess, Martin, McLeod, and Rosen in 1975 were three such events.

The 1966 Dartmouth Conference, which took place in August and early September 1966 at Dartmouth College in New Hampshire, drew together fifty teachers from Great Britain and the United States who were concerned about the state of English education. The conference was convened by the Modern Language Association and the National Council of Teachers of English, two American professional organizations, and the National Association for the Teaching of English in Great Britain. On both sides of the Atlantic, the organizers felt that it was time to rethink assumptions basic to English education. The conference participants grappled with questions such as: What is English? What is continuity in English teaching? What is knowledge and proficiency in English and language standards and attitudes?

The conference was a major force in shifting attention away from mere correctness as a goal for teaching writing. American educators were surprised to learn that their counterparts in England "were a great deal less interested in formalism, correctness and structure, and discipline than they were" (Dixon ix). Participants agreed that increasing children's perception and self-awareness should be major objectives for language arts education and the process of language learning itself, and they described new pedagogies for teaching both writing and literature. They concluded that

> *The English teacher's work, therefore has to be on two fronts. First he has to learn for himself and develop with his pupils the full potential of discussion methods and their emphasis on interplay, dialectical exchange, shared experience, group learning, and understanding. And from the very start of reading and writing he has to look beyond minimum possibilities of literacy to the profounder possibilities of a considered and extended exploration of experience, permitting slower realizations and more individual personal growth. (Dixon 112)*

The report suggested that writing could play a major role in the development of a literacy broader than one based on correctness.

The Dartmouth Conference contributed significantly to rethinking the goals of instruction in both literature and writing. Of course, almost thirty years later, many junior high and high school teachers still cling to correctness as the major goal of teaching writing. Linda Miller Cleary, in *From the*

Other Side of the Desk (18), says that many instructors who have modernized their instructional practices are still preoccupied with grammar and usage. Although they may teach students how to execute the steps in the writing process, they spend more time on proofreading and editing than on the discovery of ideas. American schools have a long history of teachers focusing on the written product rather than the process, and "giving much less attention to the writer's efforts at meaning making and more to grammatical and mechanical errors" (Lytle 49). This overemphasis on correctness has had several negative consequences for writing instruction. Teachers view writing instruction as a looming set of papers to be "corrected" and students become convinced that the process of writing is similar to walking through a mine field. Avoidance of error is the name of the game.

Another landmark event that spurred research in the teaching of writing was the establishment of an open admissions policy by the City University of New York in 1970. Before open admissions, the City University system was very selective. Only students with B averages and higher were admitted. Under the open admissions policy, all students with a high school diploma were eligible to attend the City University. Suddenly, the colleges had to create a writing program for writers who were less well prepared than previously entering freshmen. To design instructional strategies to help students learn academic writing, instructors needed more information about the composing process of novice writers. City University teachers spearheaded national research in composition for several years. Mina Shaughnessy's *Errors and Expectations: A Guide for the Teacher of Basic Writing* in 1977 was one of the earliest reports describing how underprepared students write. In the introduction she explains what happened when the "doors of City University suddenly flung open, and students wrote their first placement essays." She says,

> *Not surprisingly, the essays these students wrote during their first weeks of classes stunned the teachers who read them. Nothing, it seemed, short of a miracle was going to turn such students into writers. Not uncommonly, teachers announced to their supervisors, (or even to their students) after only one week of class that everyone was probably going to fail. These were the students, they insisted, whose problems at this stage were irremediable. To make matters worse, there were no studies nor guides, nor even suitable textbooks to turn to. . . . (3)*

Shaughnessy goes on to say that five years later teachers who had questioned the ability of any of these students to succeed "underwent many shifts in attitude and methodology since their first encounters with new students" (4). In her book she explains how she used "error as a window into the minds of her students" and tried to devise methods for helping her students learn the various skills associated with college writing. Teaching students how to identify the various stages of the composing process and the techniques for executing them was part of the new pedagogy, though Shaughnessy acknowledged that composition instructors still had much to learn about methods of teaching writing to underprepared students.

The Dartmouth Conference and open admissions at the City University of New York coincided with broad educational reforms already underway as a result of the New Education movement, inspired by the work of Jerome Bruner. The core idea of Bruner's philosophy is that "it is not enough to teach students that something was what it was, but education should teach the process of discovering how and why things were" (21). This idea led to an attack on former methods of teaching composition, such as the use of models. Gordon Rohmann, one of the composition specialists to be influenced earliest by the New Education movement, said,

> *A failure to make proper distinctions between thinking and writing has led to a fundamental misconception which undermines so many of our best efforts in teaching writing: if we train students to recognize an example of good prose (the rhetoric of the finished word) we have not given them a basis on which to build their own writing abilities. All we have done in fact is to give them standards to judge the goodness or badness of their finished effort. We haven't really taught them how to make that effort. . . . Unless we can somehow introduce students to the dynamics of creation, we too often simply discourage their hopes of ever writing at all. (106)*

Like Shaughnessy, Rohmann believed that a better understanding of the composing process was at the heart of teaching students how to write. Without such an understanding, how could they be introduced to the "dynamics of creation?"

The report, *The Development of Writing Abilities (11–18)*, by James Britton and a research team based at the University of London Institute of Education, supported the growing interest in teaching the writing process but added to it a rhetorical dimension. Britton states, in the introduction to the report, that the research team's task was to create a curriculum model that would enable them to characterize various kinds of writing in terms of the purpose and audience for which they were written, and then "go on to trace the developmental steps that led to them" (6). This research project was a reaction to the long-standing practice of using the traditional modes (narration, description, comparison, definition, and classification) rather than function categories to describe writing. The modes describe how writing is organized, whereas the major contribution of this research was to develop a series of categories to describe the purposes and audiences for which people write. When the team examined writing in British schools using function categories, they discovered that school-based writing was limited for the most part to "transactional writing," such as the typical expository essay. They found very little evidence of expressive or poetic writing, the two other major categories they identified. Expressive writing includes diary writing, biography, and the personal essay. Poetic writing includes all kinds of fiction.

Agreeing with the educators at the Dartmouth Conference, Britton's team was concerned about broadening the definition of literacy to include all forms of written expression. They defined three kinds of writing:

> *Transactional writing*—language to get things done, which is concerned with an end outside itself; it informs, persuades, and instructs.

> *Expressive writing*—language close to the self, revealing the writer, verbalizing the writer's consciousness, displaying a close relationship with the reader. Possibly not highly explicit. Relatively unstructured.

> *Poetic writing*—a verbal construct; a patterned verbalization of the writer's feelings and ideas. This category is not restricted to poems and would include such writings as short stories, plays, and shaped autobiographical episodes (88–91).

Texts that reflected new goals for the teaching of writing as well as the findings of research in composition began to appear. For example, James Moffett and Betty Jane Wagner's *Student-Centered Language Arts and Reading, K–13: A Handbook for Teachers* (1976), Donald Murray's *A Writer Teaches Writing* (1968), and Peter Elbow's *Writing without Teachers* (1973) were filled with techniques compatible with a process approach to teaching composition combined with an emphasis on writing for different purposes and audiences.

Composition Research: New Approaches

Research and the development of new theories of how writers compose explained why many of the ideas in these pioneering books worked, but taught us that there was much more to learn about a writer's behavior as he or she composes. In the early years of composition research, several studies were conducted that compared the writings of novice and experienced writers. Once teaching the composing process became a major goal of writing instruction, it was thought that if we knew how competent, confident, successful writers think and feel as they write, and if we could provide the same information to developing writers, we could bridge the gap between the two. We would be able to design methods for teaching writing that would teach the skills possessed by the experienced writers to the novice writers.

The largest number of studies were cognitively based, attempting to determine what writers think about when they are writing. For example, Linda

Flower has demonstrated that writing makes great demands on beginning writers. She concluded, "There is only so much room in the writer's conscious attention for all that needs to be accomplished due to the complex nature of writing" (29). Writing is hard work, even when it has your full attention. "The novice writer is on cognitive overload, like a 'switchboard operator' who must juggle demands on her attention and constraints on what she can do" (30). All writers experience trouble when the task becomes too hard, but novice writers often experience problems even when the task is within their reach because they do not tackle writing tasks in stages. They try to do everything at once.

Experienced writers break down the writing process into stages of planning, drafting, and revising, though these stages are not necessarily discrete; they often overlap with one another. For example, after an experienced writer has made some notes, planned her essay, and then is in the middle of drafting it, she might discover that she lacks information on a part of the subject and needs to return to the note-taking stage. Or after the writer has completed a first draft and rereads it, she might decide to reorganize the information in the essay, which requires returning to the planning stage.

Flower and Hayes documented the methods used by experienced writers to work through each of these stages, from the moment they receive a writing task, or present one to themselves, to the time it is completed. For example, experienced writers spend considerable effort during the *planning* stage, developing an image of the purpose and audience for their writing. Flower and Hayes state, "They build a unique representation, not only of their audience and assignment, but also of their goals involving the audience, their own persona [as writers] and the text. By contrast poor writers think primarily about form, such as the number of pages required" (99). Furthermore, good writers "create a particularly rich set of goals for affecting their reader which helps them to generate new ideas" (100). Good writers also continue to develop new goals as they continue to write. But, in contrast, poor writers stay with the same limited view of the writing task, which limits their ability to generate ideas. Good writers also spend more time planning than beginning writers. In one study comparing prewriting time and total writing time of high school students, researchers found that subjects spent a negligible fraction of their time planning, but experienced writers spend 65 percent to 85 percent of their writing time on the planning stage (Flower and Hayes 128–140).

Drafting, sometimes called "recording," "implementing," "writing," or "transcribing," is the process of "transforming meaning from one form of symbolization (thought) into another form of symbolization (graphic representation)" (Humes 208), or, said differently, it is the "spontaneous production of connected prose" (Lytle 52). Often the writer is working from notes or an outline, but even if this is the case, paragraphing, sentence form, and word choice require decision making. Drafting makes great demands on writers, who might be thinking about handwriting, spelling, punctuation, organization, and clarity, at the same time they are trying to translate their thinking on the page (Scarmedelia, Bereiter, and Goldman 52). We know that experienced writers have made some of these skills automatic and, therefore, have less difficulty during drafting than beginning writers. For example, they need not worry about how to write grammatically correct sentences. They can focus on other issues such as organizing the content of their messages. They also have the ability to withhold some concerns for the revision stage, such as how to create a pleasing style while they concentrate on content.

Revision usually refers to reconsidering the larger elements of an essay, its content, development, and organization, whereas the term *editing* often refers to the processes by which the writer corrects what he or she has written, focusing chiefly on sentence correctness, spelling, usage, and punctuation. Beginning writers usually revise only on the word level; they focus primarily on lower-level concerns, closer to what have been defined as editing concerns, rather than the content of their writing (Bridwell 221, Sommers 122). More recent studies of the revision process of student writers have confirmed the findings of previous studies. In a recent study of the writing of twelfth graders, Yagelski asked the question, "Do specific instructional features affect student revisions?" It was discovered that despite a classroom characterized by process-oriented instruction, in this writing program in which the teacher encouraged prewriting exercises, multiple drafts, and peer editing, what seemed to matter most was not how students were being taught to write, but the teacher's grading practices. If teachers base their grades on sentence-level issues, students will continue to confine revision to the sentence (Yagelski 237).

Another group of studies tried to understand the role that emotion and motivation play in the writing process. One of the most recent studies of the effect of attitude on the writing of high school students is Linda Miller Cleary's research on the concentration of and motivation of forty male and female eleventh graders representing different ethnic groups and different levels of writing ability. Cleary based her investigations on the work of psychologists and educators, not necessarily concerned with writing, who have studied the effect of emotion on overall student performance. She sought answers to these questions: Why do most teachers report that by eleventh grade most students resist writing? How do emotions connected with the context of writing interact with the writing process?

She interviewed students, observed them in their classrooms, and had them write several assignments using the compose aloud method. The compose aloud method requires that students explain what they are thinking and feeling when they are writing. In her interviews she asked such questions as: "What has writing been like for you from the time you first remember until the present? What do you remember of writing before you began school?

How did you learn to write? Tell me about a time when writing was really good or bad for you. What is writing like for you now? Tell me as many stories about writing as you can."

Cleary based these questions on the assumption that because writing requires an enormous amount of conscious attention, factors that inhibit concentration underlie students' unwillingness to engage in the writing process and affect the way they go about the process. Cleary's study draws on research findings about the relationship between emotion and learning, such as "Conscious attention is redirected by emotion" (Simon, quoted by Cleary 18). When a threat enters the learning environment, students cannot fully use their cognitive processes. The student concentrates on surviving, not learning. And, perhaps most important, concentration on a subject is strongly influenced by the individual's personal history with the subject.

The composing process has also been studied by researchers who favor what is called a social constructionist explanation of the development of writing ability. Social constructionist theory provides an alternative to the cognitive or affective theories about composing, although proponents of all of these theories would agree that all theories about composing have something to contribute to our knowledge of the process. In "Thinking and Writing as Social Acts" found in *Thinking, Reasoning, and Writing* by Maimon Nodine, and O'Connor in 1989, Kenneth Bruffee summarizes the social constructionist position. He says,

> *This essay assumes that there is no inherent, internal, universal mental structure that can work towards the "universals of sound reasoning." It assumes instead that what we call the universals of sound reasoning or a higher order reasoning ability is an internalization of the language use, or more broadly, the symbol use, of certain communities, in particular our own literate Western European-American culture. . . . When we write and how we write is governed by the language of the community of people within which we write, to whom we write. Writing—a form of conversation—begins in conversation and remains within that conversational community. (214)*

In other words, when we write, we use the thinking patterns and style that characterize the discourse of the community to which we belong. A writer composes according to a particular culture's inseparably linked patterns of customs and thought reflected in its unique discourse. However, to write well also requires us to learn to understand the discourse of conversation about writing, in which writing is seen as a continual process of making decisions or exercising judgment, as those decisions and that judgment are applied to our community. That is, good writing requires us to be able to talk about writing in a way agreed upon by the conversational community of which we are members.

By using examples of the kinds of questions teachers ask themselves as they try to frame goals for writing instruction, Bruffee effectively illustrates the difference between cognitive and social constructionist explanations of the writing process: "For example, a cognitivist must ask, 'What's going on in my students' heads?' and 'How can I get in there and change what's going on?' These are the questions implied when we wonder how to reach students, and how to implant in their heads what we believe is going on in our own" (216). On the other hand, when a teacher believes that only when students feel themselves to be members of the academic community will they begin to write like academics, a teacher will ask questions such as, "How do I get my students to want to give up the values of the communities they are now members of, or at least every so often their loyalty to and dependence upon those communities?" and "How do I help students join another community in ways that make that change as comfortable and fail-safe as possible?" (216). One answer is to create a transitional community that diminishes the stress that comes with change while providing the opportunity for the student to experiment with the language and thinking patterns of the new community. In classes based on the social constructionist model, conversations in the context of student writing groups and peer tutoring play an important role.

Much research related to the social constructionist theory of composition seeks to identify the characteristics of speaking and writing in different language communities and the impact of cultural differences on learning how to write. For example, the dialect spoken by African American students is the subject of an increasing number of studies. Shirley Brice-Heath's research discussed in Chapter 8 demonstrates how curriculum design and pedagogy can use cultural differences to advantage in teaching the language arts. In *Landmark Essays on Writing Process,* Sondra Perl points to the need for additional studies on all aspects of composition instruction related to social constructionism. She says

> *Researchers of writing have only begun to investigate, for example, the ways student writers choose to participate in the discourses of the communities in which they find themselves (Clark and Weidenhaupt, 1992; Sternglass, 1988), the ways teachers respond to, intervene in, challenge and support the work of students (Prior, 1991; Walvoord and McCarthy, 1991), and the ways composing is shaped by issues of difference (Lunsford and Ede, 1990; Tedesco, 1991). (xviii)*

As our school populations become increasingly more diverse, we look forward impatiently to research that answers these questions.

Technology and Teaching Writing

No chapter on new approaches to composition research is complete without acknowledging the increasing impact of technology on composition instruction.

We must agree with William Costanzo, who says that "computers are altering the way many of us read, see, and even think" (11). At the least, they offer us a new and powerful tool for producing text. My writing process has been transformed by the computer. I went from a miserable typist, dreading each writing project, to a word processor addict who imagines, often mistakenly, that when I press that magic button that turns on my computer, my work is almost done. Computers are also changing the language of texts and the nature of the environments in which language is produced. "Electronic mail talk" is one of the most dramatic examples of the medium affecting the message. I received this e-mail message yesterday from my brother in Montreal: "dear margot, no problem with dad. family is having great time skiing. off to london next week for work. regards to all." End of message. Need I say more?

Although the Internet and electronic mail are becoming an increasing presence in the composition class, most of the research that measures the impact of technology on composition instruction is focused on the link between word processing, the writing process, and the quality of the written product. Studies indicate that word processors may aid students during all phases of the writing process (e.g., Dalton and Hannafin; Joram; Owston; and others). Generating text, changing it, and deleting it are quick operations on the computer. Furthermore, composing on the computer may also help to increase audience awareness. Owston and others write that "screen displays may facilitate the young writer's development of a sense of their audience, perhaps psychologically distancing the creator from his or her work" (250). However, some studies point to possible negative effects of the computer on the writing process, and others suggest that the computer is only as effective as the writing instructor. Dalton and Owston point out that students who lack typing skills will be at a disadvantage in the computerized teaching environment. Even those students who can type may be distracted by the computer's features (Joram; Owston). In "The Role of Classroom Writing Practices in Shaping Computer Use," Cynthia Greenleaf concluded that "although many changes accompanied the use of computers, . . . the teacher's structuring of writing instruction had the greatest impact on both student writing and the ways computers entered into that writing" (46). Nevertheless, word processors are here to stay, and, as the following chapters indicate, they can play an important role in writing instruction if we use them wisely.

Conclusion

To develop effective teaching techniques, we need to take into account theories and research about the relationship between cognition and writing, between feelings and motivation and writing, and about how writing is related to learning the language of different communities and cultural differences. We also must keep up with research on the relationship between technology and composition instruction. Each area of theory and research has important implications for teaching. However, as a teacher of writing, you will need to test theory and research against your own teaching experiences. In Chapter 9, Reflection, Research, and Teaching Writing, I suggest some techniques for examining this relationship. These eight guidelines for teaching composition are supported by current research:

1. Students should learn that writing is a process, which is often recursive. The prewriting, drafting, and editing stages often overlap.
2. Strategies for executing each part of the process can be learned. Executing the process in stages helps avoid cognitive overload.
3. Students should learn how to develop rich representations of writing tasks, which include a concern for the purpose and audience of their writing as well as form and mechanics.
4. Students should learn to revise for content issues such as focus, organization, and development of ideas, as well as for sentence-level correctness.
5. We should arrange our students in small groups to talk about writing during all stages of the writing process.
6. We should try to develop environments for writing in which students are willing to take risks with language.
7. We should take cultural differences into account when teaching writing.
8. We should teach our students how to use the computer as a tool for writing.

Questions for Discussion and Writing

1. Review a composition textbook written before 1965 and compare it to your college composition textbook, or if you are presently teaching, compare it to the textbook you currently use. How are they similar? How are they different?

2. Read *Growth Through English* by John Dixon (see References). Compare the approach to teaching English in your school to the approach recommended in this report.

References

Bridwell, Lillian. "Revising Processes in Twelfth Grade Students' Transactional Writing." *Research in Teaching English* 14 Oct. 1980: 197–222.

Britton, J., T. Burgess, N. Martin, A. McLeod, and H. Rosen. *The Development of Writing Abilities (11–18)*. London: Macmillan Press, 1975.

Bruffee, Kenneth. "Thinking and Writing as Social Acts." *Thinking, Reasoning, and Writing*. Eds. Elaine Maimon, Barbara Nodine, Finbaur O'Connor. New York: Longman, 1989.

Bruner, Jerome. *The Process of Education*. Cambridge, MA: Harvard University Press, 1973.

Clark, B., and S. Wiedenhaupt. "On Blocking and Unblocking Sonja: A Case Study in Two Voices." *College Composition and Communication* 43 (1992): 55–74.

Cleary, Linda Miller. "Affect and Cognition in the Writing Process of Eleventh Graders: A Study of Concentration and Motivation." *Written Communication* (8) 1991: 473–505.

———. *From the Other Side of the Desk: Students Speak Out about Writing*. Portsmouth, NH: Heinemann-Boynton/Cook, 1991.

Costanzo, William. "Reading, Writing, and Thinking in an Age of Electronic Literacy." *Literacy and Computers: The Complications of Teaching and Learning with Technology*. Cynthia L. Selfe & Susan Hilligoss. New York: MLA, 1994.

Dalton, David W., and Michael J. Hannafin. "The Effects of Word Processing on Written Composition." *Journal of Educational Research* 80:6 (1987): 338–341.

Dixon, John. *Growth Through English. A Record Based on the Dartmouth Seminar*. Reading, England: National Association of Teachers of English, 1967.

Elbow, Peter. *Writing without Teachers*. New York: Oxford University Press, 1973.

Flower, Linda. "Writer Based Prose: A Cognitive Basis for Problems in Writing." *College English* 41 Sept. 1979: 19–37.

Flower, Linda, and John R. Hayes. "The Cognition of Discovery: Defining a Rhetorical Problem." *The Writing Teachers Sourcebook*. 2nd ed. Eds. Gary Tate and Edward Corbett. New York: Oxford University Press, 1988.

Greenleaf, Cynthia. "Technological Indeterminacy: The Role of Classroom Practices in Shaping Computer Use." Technical Report No. 58. Berkeley, CA: Center for the Study of Writing, 1992.

Humes, Ann. "Research on the Composing Process." *Review of Educational Research* 53 Summer 1983: 201–216.

Joram, Elana, and others. "The Effects of Revising with a Word Processor on Written Composition." *Research in the Teaching of English* 26:2 (1992): 167–193.

Lunsford, A. A., and L. Ede. "Rhetoric in a New Key: Women and Collaboration." *Rhetoric Review* 8 (1990): 234–241.

Lytle, Susan L., and Morton Botel. *The Pennsylvania Framework for Reading, Writing, and Talking across the Curriculum*. Harrisburg: The Pennsylvania Department of Education, 1990.

Moffett, James, and Betty Jane Wagner. *Student-Centered Language Arts and Reading, K–13. A Handbook for Teachers*. 4th ed. Portsmouth, NH: Heinemann-Boynton/Cook, 1976.

Murray, Donald. *A Writer Teaches Writing*. 2nd ed. Boston: Houghton Mifflin, 1968.

Owston, Ronald D., and others. "The Effects of Word Processing on Students' Writing Quality and Revision Strategies." *Research in the Teaching of English* 26:2 (1992): 249–277.

Perl, Sondra, ed. *Landmark Essays on Writing Process*. Davis, CA: Hermagoris Press, 1994.

Pooley, Robert C. *Teaching English Grammar*. New York: Appleton-Century Crofts, 1946.

———. *Teaching English Usage*. New York: Appleton-Century Crofts, 1946.

Prior, Paul. "Contextualizing Writing and Response in a Graduate Seminar." *Written Communication* 8 (1991): 267–310.

Rohmann, Gordon D. "Pre-Writing: The Stage of Discovery in the Writing Process." *College Composition and Communication* 16 May 1965: 106–112.

Scarmedelia, M., and Cary Bereiter, and Hillel Goelman. "What Writers Know: The Language Process and Structure of Written Discourse." *The Role of Production Factors in Writing Ability.* Ed. Martin Nystrand. New York: Academic Press, 1982.

Shaughnessy, Mina. *Errors and Expectations: A Guide for the Teacher of Basic Writing.* New York: Oxford University Press, 1977.

Sommers, Nancy. "Revision of Student Writers and Experienced Adult Writers." *The Writing Teachers Sourcebook.* 2nd ed. Eds. Gary Tate and Edward Corbett. New York: Oxford University Press, 1988.

Sternglass, M. *The Presence of Thought: Introspective Accounts of Reading and Writing.* Norwood, NJ: Ablex, 1988.

Tedesco, J. "Womens' Ways of Knowing/Women's Ways of Composing." *Rhetoric Review* 9 (1991): 246–256.

Walvoord, Barbara, and L. McCarthy. *Thinking and Writing in College: A Natrualistic Study of Students in Four Disciplines.* Urbana, IL: NCTE, 1991.

Yagelski, Robert. "The Role of Classroom Context in the Revision Strategies of Student Writers." *Research in the Teaching of English* 29 May 1995: 216–238.

3

Teaching the Writing Process

Teaching the Writing Process through Self-Reflection

A good place to start when teaching students about the writing process is to discuss your writing process and the writing process of professional writers, and give students some techniques for examining the process they use when they write their own papers. Many professional writers, especially writers of fiction, have described their writing process in diaries, journals, and sometimes in books. The *Paris Review Interviews* is a series of anthologies in which famous authors describe their methods of writing. This excerpt from the interview with Ernest Hemingway, which took place in a cafe in Madrid, Spain, comes from the *Paris Review* series.

Interview with Ernest Hemingway

Interviewer: Could you say something of this [writing process]? When do you work? Do you keep to a strict schedule?

Hemingway: When I am working on a book or story I write every morning as soon after first light as possible. There is no one to disturb you and it is cool or cold when you come to your work and warm up as you write. You read what is written and, as you always stop when you know what is going to happen next, you go from there. You write until you come to a place where you still have your juice and know what will happen next ... You have started at six in the morning, say, and you may go on until noon or be through before that. When you stop you are empty, and at the same time never empty but filling. . . . as when you have made love to someone you love. Nothing can hurt you, nothing can happen, nothing means anything until the next day when you do it again. It is the wait until the next day that is hard to get through.

Interviewer: Can you dismiss from your mind whatever project you're on when you're away from the typewriter?

Hemingway: Of course, but it takes discipline to do it and this discipline is acquired. It has to be.

Interviewer: Do you do any rewriting as you read up to the place you left off the day before? Or does that come later, when the whole is finished?

Hemingway: I always rewrite each day up to the point where I stopped. When it is all finished, naturally you go over it. You get another chance to correct and rewrite when someone else types it, and you see it clean in type. The last chance is in the proofs. You're grateful for these different chances.

Interviewer: How much rewriting do you do?

Hemingway: It depends. I rewrote the ending to *Farewell to Arms,* the last page of it, thirty-nine times before I was satisfied.

Interviewer: Was there some technical problem there? What was it that had stumped you?

Hemingway: Getting the words right.

Interviewer: Is it the rereading that gets the "juice" up?

Hemingway: Rereading puts you at the point where it has to go on, knowing it is as good as you can get it up to there. There is always juice somewhere.

Interviewer: But are there times when the inspiration isn't there at all?

Hemingway: Naturally. But if you stopped when you knew what would happen next, you can go on. As long as you can start, you are all right. The juice will come (Plimpton 221–222).

In this interview Hemingway discusses many of the behaviors and attitudes typical of professional writers. Although he is talking about writing fiction, the problems he faces as a writer are typical of all writers: finding a good place to write, focusing your attention on your subject, deciding how to get started and how to revise, and, occasionally, how to overcome writer's block. Beginning writers can benefit from reading about the methods Hemingway used to cope with these problems. Students may be even more interested in the writing process of authors who write for young people, such as those appearing in *From Writers to Students: The Pleasures and Pains of Writing* by M. Jerry Weiss. Judy Blume (*Are You There God? It's Me Margaret* and *Tales of a Fourth Grade Nothing*) and Paul Zindel (*Confessions of a Teen-Age Baboon* and *The Pigman*) are two of the popular authors who discuss their writing process in this lively text. Two more recent texts by Donald Gallo, *Speaking for Ourselves* and *Speaking for Ourselves Too,* also contain autobiographical sketches by notable authors of books for young adults.

Students may also do some research about the writing process of their favorite author. Allan Glatthorn has created a survey for this purpose (see Figure 3.1). By sharing their findings, students learn about the similarities and differences that characterize the writing processes of many authors.

Perhaps you can invite professional writers to your class. The parent of a student who writes as part of his or her profession can describe the process of writing a report, for example. Invite teachers who write for their own enjoyment or for publication to discuss their writing experiences. I have frequently called upon a colleague who freelances for several local newspapers and magazines to explain to my writing classes how she goes about writing articles. This semester she discussed the process of starting a book. (See Appendix 3a for a student's summary of her remarks.) Students in upper grades can be invited to describe how they handle writing assignments. However, make sure that they have had some experience discussing the writing process (Walvoord 33).

Your students will be interested in knowing how you write. Keep reminding them that you did not acquire your ability to write overnight. If you have saved some of your papers from high school, especially the weaker ones, you can dramatize this point. If you are currently working on a writing project, explain your motivation for writing and relate some of the problems you have encountered during the planning, drafting, and revision stages.

Once students have discussed the writing process of professional writers, and you have begun writing process instruction in your course, they can begin to develop vocabulary for discussing their own writing process. Discussion and questionnaires that invite them to reflect about their former writing experiences and the way they currently go about writing can help them to set goals to improve their writing process (see Figure 3.2).

Reviewing the writing process students followed after writing a paper is another useful method for encouraging this kind of reflection. Figures 3.3 and 3.4 are surveys designed for this purpose. The second survey should be used only after students have had considerable training in revision. Both surveys can be modified to include fewer items, if your students have not yet been introduced to all stages of the writing process.

Your Name _____ Date _____

Name of Professional Writer _____

Describe briefly the writer's accomplishments.

How often does the writer write?

What time of day is preferred?

For how long a period on a given day does the writer write?

Does the writer type, dictate, or write in longhand?

Describe briefly the physical environment in which the writer usually writes.

How does the writer usually get ideas for writing?

How much research and data-gathering does the writer usually do? What forms?

In a given period of writing, how much does the writer usually accomplish?

How much mental planning does the writer do? What kinds of written plans are made?

Describe briefly the author's revision processes. When does the writer revise? What kinds of elements are revised? How much is revised?

Identify any important behaviors that typically take place while the writer writes.

How much does the writer share early drafts with others? With whom does the writer usually share early drafts? How important a role does the editor play?

What else does the writer report about his or her composing process that is not covered in the questions above?

Indicate the source for your information.

FIGURE 3.1   Analysis of the Composing Process of a Professional Writer

Reprinted by permission of Allan A. Glatthorn.

1. How would you describe your present attitude toward writing?

2. What kinds of writing do you like to do most?

3. Briefly describe your writing history. How did you learn to write?

4. Can you remember the first thing you ever wrote?

5. Who were the people who helped you the most with your writing: teachers, parents, friends, relatives?

6. Describe the way you write. What percentage of your time do you spend on the following stages of the writing process?

   Planning _____

   Writing the first draft _____

   Revising _____

7. Tell a story about your best writing experience.

FIGURE 3.2 **"How I Learned to Write" Survey**

Process Journals

Some teachers have found process journals that students use to record their observations about the writing process throughout the semester to be useful. Students keep a separate journal for discussing their approaches to different assignments. Diane Burkehardt, an eighth grade teacher, trying to motivate her skeptical students to write process journals, began by explaining that process journals could help them to evaluate and improve their writing process: "In your process journal, you write about your writing. You pay attention to what happens. You crawl outside your body, sit on your shoulder and look at what is going on in your brain." After sharing the remarks in her own process journal, students began to get the idea (Perl and Wilson 208). It took time but, after a while, students' journals became more informative, more complex at times, and even funny. For example,

> Greg reported that he hadn't written much because he was "almost empty on thoughts for a while." Jimmy noted that in order to write he had to "block out the sound of the crickets" in the yard outside. . . . Kathy noted a "steady

Name _____ Assignment # _____

Assignment Topic _____

Title of Paper _____

The purpose of this questionnaire is to help you observe your process of writing, the way you go about a writing assignment. There are no right or wrong answers. As we talk about the writing process throughout the year, you may decide that you can improve the methods and habits you now use to approach a writing task. The first three questions and question 10 ask for a "yes" or "no" answer. Questions 5 and 6 ask you to write a response. The rest of the questions ask you to check one of the possible answers.

1. I wrote down my ideas and made some notes before starting to write my paper. yes _____ , no _____

2. I made an outline before I began to write my paper. yes _____ , no _____

3. I didn't think too much before I started writing. Ideas came to me as I was writing. yes _____ , no _____

4. I wrote zero _____ , one _____ , two _____ drafts before writing my final copy.

5. The easiest part of writing this paper was:

6. The most difficult part of writing this paper was:

7. I wrote this paper at one sitting _____ , two sittings _____ , more _____ .

8. Each sitting lasted less than an hour _____ , more than an hour _____ .

9. I worked on this paper in class _____ , at home _____ , in the library _____ , elsewhere _____ .

10. I was easily distracted while writing. yes _____ , no _____

FIGURE 3.3   Observing Your Writing Process Survey

stream of thoughts" and Nancy described the exciting experience of having an "ending just pop into [her] head." (Perl and Wilson 209)

At Friends' Central School in Wynnewood, Pennsylvania, students in Leif Gustavson's eighth grade class keep process journals called "Portfolio

Name _____ Assignment # _____

Assignment Title: _____

Title of Paper _____

1. Indicate the most demanding stage(s) of the writing process with an X. Indicate the least demanding stage(s) of the writing process with a /.

    _____ a. getting information

    _____ b. categorizing information (sorting, classifying)

    _____ c. arranging information (deciding what goes first, etc.)

    _____ d. writing the first draft

    _____ e. revising the draft

    _____ f. proofreading for grammar, punctuation, and spelling errors

2. Indicate the following revisions you made during the writing of this paper with a /.

    _____ a. I changed my topic.

    _____ b. I changed my most important idea.

    _____ c. I added information.

    _____ d. I deleted information.

    _____ e. I changed the arrangement of the material.

    _____ f. I changed the sentences.

    _____ g. I substituted new words for some of the words I had used in the first draft.

    _____ h. I corrected for grammar, spelling, and punctuation.

3. Ideas for revision came from my _____ classmates, _____ my teacher, _____ friends, etc. _____ .

Please include any additional comments about the writing of this paper on the back of this survey.

FIGURE 3.4   Reviewing the Writing Process Survey

Audits." An excerpt from Ryan Barrett's portfolio illustrates how a series of questions can be used to structure process journals. (See Appendix 3b.)

Interviews, surveys, and process journals are designed to help demystify the writing process for your students, to help them realize that ordinary mortals can learn to write competently by improving their techniques for accomplishing the various activities that are a natural part of the writing process as well as by expanding their knowledge about the elements of writing. One of my students, when reflecting back on his high school writing experiences, said that he did not like writing because he got poor grades most of the time. Even when he got good grades, he had no idea how to approach the next paper. That type of comment by students is what we are trying to avoid.

Teaching the Writing Process: Strategies for Composing

Teaching the writing process is a tall order. Like the writing process itself, teaching the writing process is recursive. In each grade students need to be reminded of general principles about the writing process, which seem to aid just about any kind of writing, and they need to be introduced to modifications of that process suitable for different kinds of writing tasks and situations. For example, the process of writing a research paper is not quite the same as writing a short personal essay, but they do have features in common. All writing tasks require planning, drafting, and revising. All writing tasks require the author to take into account the purpose and audience for the writing, especially during the periods of drafting and revising, because these considerations will influence organization and style. However, the methods used during each stage, especially the planning stage, will be quite different for each kind of writing. Planning for an essay exam may consist of jotting down key words about the content in contrast to planning an argument, which may include listing all the features of the targeted audience.

In this chapter we will review activities you can teach students to help students manage the writing process in a way that is especially useful for writing about personal experience or knowledge, a typical subject for writing assignments in the secondary grades. Many of these activities can be conducted on a computer, as I will demonstrate throughout the chapter. Prewriting strategies for writing about fiction are discussed in Chapter 7.

Regardless of the assignment, begin by creating a classroom context that provides ample time for both prewriting and revision to take place. Janet Emig's landmark study, *The Composing Process of Twelfth Graders* (1971), describes a classroom situation in which the composing process is severely constrained by the amount of time allotted to these activities. Students need sufficient time for prewriting, drafting, and revising. Tom Romano, in *Clearing the Way: Working with Teen-Age Writers*, an account of writing in his own high school classrooms, says he allows two to four days before a draft must be created, "although students may, of course, write any time they are ready" (60). "Furthermore, your students should know from the day classes begin that they can expect your support, assistance, and feedback throughout the process of writing a paper, but that you will not over-correct and over-manage their writing once the process is underway" (60). Students should expect that you will explain all assignments clearly, and you should give students ample class time to ask questions about each writing assignment.

Prewriting and Planning Techniques

There are two kinds of prewriting techniques, those that work by free association such as brainstorming and freewriting, and more structured prewriting methods such as questions. Either group of techniques can be executed independently or in small groups. *Brainstorming* usually means making a list of all the details and ideas that come to mind as the writer begins to think about the topic, whereas *freewriting* has come to mean writing connected sentences about the topic. In both cases the writer tries not to censor the ideas and details he or she is generating through free association. This method is one useful way of reducing the cognitive overload we discussed earlier in the chapter. The writer tries to shut down concerns about form, style, correctness, and even organization while brainstorming or freewriting.

Here are several ways to encourage brainstorming and freewriting: Brainstorming can be modeled as a class activity. Beth Neman asks students to select a topic about which everyone may have some knowledge, such as George Washington or Abraham Lincoln. She then asks students to contribute an idea or a detail, which she lists on the blackboard (see Figure 3.5). Once a fairly healthy list is generated, Newman recommends that the class begin to connect those bits of information that seem related and observe patterns of meaning that seem to be emerging from the list. She urges them not to be overly concerned about the lack of orderliness in the original list of details or ideas (40).

FIGURE 3.5   Group Brainstorming

George Washington	*Abraham Lincoln*
First president	Self-made man
Man on a white horse	Assassinated
Crossing the Delaware	Grew up in a log cabin
Mt. Vernon	Freed the slaves
Chopped down a cherry tree	The Gettysburg Address
Valley Forge	Humble, eloquent
Great general	The Lincoln Monument

Although these lists are a true hodge-podge of information at this stage, some categories for organizing a comparison are already emerging, for example, Washington's and Lincoln's childhood experiences, their great accomplishments, and their public image today.

Clustering

Jackie Proett and Kent Gill, among others, recommend clustering, a kind of brainstorming, which, as they point out, "retains the rich development of data or ideas brainstorming offers, while adding an organizational element to the collection" (6). They believe that its visual element may stimulate "the flow of association" (6) for some students more effectively than the linear kind of organization usually used in brainstorming. The writer records the topic in the middle of the page, and then, using lines and circles, records related topics (see Figure 3.6). For some students the visual image is very useful for moving to the organizational stage of their planning.

Freewriting

Freewriting is more effective than brainstorming for generating connecting ideas early in the prewriting stage of the writing process. Peter Elbow describes freewriting this way:

The idea is simply to write about ten minutes (later on, fifteen or twenty). Don't stop for anything. Go quickly without rushing. Never stop to look

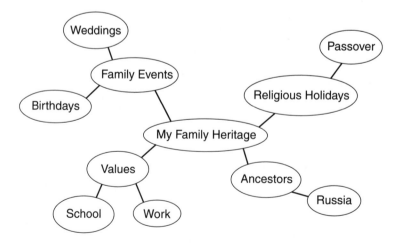

FIGURE 3.6   (Sample of Clustering) Topic: My Family's Heritage

back, to cross something out, to wonder how to spell something, to wonder what word or thought to use, or to think about what you are doing. If you can't think of a word or a spelling, just use a squiggle or else write "I can't think of it." Just put down something. The easiest thing is just to put down whatever is in your mind. If you get stuck it's fine to write "I can't think what to say, I can't think what to say" as many times as you want, or repeat the last word you wrote over and over again, or anything else. The only requirement is that you never stop. (3)

Donald Murray suggests that students take freewriting through a series of stages, asking different questions after each stage. I attended a seminar with Murray and the first thing he did was distribute 3 × 5 index cards. We "free wrote" until we completed one side of the card, and then he asked us, "What appeared on the card that you did not expect, or that you believe is the most significant idea on the card?" Then we wrote about that idea on the other side of the card for three minutes, and so on. The index cards help students to scrutinize their writing in small chunks for good ideas. The italicized sentences on the cards become the prompts for the new cards (see Figure 3.7).

The last sentences on the first two index cards contain the surprising information that the student chooses to develop further. Notice how the writer is closing in on a narrower version of the topic ("my family tradition") than she wrote about in her first freewriting. Her essay will focus on the role her parents play in keeping family traditions alive.

Heuristics

Systematic questioning, which is a very different approach to prewriting, can be more beneficial for some writers than brainstorming or freewriting techniques. Systematic questioning is based on the use of heuristics. A heuristic is defined by Linda Flower and John Hayes as "the codification of a useful technique . . . as an alternative to trial and error [which] can operate as a discovery procedure"(quoted in Neman 48). Richard Young and Alton Becker describe heuristics as: "A method of solving problems, a series of steps or questions which are likely to lead an intelligent analyst to a reasonable solution to a problem" (quoted in Neman 48). In plain language a heuristic is a set of guidelines, not to be followed slavishly, but to be applied to the problem in ways that help the problem solver arrive at a solution. For example, the five W's of journalism (who, what, when, where, and why) are powerful questions for gathering the information required by the typical news story. The five W's are called a heuristic because all five questions might not apply equally well to all news events. For example, the people element ("who") of some stories may require more details than the setting element ("where") of an event. These same questions can used as a heuristic for writing the personal essay.

Index Card 1

My family heritage is tied up with celebrations related to holidays and important family events, such as birthdays, weddings, and new additions to the family,—that is new babies. Although we do not all live near one another anymore, we always get to together as often as we can in addition to these celebrations. I am the youngest. My older brothers and sisters are married and have children. <u>My parents are still the hub of our family wheel.</u>

Index Card 2

My parents keep our family traditions alive. When we were young, they taught us the importance of being together for all events, happy or sad, which members of our family might experience. We learned to share in each other's happiness and sadness. But they also taught us the importance of celebrating religious and national holidays together. Thanksgiving is such a great time. My brothers come with their wives and children to meet us at my parents' home. <u>They still live in the same house where we all grew up.</u>

Index Card 3

One of the main reasons we are able to keep our family traditions alive is that my parents still live in the same house where we all grew up. Our house is filled with things that remind all of us of important family traditions. As you enter the house, you are reminded of all the wonderful times we have spent around the dining room table on holidays, birthdays, before weddings, and, yes, even before funerals.

FIGURE 3.7   Sample of Freewriting, Donald Murray's Approach

There are other heuristics that are far more complicated than the five W's, but students may have difficulty applying them. William Irmscher warns that "two conditions are important" for any heuristic to be useful as a prewriting device. First, it must be relatively simple so that we can readily keep it in mind as the need arises. A series of questions should probably be limited to five or seven. The second important condition is that the terms apply to more than one topic" (90). Edward Corbett's adaptation of Richard Larson's list of questions according to general topics, useful for students at all grade levels, meets this requirement (see Figure 3.8).

FIGURE 3.8   Larson's List of Questions

A. About Physical Objects

1. What are the physical characteristics of the object (shape, dimensions, materials, etc.)?
2. What sort of structure does it have?
3. What other object is it similar to?
4. How does it differ from things that resemble it?
5. Who or what produced it?
6. Who uses it? for what?

B. About Events

1. Exactly what happened?
2. What were its causes?
3. What were its consequences?
4. How was the event like or unlike similar events?
5. To what other events was it connected?
6. How might the event be changed or avoided?

C. About Abstract Concepts (e.g., democracy, justice)

1. How has the term been defined by others?
2. How do you define the term?
3. What other concepts have been associated with it?
4. In what ways has this concept affected the lives of people?
5. How might the concept be changed to work better?

D. About Propositions (statements to be proved or disproved)

1. What must be established before the reader will believe it?
2. What are the meanings of key words in the proposition?
3. By what kinds of evidence or argument can the proposition be proved or disproved?
4. What counterarguments must be confronted or refuted?
5. What are the practical consequences of the proposition?

Source: Edward P. J. Corbett, *The Little Rhetoric* (New York: John Wiley, 1977) 42–43. Copyright 1977. Reprinted by permission of Addison-Wesley Educational Publishers, Inc.

Instructors can develop their own prewriting questions. For example, here is a list of questions I give my students for writing about a person who has had a significant influence on their lives (see Figure 3.9). I explained that some of the questions might be more meaningful than others, and it is not necessary to use all of them.

The Computer and the Writing Process

For some students the computer can be a strong motivating device during the prewriting stage. Rick Monroe, in *Writing and Thinking with Computers: A Practical and Progressive Approach* (1993) says, "As a tool, the computer has increased the fluency of my reluctant writers. And as an ally, the computer has led ordinarily apathetic students to enjoy their work in the lab" (2). After Monroe assigns a paper, he gives his students an hour in the computer lab for prewriting. They can use any of the forms of prewriting we have discussed, brainstorming, freewriting, or systematic questioning. Monroe has created his own "heuristic lesson file," which includes many of the questions listed earlier. He says that some students like "invisible writing," which involves turning off the monitor and turning it back on to see what they have written. This technique is especially effective with students who may be too quick to edit when they are freewriting on the computer.

Other Prewriting Activities

Other activities, such as small group discussions, interviews, and debates, can help students during the prewriting stage. But for these approaches to be effective, students need some preparation. They must learn how to ask questions and how to be very tolerant of one another's ideas. Perhaps most important, they need to learn to be good listeners. Small group discussion, for example, can have several benefits. Conversation helps us to know what we

FIGURE 3.9   The Essay on a Person of Influence

1. Think of someone you admire. Is this person a family member, a friend, or a celebrity? Why have you chosen this person?

2. Discuss three admirable traits of this person.

3. How did this person influence your life? Did he or she influence your values, what you would like to do for a career . . . other important choices or decisions?

4. Describe one situation that shows how this person has had an important influence on your life.

5. Describe your present relationship with this person.

want to say. If students are all working on the same assignment, they will often stimulate each other's thinking about the topic. Group work can also help students to practice brainstorming, freewriting, clustering, and systematic questioning. Although we want our students to be able to use these techniques independently, they can become more comfortable with these techniques by experimenting with them in small groups.

Students can also interview one another about a particular topic as a technique for prewriting. In this case, they create the questions. The advantage of this approach is that the questions will reflect the students' interests. Other members in the group can take notes for the interview as they respond to the questions. An excellent discussion on interviewing techniques can be found in *Student-Centered Language Arts and Reading, K–12* (366–368) in which Moffett and Wagner advise students to prepare a list of questions before the interview. The questions in Figure 3.10 were prepared by one seventh grader who, with the aid of her classmates, interviewed her grandmother on the topic of childhood.

Group interviewing might work something like this. Bob says to his group: "Please interview me about my topic. I'm thinking of writing about my neighborhood. Ask me some questions. Take ten minutes to prepare a list of questions." As with other activities suggested throughout this text, teachers can help students learn how to use the interview during the prewriting process by modeling the process themselves. The instructor can offer to be the interviewer or the interviewee in the mock interview.

Debates and panel discussions on controversial topics can also stimulate ideas for writing. If you try this approach, be sure to give the participants a

FIGURE 3.10   Life Stages Interview Questions

1. What is your earliest memory?
2. What are some of your outstanding childhood memories?
3. What kinds of things made you happy during your childhood? What kinds of things did you enjoy doing?
4. What kinds of things made you sad? What kinds of things did you not like to do?
5. Do you have any brothers or sisters? If so, what is your relationship like with them?
6. Who were some of your favorite teachers? Subjects? Friends? Other? Why?
7. Did you have a nickname? Where did it come from?
8. Did you have a favorite song, poem, or book?
9. Where did you live? Did you like your house?
10. Any additional comments?

Sarah Lytle, "Life Stages Interview," n.d.

chance to prepare their opening remarks before the class and provide some training in the art of debate. Students are always somewhat apprehensive about performances before the entire class. Perhaps you can ask for volunteers if you choose this format. Other students can take notes and participate by discussing the merits of the arguments presented.

I will close this brief discussion on classroom activities and prewriting with an example from my own class on methods of teaching writing. Students in my course, Understanding the Composing Process, which I teach at La Salle every spring, were corresponding with students in an eighth grade classroom at St. Athanasius School in Philadelphia. The letters we received early in the semester were short and not very informative or lively. We guessed that a lesson on letter writing with a strong prewriting component might help. With the permission of their teacher, we arrived at St. Athanasius School one spring afternoon to conduct this lesson.

First, we asked the eighth graders to describe their reactions to the letter writing activity. Were they enjoying it? Was it a chore? They seemed very positive about the project, but said it was hard to know what to write about. We divided into small groups and talked about the kinds of letters we like to receive. Students were asked to discuss the topics of their favorite letters. Boys said they liked letters about sports, and girls mentioned popular music as a favorite topic. The La Salle students asked them if they would like to know more about us. We asked them to list the kinds of things they would like to know, and we, in turn, listed the kinds of things we would like to know about them. Some students were more shy than others, but everyone was intensely engaged by the discussion, even when they were just listening. Keep in mind that even when students are not saying much in group prewriting exercises, they still may be reaping the benefits of talk as a preliminary stage for writing. Much to our delight, the letters we received in future weeks were much longer and more interesting than the letters we received prior to the prewriting lesson.

The Process of Teaching Prewriting

You can use the same steps for teaching prewriting techniques regardless of which technique you introduce to your students.

- Explain the purpose of the technique.
- Illustrate the technique.
- Give students an opportunity to experiment with the technique and ask for feedback. (How did it feel to use the technique?)

Don't get discouraged if your students do not catch on to the prewriting activities immediately. Even after classroom practice, students' initial prewriting efforts may not be successful. Some students may not gain any benefits from prewriting activities for a particular assignment. Maybe they already have a headstart on their topic, or the type of prewriting activity suggested was not useful to them.

Assure your students that the same techniques do not work for all writers. Some writers prefer free association kinds of techniques, like brainstorming and freewriting, whereas others prefer systematic questioning (probably less popular with beginning writers). Some writers prefer isolation and quiet when they begin a paper, whereas others need the company and support of others. I prefer conversation. I cannot begin a new writing project without first discussing my ideas with a colleague, a sympathetic friend, or my husband. Not only do I need some reassurance that I am on the "right track," but they often help me to rethink some ideas and add new ideas that I had not thought about before our conversations took place.

Do not forget that all prewriting techniques require students to delay gratification and accept the idea that they cannot proceed immediately to writing the final paper. We all have the impulse to start writing, to try to complete our writing projects as soon as possible. It is only through repeated modeling and practice that students may begin to see the benefits of prewriting strategies. When students use prewriting techniques, if drafting becomes easier and if the quality of their papers begins to improve, then you have a fighting chance to convince your students of the benefits of using prewriting strategies. Daniel Sheridan, in *Teaching Secondary English: Readings and Applications*, offers some good advice about teaching writing, which especially applies to teaching prewriting techniques:

> When we teachers make an assignment, we are often working from a generalization about what most students need to get the job done. This is inevitable. But just as inevitable is variation from that norm, the different ways that students will work out the process in their real lives. And this disparity between the teacher's agenda and the student's individual needs applies everywhere: in the kinds of topics students choose, in the ways they explore those topics, in whether they find a particular prewriting activity useful or a waste of time, in the time needed for deadlines, in everything.
>
> There is a difference between the process suggested by the classroom situation and the real process of writing. There is no ideal solution to the problem. It is, in one way or another, part of every writing situation. (186)

Writing Time: Drafting and Revising

It is not easy to move from the prewriting stage to the drafting stage. The classroom, once lively and buzzing with interaction, now becomes a quiet place. If students have been in writing groups, they must now return to their desks and begin the lonely business of drafting. In "Helping Children Start to Write," Phillip Lopate stresses the difference between the drafting stage and prewriting class activities. He says that writing is an "entirely different activity" than discussion and urges teachers not to "fail to take into account the wide gulf that separates the social euphoria of the collective poem from the lonely individual effort" (138–139). Though he is discussing the writing process in the context of writing poetry, the same is true for all kinds of writing. At some point the writer must be alone with his thoughts, his feelings, and his notes, if he has them. Lopate suggests trying to make the classroom environment as comfortable as possible during the drafting process, freeing up students to sit wherever they wish, even on the floor.

Tom Romano agrees:

> *I seek to establish in my classroom a "studio atmosphere". . . a place conducive to making writing. Noise level and movement will vary, depending on what students are doing . . . "Class," I say, "find your spots." I've talked about each of them finding that special place in the room where they are safe and comfortable, where they feel naturally happy and strong, a place where they can write well. Their spot. . . . Terry moves his desk so it faces the wall. Cheryl and her friends seek out a piece of carpet in the front corner of the room. They lie on their stomachs, writing pads before them. Three or four students move their desks closer to the windows where the light is better . . . Bonnie and Kristi, two of the best writers in class, have written passes to the library, where they like to work. I sign them out and they're on their way. "May the Muse be with you, I call after them." (63–64)*

Romano permits students to speak to each other, but tries to discourage them from doing so. He says, ". . . I want to ensure that my students have extended time to concentrate fully on creating a draft. Students who are idly talking fail to begin that concentration" (63–64).

But "finding one's spot" is hardly the only problem writers face when they begin to draft. As we have learned from research, cognitive overload during the drafting stage can paralyze the writer even when the writer has sufficient material to start writing. You can help your students overcome cognitive overload ("I must think about my sentences, the organization of the paper, etc.") by reminding them that most professional writers realize the impossibility of writing the perfect first draft. On the contrary, most experienced writers view the first draft as an opportunity to transfer notes and thoughts into connected prose. They worry about the "big picture" rather than choosing the right word. Flower and Hayes call the first draft "writer based prose." The writer is writing to herself to make sure she knows what she is trying to say.

However, experienced writers do begin to establish an organizational pattern during the first draft, although they keep in mind that the organization of ideas can always be modified. Some teachers believe that students should be taught some basic organizational schemes, such as the comparison/contrast framework, before they need to use them. If, for example, a student knows the two formats for a comparison paper—divide the paper in half, and discuss all of A and then all of B, or compare and contrast similar features of A and B (A/B A/B A/B pattern)—then decision making about organization during the drafting stage may become more automatic.

Outlines can also help to relieve cognitive overload. Although formal outlines are often not necessary for short papers, some kind of outline may be helpful to your students, even if they have a general idea as to how they want to organize their papers. Simply a list of items indicating which goes first, second, and third may help, if the paper is very short. The block outline is another technique for organization that is not as structured as the traditional Roman numeral style outline. The student using a block outline asks, "How many blocks of material will I need?" and "What material goes into each block?" This strategy for planning requires that the student "chunk" material (Lindemann 163–165). For example, in an essay comparing George Washington and Abraham Lincoln, the blocks might look like this:

Paragraph 1 Open with a story about each president that demonstrates a particular quality.

Say something about the different times in which they lived.

Paragraphs 2 and 3 Use paragraphs 2 and 3 for comparing their childhoods, especially their educations. Explain how they had no formal education.

Paragraphs 4 and 5 Describe their early careers.

Paragraphs 6 and 7 Describe their major achievements.

Paragraph 8 Sum up. Who has more prestige in the eyes of Americans today?

Drafting will also seem less formidable for students if they know they can receive help from their instructors during the drafting process, whether they write at home or at school. However, for some students, composing the first draft in class is not possible. In the collaborative letter writing project referred to earlier between the students at St. Athanasius and La Salle University, everything was going fine during the prewriting phase of the lesson. However, the drafting phase of the lesson was not as successful. The eighth graders had difficulty making the transition from prewriting to drafting. They seemed very self-conscious about writing in class, although their teacher was not present. We reassured the students that they could complete their drafts at home. The lesson to be learned from our experience is that, although you may want to have students begin a draft in class in order for them to receive immediate feedback and encouragement, be sure to give them the option of completing it at home. Especially in the junior high grades, where some students may still have handwriting problems, writing in class may be laborious. We noticed that several students wrote very slowly. Each sentence required considerable effort. In schools that have computers available to students, writing drafts in class may be more practical, though some students will still want to write their drafts in the privacy of their own homes.

Revision

Revision, as research has demonstrated, is part of the writing process, from the moment we start to write. Writers are always revising; as we write a sentence, we often change it before we complete it. Some research shows that students revise more frequently when they are writing using the computer as a word processor. They often make minor changes as they write. However, once a first draft is completed, revision takes on new meaning. Experienced writers start reviewing their drafts for holistic issues, such as the organization and the development of their ideas. Yet, in a study by the National Association of Educational Progress (NAEP), which periodically tests the writing abilities of students aged nine, thirteen, and seventeen, when students were asked to write for a given period of time and then rewrite for another given period of time,

> *approximately 90 percent of the students did nothing during the rewrite time. Only five percent of the few who tried to revise their writing improved their writing to a measurable degree; another five percent downgraded their writing to a measurable degree; all other students who attempted revision made no measurable change in their writing. This data holds true across age levels. (Weaver 44)*

Revision should be the stage of writing when writers begin to transform their work for an audience, if they are confident about what they want to say. Writer-based prose must be converted to reader-based prose. However, students, like all writers, are reluctant to revise for several reasons, all too familiar to any writer.

Reason 1
For all writers the greatest stumbling block to revision is that writing is hard work. Every sentence requires effort. To actually delete any of those sentences,

after all of the effort that went into crafting them, is too hurtful. We hate to delete what took so much trouble to write in the first place. As I wrote the draft of this text, although I kept reminding myself that it was only a first draft, I kept secretly, illogically hoping that it would be the last. Maybe just this one time, I would strike it rich. No such luck. I have rewritten this chapter three times as of this morning, and will probably rewrite it again. If you keep writing with your students, you will remind them that they are in good company if they find revision painful.

One of my favorite stories about students' reluctance to revise involves a perplexed freshman I taught quite a few years ago. When reviewing Jodi's draft I remarked, "Jodi, either the first paragraph or the second paragraph probably needs to be eliminated. They seem to be about different subjects." She did not answer me at first, but just stared at her paper. I mistakenly thought she was trying to decide what she wanted to say in her essay, but, when she finally looked up she said, "Well, I guess I will keep the second paragraph because it is longer." My student could not bear to part with her sentences.

Reason 2

A writer's response to his or her writing is very much conditioned by what he or she has already written. We fall in love with our own words. It's hard to resee the material from the point of view of the audience. As Flower and Hayes have demonstrated, reseeing the material from the reader's perspective requires much practice. Writing my first grant proposal several years ago to the National Endowment for the Humanities (NEH), a government agency that funds faculty development programs among its other projects, taught me this lesson. Although this was a collaborative project, my coauthor and I were surprised when, after sending a draft of the proposal for review to the NEH, the program officer made extensive recommendations for revising the proposal. When we originally sent it to him, we were very confident that we had a good proposal. It took us several weeks before we could admit that we had to revise to meet the requirements of the NEH audience.

Reason 3

Beginning writers often do not like to read their own writing. They make such statements as "I'm such a bad writer, I hate to read my own writing," or "My first draft is the best I can do. I can't improve it." This is when they need lots of reassurance about their writing. You may need to undo their own negative attitudes toward their writing abilities developed as a result of many past failures. I wish I had a dollar for every student who has told me during our first writing conference, "By the way, writing is my worst subject." One of my students, commenting about his high school writing experience, said, "I felt that expectations were too high and that I could never be a good writer" (Daniel File). Students will not reread their papers if they believe that their writing is terrible to begin with and beyond help.

Reason 4

Beginning writers often don't know what to think about when they are revising. Simply asking them to "demonstrate revision," as one of my own children's teachers in ninth grade optimistically recommended, is hardly sufficient. My daughter conscientiously crossed out several words in her essay in very visible black ink to meet the revision requirement. To revise students need to know the general issues writers think about when they revise, and they must be able to evaluate what they have written. The National Association of Educational Progress has identified a series of categories that can serve as a basis for discussing the kinds of revision that are possible (Weaver 45, see Figure 3.11). Of course, these categories would need to be introduced gradually, with many opportunities for practice in each category.

FIGURE 3.11   NAEP Categories for Revision

1. Total or Holistic Revision: A totally different response is written, or revisions are so major that the difference between the original and revised papers cannot be described by other categories.

2. Informational: Additions are made in the form of facts, ideas, attitudes, qualities, details, comparisons; irrelevant information and unnecessary repetition are deleted.

3. Organizational: Sentences, parts of sentences, groups of sentences, or paragraphs are rearranged, or reordered. A sentence or section is moved to another location in the paper.

4. Connectional or Transitional: Connectives or short transitional sections are added or deleted. One kind of transitional link or connective is substituted for another.

5. Continuational: The original paper is extended by adding to the end of the paper.

6. Stylistic: In an attempt to achieve greater accuracy, precision, concreteness, emphasis, or euphony, the writer substitutes a word, phrase, or sentence for another.

7. Grammatical: A change is made in verb forms, subject/verb agreement, pronoun/antecedent agreement, and so on to conform to grammatical conventions.

8. Mechanical: A change is made in spelling, punctuation, underlining, or capitalization.

There is no point asking students to revise for features of writing they have not yet learned. For example, if students are to revise introductions and conclusions, they need to know the characteristics of a good introduction and conclusion to an expository paper as well as several alternative approaches for writing introductions and conclusions. In the early stages of teaching revision less stress should be placed on categories 7 and 8 in Figure 3.11 (grammar and mechanics) because, as we have said perviously, students tend to think of revision only in these terms.

Reason 5

Beginning writers often don't know how to approach revision. They are surprised to discover that experienced writers rarely revise alone but often ask a trusted colleague, friend, or family member to read and respond to their writing. Experienced writers often belong to a writer's group. One of my friends, who is a freelance writer, says her writing group, which meets once a week, is an invaluable part of her writing life. Group members take turns submitting their drafts for review prior to each meeting. Beginning writers should be taught how to benefit from responses to their writing both in and out of school.

Techniques for Encouraging and Teaching Revision

There are several strategies for encouraging revision. Some of them are the same ones you will use to motivate your students to use prewriting and drafting techniques.

1. Keep writing with your students and sharing your drafts and the drafts of other writers. Students must be reminded that revision is a natural part of the writing process.

2. Positive feedback is a must during the revision process. Compliment your students for even minor revision efforts at the beginning of the semester.

3. Isolate particular features of writing for revision rather than asking students to revise the whole essay. For example, focus on revising introductions and conclusions after a lesson on how to write introductions and conclusions.

4. Assign fewer papers with the understanding that each paper will be written two or three times. If emphasis is placed on revising a few papers rather than writing many papers, students may be more positive about revising.

5. Have students read each other's writing. Students can help one another improve their writing and can often see the problems in another student's writing more easily than they can see problems in their own writing.

Peer Writing Groups

One of the most popular strategies for encouraging revision is the student writing group, often called the peer writing group or writing workshop. Zemelman and Daniels say, "Of all the instructional strategies developed during the first wave of writing-process pedagogy, the writing workshop is probably the best developed, most fully tested and widely proven method" (89). Some composition specialists, such as Nancy Atwell, recommend that the student writing workshop should be the primary format for writing instruction.

Instructors often become quite discouraged when they first attempt peer review. The use of writing groups is one of the most frequently abandoned strategies of writing process instruction; many teachers will tell you that they tried peer editing and it just does not work. They often cite two reasons: Student comments are not sufficiently specific, and they do not stay on task. Instead, they tell their classmates that their essays are fine and they let the conversation wander to subjects such as lunch, the movies, and so on. They find it hard to concentrate on writing. One reason offered for their vague responses is that students are reluctant to critique one another's work, especially to say anything that could be interpreted as a negative comment. Although I would agree that students are afraid to hurt their classmates' feelings, I believe that students' lack of confidence in their ability to judge another student's work is probably more often the reason for their vague comments rather than embarrassment. Students can often be heard saying, "Yeah, that's really good," or "I think you wrote an interesting paper" because they are reluctant to pass judgment.

There are several strategies that instructors can use to make these groups operate more effectively. Providing checklists to direct the work of the peer group can help students be more specific. These checklists can be comprehensive, they can include criteria for evaluating the whole essay, or they can be limited to specific features of writing under discussion. The checklist in Figure 3.12 was designed for reviewing the summary, the one in Figure 3.13 for reviewing the personal essay.

Eventually, students need to be weaned from checklists. Neil Elman from Hanover Park Regional High School District in New Jersey recommends a four-stage checklist weaning process. In the initial phase of responding to student papers, students respond only to the presence or absence of specified qualities. They do not illustrate or explain their responses (see Figure 3.14).

At the second stage students support their comments with specific references to the text. At the final stage, when they have internalized the qualities of effective written composition and formed the concepts necessary for effective feedback, students no longer need a checklist. While they are listening to the paper as it is read aloud, they take notes in three columns labeled "strengths,"

FIGURE 3.12 Comprehensive Checklist: The Summary

1. Has the document to be summarized been identified appropriately (title, author, publication information)?
2. Are the main ideas in the original document clearly stated?
3. Are the relationships between the ideas clearly indicated?
4. Are important examples and explanations included?
5. Is all basic information (names, costs, places, dates, etc.) included?
6. Is the length of the summary appropriate, in view of the purpose of and audience for the summary?
7. Has the author avoided interjecting his or her own opinion or additional information?
8. Is sentence structure, spelling, and punctuation correct?

FIGURE 3.13 Limited Checklist: The Development of Ideas in a Personal Essay

1. Does the introduction include background material? Underlines sentences that include background material?
2. Does the middle of the paper include sufficient detail (names, costs, places, dates, etc.)?
3. Does the middle of the paper include anecdotes or short stories?
4. Does the conclusion include a summary of important ideas in the essay?

FIGURE 3.14 Checklist Response without Comments

1. After reading the introductory paragraph, do you have a good idea of what the author intends to say in the composition?
2. Does the beginning of the composition make you want to continue reading?
3. Do you think that the author has said enough about each subject in the paper?
4. Do you think that the paper has an effective ending?

"weaknesses," and "questions." The video *Beginning Writing Groups* (Hale, Mallon, and Wyche-Smith) models this approach. Students read their papers aloud twice while the other students in their group take notes. After the student reads, the group tells the author their reactions. After seeing the video, students in my composition class voiced surprise at the honesty of the students in the film and their ability to be specific. They also observed in the film the student-author telling his peers that he disagrees with some of their suggestions. The student-author can accept or reject recommendations by his peers. The paper is always his. I have found this film to be one of the most effective tools for training writing groups.

The composition of the groups can also contribute to their success. Groups should be fairly small to ensure that all students receive responses to their drafts during a typical class period. Three students in a group works well. Although some instructors favor assigning the students to groups, I find that when students choose their own group, they work more effectively. To give them even more control over the writing groups, I give them the option of switching groups, though they rarely do.

As with other practices we teach students, peer review must be practiced for students to learn how to do it well. If you use small groups for other kinds of instruction, such as for teaching literature, then students will naturally be more at ease in writing groups than in classrooms in which there is relatively little group work. When writing groups meet frequently, students become more adept at responding to their peers' work.

For example, in Len Schutzman's twelfth grade class, one writing group's progress illustrates the benefits of long association. Schutzman reports:

> Like others in English 12, Kim, Katherine, Teresa and Terry were wary of writing—school writing at least—when they entered Len's class. In their case study interviews Kim and Terry said they liked writing in journals, for themselves, but only as Terry wrote about Kim, "where people won't see it." Teresa wrote that Katherine "tends to dislike writing;" "when words flow she doesn't mind it." And Teresa herself had come to "hate" it—even "writing letters." Yet together they wrote, encouraged one another to write about what mattered to each, and developed a group style that supported each individual's struggle.
>
> Part of the strength of the group we all agreed, came from long association. Theirs was the only group in the class that stayed together. "We know each other's ways of working," said Terry in May. "For instance, Teresa sometimes drops characters in a story—she just forgets about them—but we know to watch for that. We remind her to pick them up again . . ."
>
> Kim was the most painfully shy about reading her work out loud, and Teresa most sharply self-critical, but all understood shyness and self-doubt. They calmed each other. When one prefaced her reading with a ritual disclaimer ("It's dumb," or "I just dashed this off ten minutes last night—it's no good"), the others would wait patiently for her embarrassment to subside, then gently encourage her to go on. . . .
>
> Once discussion of a piece got under way, separate voices blended in a murmur of encouragement and helpful questioning. Nods and a chorus of

*"yeah" and "uh-huhs" punctuated discussion: questions moved it along.
"What's going to happen next?" "Is it from your point of view?" (163–164)*

Peer review can also be conducted on the computer. Assuming you are teaching your writing class in a computer lab, you can conduct what Rick Monroe calls an "electronic read-around." Monroe explains that students bring their text to the screen and then move over two or three chairs to a classmate's computer. They read the whole text and then add their comments to the right on the screen, using the Cap Lock key. They shift seats every ten minutes, and by the end of the period, each student has several students' responses to his or her draft. Monroe cites these advantages: Students read pieces from classmates not in their writing groups; premature editing is delayed. Students need to print out their files and review them before editing.

Perhaps this comment by a Japanese student, who is still struggling to learn how to speak and write English, best sums up some of the advantages of peer groups, whether they are on-line or not: "In this class I actually learned to use revision, which is the most helpful skill for improving the paper assignment. This technique was from my classmates. I also could listen to other students' papers and could compare my paper to others and realize the level of my paper and writing."

Publishing

Publishing is the last stage of the writing process. Professional writers want to publish, whether it is an article or a whole book. One of the most valuable techniques for encouraging good writing is giving students the opportunity for publication. Publication as a way of motivating writing seems to work at all levels, from first grade or second grade when students write "books" for students in other grades, to the junior, senior, and college levels with students writing for school publications or the local newspaper.

Although publishing student writing is certainly not a new idea, it has often been limited to the writing of our best students. We are all familiar with essay contests, schoolwide contests, and writing contests. Many are conducted by organizations such as the National Council of Teachers of English. Also there are many young adult periodicals that welcome student submissions. In *Market Guide for Young Writers,* Henderson includes lists of such periodicals. Perhaps the easiest way for students to publish their work is to get a list of electronic places to publish. These are growing in number. For example, *Edge* is described as "a magazine for sophisticated teenagers who are serious about information opportunities. This e-zine [computer talk for magazine] also provides opportunities for teens to publish stories, articles, etc."

Mid-Link—The Electronic Magazine for Kids in the middle grades invites students, ages ten to fifteen, to contribute their writing and art (Bread Loaf School of English Educational Resources 4).

For publication to be effective as a strategy for motivating writing, the opportunity should be available to all students. In recent years I have been incorporating "publication" in several of my writing courses. At the beginning of the semester, I suggest that we focus our essays on a theme of interest to a general audience and produce a class publication for distribution to the school on the topic. For example, one class chose "Philadelphia Rediscovered" as its theme. I point out that everyone has an opportunity to revise one of their papers for the publication, and the class will be responsible for developing the book and editing it. My students greet the idea with enthusiasm. They like working toward the goal of seeing their work in print. Students help each other choose the papers targeted for publication. Eventually they design the cover and write the introduction to the booklet and to each essay. Class time used at the end of the semester for editorial meetings is time well spent.

The opportunity for publication influences the class's attitude toward the writing process at all stages but especially during the prewriting and revising stages. Students choose their topics carefully, trying hard to find topics that will have wide appeal, and after writing their essays and receiving feedback from the class and me, they revise and then revise again. Knowing that the audience is made up of students, faculty and administrators, family and friends, as well as me and their classmates is a strong motivator. Suddenly they are no longer just students but a team of writers working together to publish their work. As I work on this book, the second edition of "Philadelphia Rediscovered" is going to press. (See Figure 3.15 for the cover and table of contents of the first edition of "Philadelphia Rediscovered.")

Conclusion

The techniques presented in this chapter are based on theoretical understandings that explain how writers think and how they feel as they become a part of a writing community. As teachers we should introduce our students to options, and we should do everything in our power to encourage them to learn the behaviors and strategies that will serve them well as writers. When we get stuck, when we feel as if we are failing, we should praise our students for what they have accomplished thus far, for trying to employ even one strategy we have taught them, and then we should be patient. The writing process is a set of behaviors, a way of thinking, doing, and feeling about writing. All of these behaviors take time to develop.

PHILADELPHIA REDISCOVERED

Advanced Composition

January 1995—May 1995

Continued

FIGURE 3.15 "Philadelphia Rediscovered"

Philadelphia Rediscovered

Rocky. Cream Cheese. Brotherly Love. The Liberty Bell. Especially for us out-of-towners, these phrases once rang in our ears upon hearing any mention of Philadelphia. The *City as Classroom* project forced us to go beyond these cliches and discover what makes Philadelphia tick.

The papers that follow, written for our Advanced Composition class, were not dreaded, last-minute assignments thrust upon us in the name of conventional teaching. Instead, they are the result of our own questions and research, developed within guidelines, through individual choice and personal intrigue.

Sports, music, history, architecture, movies, schooling, current issues, and Philadelphia neighborhoods were just a few of the paper topics written about in our class relating to Philadelphia. The topics that each student chose to write about proved to the class that behind the everyday tourist attractions, there is much more to be rediscovered within the city.

The *City as Classroom* project was a cohesive element in Advanced Composition. This booklet is a presentation of our new knowledge, our rediscoveries in Philadelphia.

Alicia Bessette and Shelly Halloran

FIGURE 3.15 *Continued*

Table of Contents

FIGURE 3.15   *Continued*

Adapted and reprinted by permission of Alicia Bessette and Shelly Halloran.

Questions for Discussion and Writing

1. How did you learn to write? Complete the survey in Figure 3.2. What role did school play in the development of your writing ability? (Read Eric Kellich's report on "How I Learned to Write," Appendix 3c).

2. Discuss your present attitude toward writing and your writing behaviors. How do you feel about writing? What kinds of assignments do you like best? How do you use writing apart from school? Do you keep a diary or a journal?

3. Describe your composing process. You may want to use one of the questionnaires in the chapter for this question.

4. Describe your composing process for a paper that you have been assigned recently.

5. What kinds of prewriting strategies work best for you? Choose a topic you can write about without doing research and try several of the prewriting strategies for retrieving information from memory. Which prewriting strategy helped you to generate the most information?

6. Write about your past experiences in student writing groups. What were the benefits and limitations of student writing groups? How could the limitations have been avoided?

7. Discuss an idea in this chapter that is new to you. Discuss parts of the chapter that can help you to improve your own writing.

8. Read a book by an author who describes his or her development as a writer (e.g., *Growing Up* by Russell Baker, or *One Writer's Beginnings* by Eudora Welty).

References

Atwell, Nancy. *In the Middle: New Understandings about Writing, Reading and Learning.* Portsmouth, NH: Boynton Cook, 1998.

Baker, Russell. *Growing Up.* New York: Penguin, 1995.

Blume, Judy. *Are You There God? It's Me Margaret.* New York: Dell, 1991.

—. *Tales of a Fourth Grade Nothing.* New York: Dutton, 1972.

Bread Loaf School of English Educational Resources. *Electronic Places to Publish.* Online posting. http://tigger.clemson.edu/bnet/resources/comp.html. Internet. 18 Dec. 1997.

Bruffee, Kenneth. "Thinking and Writing as Social Acts." *Thinking, Reasoning, and Writing.* Eds. Elaine Maimon, Barbara Nodine, and Finbarr O'Connor. New York: Longman, 1989.

Burkehardt, Diane, Diane Burkhardt, Eighth Grade. *Through Teacher's Eyes. Portraits of Writing Teachers at Work.* Eds. Sondra Perl and Nancy Wilson. Portsmouth, NH: Heinemann, 1986.

Cleary, Linda Miller. "Affect and Cognition in the Writing Process of Eleventh Graders: A Study of Concentration and Motivation." *Written Communication* 8.4 (1991): 473–505.

———. *From the Other Side of the Desk: Students Speak Out about Writing.* Portsmouth, NH: Heinemann-Boynton/Cook, 1991.

Corbett, Edward P. J. *The Little Rhetoric.* New York: John Wiley and Sons, 1977.

Elbow, Peter. *Writing without Teachers.* New York: Oxford University Press, 1973.

Emig, Janet. *The Composing Process of Twelfth Graders.* NCTE Research Report No. 13. Urbana, IL: NCTE, 1971.

Flower, Linda, "Writer Based Prose: A Cognitive Basis for Problems in Writing." *College English* 41 (1979): 19–37.

Flower, Linda, and John R. Hayes. "The Cognition of Discovery: Defining a Rhetorical Problem." *The Writing Teacher's Sourcebook.* 2nd ed. Eds. Gary Tate and Edward P. J. Corbett. New York: Oxford University Press, 1988.

Gallo, Donald, compiler and editor. *Speaking for Ourselves.* Urbana, IL: NCTE, 1991.

———. *Speaking for Ourselves Too.* Urbana, IL: NCTE, 1993.

Glatthorn, Allan. "Analysis of the Composing Process of a Professional Writer." Unpublished materials, 1976.

Hale, Connie, Tim Mallon, and Susan Wyche-Smith. *Beginning Writing Groups.* (Video) Tacoma, WA: Wordshop Productions, 1991.

Hemingway, Ernest. (Interview) *Writers at Work: The Paris Interviews.* Ed. George Plimpton. New York: The Viking Press, 1963.

———. *A Farewell to Arms.* New York: Scribner, 1995.

Henderson, Kathy. *Market Guide for Writers.* White Hall, VA: Shoe Tree Press, 1990.

Irmscher, William. *Teaching Expository Writing.* New York: Holt, Rinehart and Winston, 1979.

Lindemann, Erika. *A Rhetoric for Writing Teachers.* 3rd ed. New York: Oxford University Press, 1987.

Lopate, Phillip. "Helping Children Start to Write." *Research on Composing: Points of Departure.* Eds. Charles Cooper and Lee Odell. Urbana, IL: NCTE, 1978.

Lytle, Sarah. "Life Stages Interview." n.d.

Lytle, Susan L., and Morton Botel. *The Pennsylvania Framework for Reading, Writing, and Talking across the Curriculum.* Harrisburg: The Pennsylvania Department of Education, 1990.

Moffett, James, and Betty Jane Wagner. *Student-Centered Language Arts and Reading, K–12.* Portsmouth, NH: Heinemann-Boynton/Cook, 1992.

Monroe, Rick. *Teaching Ideas and Topics: Electronic Read-Arounds and Other Computer Writing.* Email:webmaster@ncte.org.

———. *Writing and Thinking with Computers.* Urbana, IL: NCTE, 1993.

Murray, Donald. *A Writer Teaches Writing.* 2nd ed. Boston: Houghton Mifflin, 1985.

Neman, Beth. *Teaching Students to Write.* Columbus, OH: Charles E. Merrill Publishing Co., 1980.

Perl, Sondra, and Nancy Wilson. *Through Teacher's Eyes: Portraits of Writing Teachers at Work.* Portsmouth, NH: Heinemann, 1986.

Plimpton, George, Ed. *Writers at Work: The Paris Interviews.* Second Series. New York: Viking Press, 1963.

Proett, Jackie, and Kent Gill. *The Writing Process in Action: A Handbook for Teachers.* Urbana, IL: NCTE, 1986.

Romano, Tom. *Clearing the Way: Working with Teen-Age Writers.* Portsmouth, NH. Heinemann, 1987.

Schutzman, Len. "Twelfth Grade." *Through Teacher's Eyes: Portraits of Writing Teachers at Work.* Eds. Sondra Perl and Nancy Wilson. Portsmouth, NH: Heinemann, 1986.

Shaughnessy, Mina. *Errors and Expectations.* New York: Oxford University Press, 1977.

Sheridan, Daniel. *Teaching Secondary English: Readings and Applications.* New York: Longman, 1993.

Sommers, Nancy. "Revision of Student Writers and Experienced Adult Writers." *The Writing Teacher's Source Book.* 2nd ed. Eds. Gary Tate and Edward Corbett, New York: Oxford University Press, 1988.

Walvoord, Barbara. *Helping Students Write Well.* New York: MLA, 1986.

Weaver, Francis E., and M. Lynn Smith. *Expressive Writing: A Workshop Manual.* Cincinnati, OH: Cincinnati Public Schools, 1985.

Weiss, M. Jerry. *From Writers to Students: The Pleasures and Pains of Writing.* Newark, DE: IRA, 1979.

Welty, Eudora. *One Writer's Beginnings.* New York: Warner Books, 1984.

Zemelman, Steven, and Harvey Daniels. *A Community of Writers.* Portsmouth, NH: Heinemann, 1988.

Zindel, Paul. *Confessions of a Teen-Age Baboon.* New York: Bantam, 1984.

———. *The Pigman.* Glenview, NY: Harper Collins, 1984.

APPENDIX

Appendix 3a: Summary of Judy Trachtenberg's Writing Process

Eric M. Kellich   January 23, 1997

English 300   Margot Soven

   Professor Judy Trachtenberg's discussion on the
writing process brought life to the ideas examined in
the readings. In the beginning of the discussion,
Trachtenberg explained how she prepared herself for the
demands of writing a book about families with behavior
disorder children. In order to become familiar with her
subject, she had to interview afflicted families and
research relevant data. What is enabling Trachtenberg
to pursue her writing ambitions is her desire and
discipline. She also stressed the need for writers to
become involved in writing groups. These groups allow
the writer to become more comfortable with both giving
and receiving criticism. Writing groups are a helpful
source for important comment that writers may overlook
in their own writing. When writing, she suggests that
the writer give himself or herself ample time to warm up
mentally and block out all distractions. It is crucial
for writers to discover the best time for their optimal
writing. Trachtenberg mentioned the importance of
revision as the key to successful writing. The coherent
readability of a writer's work is the by-product of
quality revision.

Adapted and reprinted by permission of Eric M. Kellich.

Appendix 3b: Portfolio Audit

Ryan D. Barrett
September 25, 1995
Portfolio Audit #2

What's in stock?—In my writing section, I have 2 drafts of my absurd short story called First and Last Memories. I have a snapshot first draft called Picture of Chaos that I wrote about a picture that I took where everything looked wrong, or distorted, in some way. I have a few pieces that have no name. Two I wrote when I was really angry at my father, and I couldn't get the anger out in any other way than writing. I have one Quicky, the first one that we did, the first day of class. You commented on it and handed it back, so I put it in my portfolio. I have two poems about completely different things. One (which I read in class) is about how "artificial" our world is. The other is about this girl who was staring at me when I went into Temple University with my mom. In my logs section, I have one that I wrote on There's a Man in the Habit of Hitting Me Over the Head With an Umbrella. I am planning on writing some more on a few short stories, one of which being Mother. Maybe I'll do that tonight. And, I have one Inquiry on the tours that we took for on of our Quickies. It isn't finished yet, but it's a short story about a crazy principal.

What's on the Backorder?—I have to finish my short story about the crazy principal. I'm not really sure where I'll go with that, but I think that I have made a great start. I've really been thinking about the story, Mother. I think that if i have time, I'll write a log on that tonight.

<u>Which Pieces are Working?</u>—I really want to continue my crazy principal story. The beginning part that I have is kind of comical and strange, and I like that. When I have some extra time, I'll sit down and really go to town on that story. I have some really solid poems, but I don't think that they are going to grow. I love the way they are right now. However, I might use bits and pieces of them in other stories that I might write.

<u>How are Your Work Habits?</u>—I spend a great deal of my time writing. I probably spend about 75% of my day writing. It's kind of a habit. I always doodle, and write little things all over everywhere. My mother always comments on this, she says that I'm destined to be a writer. When I'm writing a story, I'll usually write at the computer. But when I write a poem, it's usually very spontaneous, and sometimes there isn't a computer near. So, I'll hand write them. Today in study hall, we were reading short stories. I got almost everyone there to read <u>Dinnertime.</u> Everyone kept asking me if they could read it; the book circulated around the whole room. I have been reading A LOT of short stories from both of my <u>Sudden Fiction</u> books.

<u>Is Your Log Up To Date?</u>—I have read all the excerpts, but haven't responded to all of them. Some of them just don't grab me like others. I hope to respond to <u>Mother</u> and maybe <u>Dinnertime</u> or <u>Snapshot: Harvey Cedars, 1948,</u> soon.

<u>How Have You Contributed To the Studio?</u>—I participate and contribute to the studio a great deal. I read my poem to the class a few days ago, therefore sharing it and putting it into the studio for others to talk and to think about. I comment on, and give suggestions on other peoples writing. I share my writing and read others writing. I give constructive criticism to writing by anyone. I like how I am in the studio, and I have fun doing it, too.

Appendix 3c: How I Learned to Write

Eric M. Kellich   January 21, 1997
English 300   Margot Soven

My recollection of how I learned to write is quite
vague. What I can remember from my elementary Catholic
school days is that penmanship was of vital importance.
I distinctly recall that how well you wrote in cursive
was just as important as the content of your assignment.
I quickly developed a disdain for writing because of the
pressure. My mother and older sister did a little more
than just help me through my assignments. They virtually
wrote most of my assignments for me. In retrospect, I
realize how much damage this caused because I never gave
myself the opportunity to acquire basic writing skills.
When tracking came along I was in sixth grade and, not
surprisingly, I found myself in track three. All of my
fears of inadequacy were reinforced, and I withdrew
further into an academic abyss. My English grades were
straight Cs, up to and including high school. What
really makes me mad is that instead of passing me along
to higher grades, my teachers should have considered
ways to help build up my skills and confidence.

In all honesty, my first real learning experience
with writing occurred in college. I really felt as if I
was learning everything for the first time. My grades at
the undergraduate level were virtually the same as my
grades in high school. I never considered planning,
drafting, and revising when I was writing my papers.
When I think about how I wrote papers, the first draft
was the final draft.

Writing did not make sense to me until about six
years ago. I started to become interested in reading
plays and novels. It was at this point that I started

to admire the craft of writing. I moved to London to
study communications and theater and found myself an
internship with United Press International. The position
just fell into my lap, and I was immediately
overwhelmed. I certainly did not consider myself to be
much of a writer when I started, but I quickly learned
from professional journalists. I have to say that one of
my most memorable writing experiences happened when my
editor showed me a copy of one of my articles published
in a newspaper. It proved to me that I was capable of
anything if I worked hard enough. No one seemed to
believe in me until I worked at UPI, and I have them
to thank for my wanting to teach language arts in
high school.

Adapted and reprinted by permission of Eric M. Kellich.

4

Teaching about Sentences

I frequently conduct workshops on teaching writing for secondary school and college instructors. A typical workshop begins with discussion about the writing process. Almost immediately, participants become impatient. They ask, "When are we going to get to sentence problems? Why do my students write short sentences? Why do they still make so many mistakes, after I have gone over these rules repeatedly?" These questions come from teachers at all levels. Sentence instruction is the most baffling part of teaching writing. Yet, teachers know that students' ability to write will be judged by the way they write sentences. The ideas of a good essay will be often be overlooked if the essay contains glaring mistakes, such as misplaced commas, a mistake in agreement between subject and verb, or a sentence fragment. High school guidance counselors know that a college application accompanied by an essay riddled with errors will most likely not be accepted.

There is little consensus about how to teach students to write good sentences. There are no definitive answers to questions about which is more effective—direct teaching techniques, such as exercises and modeling, or indirect instruction, such as more reading assignments with the hope that student writing will improve by continuous exposure to good literature. And what kinds of direct teaching techniques are most effective, and at what stage in the development of a writer should they be introduced? Where does grammar instruction fit in? How do we help students improve their sentences in ways that are compatible with a process approach to teaching writing?

You will confront these questions as a new teacher of writing and, indeed, throughout your teaching career. To answer them, we will try to understand the reasons students have difficulty writing good sentences and then review the benefits and limitations of various approaches, both old and new, for teaching sentence skills. Our discussion will force us to question, though not ignore, the simple dictum of the past: The cure for sentence problems is simple—more grammar instruction. If only that were the case!

The Development of Sentence Skills

John went to the store and *John bought some apples* are grammatically correct *simple* sentences. Each one is an independent clause. *John went to the store, and he bought some apples* is a grammatically correct *compound* sentence. This sentence contains two independent clauses joined by *and*. A child learns to write simple sentences in elementary school. There is nothing wrong with these sentences, but a writer restricted to elementary sentence constructions will write dull, immature sounding prose. In the secondary school years our goal should be to teach students to write increasingly more elaborate sentences. By this time they should be adding modifying constructions to their sentences and expressing other kinds of relationships in the sentence besides the simple *and* relationship often used to create more elaborate sentences.

Walter Loban, author of *Language Development: Kindergarten through Grade Twelve,* gives us a useful working definition of *elaboration.* His research suggests that elaboration should be defined as "the use of various strategies of syntax through which the communication unit is expanded beyond the simple subject and predicate" (15). For example, the simple and compound sentences in the previous paragraph, when elaborated, become *John went to the store, learned the time of day from Peter whom he met on the way, and bought some freshly picked apples, just brought in by truck.* The new sentence includes several modifiers: *learned the time of day from Peter whom he met on the way, freshly picked,* and *just brought in by truck.* A further development occurs when students begin to consolidate modifiers into fewer words. Loban uses the term *syntactic maturity* to describe the progression from sentences with simple modifiers to sentences that contain a relatively high number of underlying propositions in relatively few words (68). He says,

> As they [children] mature, the low group increases its ability to use dependent clauses, whereas the high group shifts to that tighter coiling of thought accomplished by infinitive clauses, participial, prepositional and gerund phrases, appositives, nominative absolutes, and clusters of words in cumulative sentences. (62)

For example, *I went to the school* becomes *I went to the school, which is in my neighborhood,* when a subordinate clause is added, but the sentence *I went to the neighborhood school* consolidates the subordinate clause *which is in my neighborhood* into a possessive adjective, *neighborhood.*

Here are several other examples in *Language Development* (12) of what Loban calls a "tighter coiling of thought." In the more mature sentences phrases have replaced dependent clauses.

Less Mature	*More Mature*
When Nina fed the baby, she hurried after her father.	*Having fed the baby, Nina hurried after her father.* (participial phrase)
Literature is written so that it can clarify the real world.	*Literature is written to clarify the real world.* (infinitive phrase)
The dog was in such a wild fury that he bit his master.	*In his wild fury, the dog bit his master.* (prepositional phrase)

Junior high and high school instructors expect students to progress rapidly from writing simple correct sentences to writing more elaborate correct sentences. However, when students begin writing more complex sentences, their new sentences often contain errors not present in the simple ones. Their teachers become frustrated when students seem to be regressing. Simply pointing out the offensive error and demonstrating how to repair it usually does not work.

Students master many other writing skills more rapidly than they learn to write complex sentences. For example, most students who write essays with poorly developed ideas can learn to add more information, once they understand that expository writing requires detailed explanations. Other rhetorical skills, such as the ability to write good introductions and conclusions, can usually be taught by explaining their logical rhetorical features. However, we cannot assume that modeling effective sentences or explaining their characteristics will result in students writing effective sentences. The sentences they write, more than any other aspect of their writing, are related to cumulative language experiences, such as long established patterns of speech and the amount and kind of written materials to which they have been exposed in and out of school.

What are some of the variables that affect sentence development? Students from homes in which conversation is a significant part of family life are at an immense advantage when it comes to writing effective sentences. Students who have been encouraged to read from an early age have an easier time with sentence construction than those of their peers who, in contrast, have spent many of their waking hours watching television. Television encourages passivity; reading and conversation encourage active language learning. Psychologists tell us that "massive amounts of language processing are required to internalize the codes of written language" (Strong 2). Children must have both oral language experiences as well as written language experiences to become good writers.

Unfortunately, an increasing number of children, regardless of ethnic background or socioeconomic class, are not talking very much to adults or reading. We know that parents at all socioeconomic levels are spending less time with their children. Increasingly, the adult members of a family are overburdened with work schedules that permit little time for the informal conversation with their children so crucial to language growth. Mothers as well as fathers are immersed in hectic schedules, trying to raise a family while at the same time holding down a full-time job. The kind of language learning that goes on outside of school and serves as a foundation for writing good sentences may be absent from the lives of many of our students.

On the other hand, many experts agree that although students gain considerable benefit from oral language experiences, it is the difference between spoken language and written language that explains why students often write weak, incorrect sentences. They would argue that having rich and varied language experiences outside of school does not guarantee that students will write well. They theorize that students often have a rich set of inner language competencies that they do not use when they write. Erika Lindemann and others say that students do not use their entire "repertoire of syntactic constructions" when writing; they tend to write the way they speak and oral language in which we have gestures and facial expression to help us is less specific than written language. One reason these students rely on their spoken language is that they are afraid of taking risks when they write. Each additional word increases the possibility of making errors in punctuation or grammar. So they play it safe (132).

In the second half of this chapter I will discuss a variety of techniques to encourage students to use these inner language competencies when they write. But having some understanding of the reasons that prevent students from reaching their potential for writing effective sentences should help us make decisions about the kind of sentence-level instruction we want to implement in our classes.

How Error Analysis Can Contribute to Teaching Sentence Skills

We take the same approach to error that we used in addressing the development of sentence complexity. If we understand why students make "mistakes," we can devise better strategies for helping students avoid them.

From the student's point of view, teachers seem to become impatient with error sometime during the fifth or sixth grade. The "fun" days of writing in elementary school, when the teacher ignored mistakes, come to an end. Elementary teachers often ignore spelling errors to encourage fluency, to help students see writing as a form of expression rather than a test. For example, this book report and short story were written by my nephew, then in second grade:

A book report by Shai
Rosie's Walk.
By Pat Hutchins
My favorite part of Rosie's Walk was wen the fox was being chaste by the bee's.

A short story by Shai

Wans there was a kasl there was difint colors The kasl was abandoned No wan kame An old man livd in there. That old man lived there whan he was a yog man The old man dide.

The happy face sticker on both papers demonstrates that my nephew's teacher wants to praise his efforts, not comment on his errors, which she will overlook for the present.

But as soon as capitals and periods are introduced, it's expected that students will use their new knowledge. Unfortunately, this is often not the case. The egocentricity of young children is one explanation for the mistakes they make when they first begin to learn to write. Weaver says, "Language learners initially attend much more to deep structure (meaning) than to surface structure (form). Specifically they attend more to basic elements of underlying propositions than to other words and elements of the sentence" (13).

They write primarily for themselves, producing the kind of prose we call expressive writing, and they need all their powers to transfer what they are thinking onto the paper. At this stage they pay little attention to audience because developmentally they are not ready to worry about communicating with others. For example, in this short story, written by my daughter in fifth grade, her use of capitals and her spelling are erratic as she becomes absorbed in her story (though her quotations for dialogue are in the right place!):

Ruthy, 5th grade

On a street named 5th Avenue lived a very rich family. There was a mother, father a girl 8 and some servants one night the mother and father decide to go out the little girs was thrilled when here parents went out because she just loved to spend time with the servants which her mother did not allow. The little girls was about to go down when she heard the servants fighting and new that all was not well she wondered what could be wrong. she always thought the servants liked

each other alot. so she quietly wnet down and tip toed into the kitchen the ser-
vants did not hear and kept right on fighting the little girl did not know what to
do, so she finally said, "what are you fighting about?". . .

When writers begin to pay attention to audience, which generally happens at some point in high school, they become more concerned about punctuation. However, they continue to make mistakes for other reasons. For
example, consider the following sentences, each written by a first-year college student:

Sentences by first-year college students

The time of my life when I learned something, and which resulted in a change in
which I look upon things. This would be the period of my life when I graduated
from Elementary School to High School.

   So what did you do this week-end? I went to my sisters house and helped her
with her house because I remember I told you that she moved and that all her
stuff was not there well that's what I did I helped her. Did you go to the mall?

In the first paragraph, the first sentence is a fragment because the relative
pronoun *when* makes the whole construction an introductory phrase. The
second group of sentences includes a comma splice. (A period should appear
after *there.*) In the past we would have assumed that these students are confused about sentence boundaries, that they do not know the meaning of the
word *sentence.* But we now know that this is only one possible explanation for
sentence problems. These errors could be performance based rather than
competency based, which means that students may understand the concept
of the sentence but in certain writing situations they will slip up. Students are
often inconsistent when it comes to error. They may produce three or four
sentence fragments or comma splices in an essay in which most of the sentences are correct. Interestingly, the number of sentence fragments and
comma splices often increases precisely at the time when students begin to
write more complex sentences.

   Error analysis, a method long used for understanding error in reading
and second language learning, and now being applied to writing, offers several explanations for why errors occur. David Bartholomae wrote one of the
earliest essays on error analysis as it could be applied to writing. In "The
Study of Error" he says,

Error analysis begins with a theory of writing, a theory of language devel-
opment that allows us to see errors as evidence of choice or strategy among
a range of possible choices or strategies. They provide evidence of an indi-
vidual style of using the language and making it work; they are not a simple

record of what the writer failed to do because of incompetence or indiffer-
ence. Errors are seen as necessary stages of an individual's development and
as data that provide insight into idiosyncratic strategies of a particular lan-
guage user at a particular point in his [her] language acquisition. They are
not simply "noise in the system." (quoted in Graves 315)

If we understand the reason for error, then we can identify instructional techniques most useful for each student. Following Bartholomae, we can identify four possible reasons for error:

1. An error is just a slip of the pen. Students know the correct rule but as their thinking races ahead of their writing, they do not apply it. Such errors can be corrected by lessons in proofreading and by making sure that students have ample time in the writing process for editing.

2. Students have gotten in over their heads and are attempting a syntax with which they are unfamiliar. For example, students experimenting with longer sentences, using various kinds of modifiers, may in fact write a dangling participle. Many students become nervous and unsure about punctuation as sentences get longer, and their new sentences may be dotted with commas in the wrong places. In this case errors are seen as a necessary stage of individual development. The instructor may not want to call students' attention to many of these errors or penalize students for writing them.

3. The error may be the result of students having created an intermediate system or an idiosyncratic dialect. In other words, many errors are the result of students attempting to approximate the kind of language and mechanics they think are appropriate. They create their own rules—when sentences are long, they need periods. We can find out about their rules by simply asking, "Why did you put a period there?"

4. Errors occur because of problems in language transfer or, more commonly, because of dialect interference. In the attempt to produce a new dialect (in this case, the written dialect), the writer introduces forms from the first or native language (in this case, the spoken language). Some of these errors can be avoided if instructors make students aware of the differences between spoken and written language.

Bartholomae says, "By charting and analyzing a writer's errors, we can begin our instruction with what a writer does rather than with what he fails to do. For example, it makes no sense to teach general spelling rules to a student who has trouble spelling principally words that contain vowel clusters. Error analysis, then, is a method of diagnosis" (quoted in Graves 316).

Perhaps the major benefit of error analysis is that it changes our attitude toward error. It forces us to abandon the moral attitude that assumes that students who make errors are either lazy or stupid. Error analysis assumes that most errors are developmental: Students either do not have the knowledge needed to identify the error, or they are following a system for writing that they have invented but is at odds with Edited American English.

Mitzi Renwick, who teaches English at Fairfield Middle School in Winnsboro, South Carolina, uses error analysis and follow-up exercises to identify and correct common problems in her students' writing. After surveying the writing in her class, the most frequent areas of misuse she found were:

1. irregular verb forms (eat, eating, ate, eaten; go, going, went, gone)
2. s, *ed*, and *ing* endings (problems with tenses)
3. double negatives (*we don't have no money*)
4. pronoun usage (agreement problems in gender, number, case)
5. homophones (words that have the same sound but are spelled differently, e.g., *hear* and *here*)

Renwick discovered that the first three problems were related to students using forms from their speech in their writing—for example, *I seen, I ain't got, I seen her, I got no money,* and *me and my brother* sounded right to them because they had heard these expressions all of their lives and routinely used them. Students were also developing "intermediate" hypotheses for how to use verb forms. They were applying the rules for standard verbs to irregular verbs. For example, when asked the forms of *bring,* they replied automatically *is bringing, bring,* and *have bring.* Once having discovered the causes of their verb problems, Renwick developed a series of techniques to focus students on these errors. First, she discussed the differences between the conventions of everyday speech and writing. To tackle the wrong "intermediate hypothesis," she explained the past participle form without using grammatical terminology, but instead called it the form that takes a "helper." Then she presented the students with a well-written paragraph with the exception of one wrong sentence: *I had did my homework, but I lost it.* When her students were able to recognize the incorrect sentence, they wrote ten sentences with the verbs they found most confusing. Afterward, they wrote an essay in which they were required to use the past participle form of the verb. At the end of the term, Renwick was quite confident that by recognizing the reasons for their errors, working through a series of exercises, and finally using the correct verbs in their essays, they learned to improve their use of irregular verbs.

Techniques for Helping Students Improve Sentences

Now that we have considered some of the reasons students' progress toward syntactic maturity is often slow, and we have reviewed several explanations for the errors in their writing, we need to connect that information with teaching methods for developing sentence-level skills. We will begin with a review of the most traditional methods, teaching grammar and sentence exercises, and then discuss more recent approaches to sentence instruction, such as sentence combining and generative rhetoric. The last sections of the chapter will include special topics related to sentence instruction.

Where Does Grammar Fit In?

Before we talk about the role of grammar in sentence instruction, we must be clear about terms, though this is not an easy task given the variety of definitions commonly assigned to the term *grammar*. W. Nelson Francis's discussion in "The Three Meanings of Grammar" can help us clarify the issue.

Grammar I denotes the set of formal patterns in which the words of a language are arranged in order to convey larger meanings. It is not necessary that we be able to discuss these patterns self-consciously in order to be able to use them. In fact, all speakers of a language above the age of five or six know how to use its complex forms of organization with considerable skill; in this sense of the word speakers are thoroughly familiar with grammar.

Grammar II is the branch of linguistic science that is concerned with the description, analysis, and formalization of language patterns. Grammar II gives us the terminology often used in traditional grammar instruction, such as *noun, verb,* and so on.

The third sense in which people use the word *grammar* is to describe linguistic etiquette or usage. This Francis calls Grammar III. The word in this sense is often coupled with a derogatory adjective. For example, we say that the expression *he ain't here* is "bad grammar." But if I were to call my students *kids,* I could be accused of using "bad grammar" by anyone who thinks that *kids* is too informal a word to discuss students. (Francis's definitions are summarized in Lindemann 99.)

Many teachers still cling to the belief that teaching students grammatical terminology, Grammar II, will help them write correct complex sentences. They believe that if students can identify parts of speech—constructions such as participles, infinitives, and so on—they will write better sentences. The notion that grammar is "good" for a person has become a part of our hallowed cultural mythology and is probably related to the continued support for the correctness approach to writing discussed in Chapter 9. Because this approach assumes that writing instruction begins with sentences, it seems to follow that learning the names of the elements of a sentence and being able to dissect sentences into these elements will enhance writing ability. Another reason for the emphasis on grammar instruction is that many instructors, who recall the positive effect of learning grammatical terminology as students of foreign languages, mistakenly conclude that their students will reap the same benefits from grammar instruction when learning how to write in their native language. However, as early as 1939, research in the teaching of writing forced English teachers to seriously question the effectiveness of instruction in grammar. The Curriculum Commission of the National Council of Teachers of English recommended that "all teaching of grammar separate from manipulation of sentences be discontinued . . . since every scientific attempt to prove that knowledge of grammar is useful has failed" (*Encyclopedia of Educational Research* 392).

Although it has been proven that knowledge of grammatical rules is not sufficient for learning how to write well, knowledge of grammar may be beneficial to some students, especially when it is connected to their own writing. Having a common vocabulary for discussing the elements of a sentence can be very helpful. If I can say to a student that one may not begin a sentence with the relative pronoun *which*, I may be able to use that explanation to help the student to avoid writing sentence fragments. However, because many students have difficulty learning grammatical terminology, teachers must question whether it is worth spending very much instructional time teaching it in their writing programs. Furthermore, emphasizing grammar can be counterproductive. Students who cannot learn to identify grammatical elements may turn off from all writing instruction because of their frustration.

If you are interested in teaching grammatical terminology, take advantage of the new books that try to make grammar "fun" and accessible. For example, *How to Make Grammar Fun—and Easy!* by Elizabeth Ryan, defines grammatical terms without sounding too technical and explains them with clear, concrete examples. The introduction, "Why Grammar Seems So Hard," illustrates the book's conversational style:

> *Believe it or not, you already know quite a lot about grammar. For example, can you tell the difference between these two sentences?*
>
> Wilbur ate the lobster.
> The lobster ate Wilbur.
>
> *Both sentences use exactly the same words. Yet the way words are put together makes a big difference in what they mean. Grammar is no more than the structure of a language, the way to put words together in order to make sense. If you can tell the difference between these two sentences, you already know a great deal about English grammar.*
>
> *When it comes to talking and making yourself understood, you probably don't have any trouble. When you talk, you have your tone of voice and the expression on your face to help your listener to understand you. Everyday conversation does not require you to follow a set of formal rules. How-*

ever, there is a basic set of formal rules for writing (although these "rules" have a lot of exceptions and variations, and they keep changing). The grammar for both speaking and writing that fits this uniform set of rules is known as Standard English.

Nobody is born knowing how to speak and write Standard English, just as nobody is born knowing how to talk. You can learn to follow the rules of Standard English grammar just as you learned to talk—by practice and by getting a feel for what sounds right. Just as you know the difference between "Wilbur ate the lobster" and the "The lobster ate Wilbur," you can learn the difference between what is and is not correct in Standard English.

The next section in the book, The Eight Parts of Speech (The Building Blocks), goes on to explain that the "art of speech is the name for how a word is used in a sentence" before defining the parts of speech and giving examples of each. For example, the adverb is defined as a word that "tells more about a verb, adjective, or another adverb." These examples follow: *slowly, fast, tomorrow, down, very, hardly, so, happily* (7). Books like this one can help students understand that knowledge of grammatical terms is a tool for learning to write, but not the only tool.

Sentence Exercise Books

Sentence exercise books have two goals: to help students eliminate error and to reinforce their knowledge of grammatical terminology. The exercise books used from middle school through college differ in terms of difficulty but usually follow a similar pattern. Here is the table of contents for the first half of Larry Mapp's *Harbrace College Workbook: Form 12A,** a typical sentence exercise text.

1. Sentence Sense (includes a review of terminology such as subjects, objects, parts of speech, phrases, and clauses)
2. Sentence Fragments (the difference between phrases and sentences, between subordinate clauses and sentences)
3. Comma Splice and Fused Sentences (the punctuation of two main clauses)
4. Adjectives and Adverbs (uses of adjectives: to modify verbs, nouns, as complements)
5. Case (the case of pronouns in different constructions, such as the possessive case, the objective case for direct and indirect objects)

*Excerpts adapted from *Harbrace College Workbook,* Twelfth Edition, Form 12A, by Larry G. Mapp, copyright © 1994 by Harcourt Brace & Company, reprinted by permission of the publisher.

6. Agreement (between verbs and subjects of different kinds)
7. Verbs (different tense forms)

Mechanics

8. Manuscript Form
9. Capitals
10. Italics
11. Abbreviations, Acronyms, and Numbers

Punctuation

12. The Comma
13. Superfluous Commas
14. The Semicolon
15. The Apostrophe
16. Quotation Marks

The pedagogy of exercise books requires students to identify a problem in a sentence and correct it, as in these sentences from an exercise in the Instructor's Edition of Mapp's *Harbrace College Workbook* (71) on fragments, comma splices, and fused sentences.

Comma Splices, Fused Sentences, and Fragments: A Review

Directions: Classify each of the following word groups as a fragment (frag), a comma splice (CS), a fused sentence (F), or a correct sentence (C). Revise each faulty word group.

Example: Irving Howe writing about Ellis Island in his book, *The World of Our Fathers.* frag

Correct: Irving Howe wrote about Ellis Island in his book, *The World of Our Fathers.*

1. European immigrants who entered the United States between 1892 and 1943 and who had to be processed through bureaucratic red tape at Ellis Island. frag

Correct: European immigrants entered the United States between 1892 and 1943 had to be processed through bureaucratic red tape at Ellis Island.

2. Howe vividly evokes the anxiety that immigrants experienced as their ships neared Ellis Island, each of them wondered if he or she would be sent back. cs

Correct: Howe vividly evokes the anxiety that immigrants experienced as their ships neared Ellis Island. Each of them wondered if he or she would be sent back.

3. "On Ellis Island they pile into the massive hall that occupies the entire width of the building," writes Howe, they break into dozens of lines, divided by metal railings, where they file past the first doctor." <u>cs</u>

Correct: <u>"On Ellis Island they pile into the massive hall that occupies the entire width of the building," writes Howe. "They break into dozens of lines, divided by metal railings, where they file past the first doctor."</u>

Unfortunately, we cannot be sure that by simply completing this exercise successfully students will eliminate sentence errors from their own writing. The ability to identify and correct errors in exercises does not necessarily lead to better writing, especially if these activities are divorced from student writing. Error analysis should remind you that there are many reasons for student writing to still contain mistakes, even after direct instruction.

However, when exercises are related to students' mistakes, they seem to have greater benefit. For example, some students may become more proficient at identifying the errors in their own writing after completing an exercise on that topic. Although exercises make up only a small fraction of my writing program, I find them useful as one strategy for focusing attention on sentences. After completing the assigned exercises, usually at home, students compare their responses in small groups, and, as a class, we review those sentences in the exercise that puzzled them. I have them check the essay that they are currently writing for the kinds of errors highlighted in the exercise. This approach seems to awaken them to some of the idiosyncrasies in their own writing. Exclamations such as "Why do I always make the same mistake!" tell me that something is indeed sticking.

Sentence exercises are bound to have even more impact if you refer to them during conferences and when you grade the essay. For example, you might say, "This sentence has the same problem as the exercise we did last week on agreement. Check sentence 4 in that exercise." At the end of the semester, my students choose ten sentences from their essays that needed to be revised and try to explain their reasons for revision. Doing the exercises helps them to understand the reasons for revising their sentences (see Appendix 4a: "Sarah" and "Christina").

Exercises have yet another advantage. They often provide an opportunity for students who are weak writers but who do well on the exercises to experience some measure of success in the writing classroom.

Sentence Combining and Generative Rhetoric

Teaching grammatical terminology and using traditional exercises aim at eliminating error. During the last twenty years, sentence combining and generative rhetoric have emerged as methods of focusing sentence-level instruction on fostering growth rather than getting rid of mistakes. In the first case, sentence combining, students are presented with two or more sentences and asked to combine them into one sentence. In the second case, generative rhetoric, students are presented with a sentence and asked to add modifiers at various points in the sentence, possibly at the beginning, the middle, or the end. The goal of both methods is to enlarge the students' repertoire of sentence options, to try to force their sentence development through exercises beyond what it would be if the exercises had not been performed—to in effect speed up syntactic maturity, the adding of modifiers and the tightening of the recoiling of thought. For example, the two sentences, *The girl is pretty* and *The girl went to school* can be combined to form the sentences *The girl who is pretty went to school* or *The pretty girl went to school*. The second sentence, *The pretty girl went to school*, demonstrates a tight coiling of thought. Fewer words have been used to express the same ideas.

Sentence combining is based on generative transformational grammar theory. Unlike descriptive grammar, which describes the structure of sentences, generative transformational grammar describes the process of forming sentences without formal instruction. Transformational grammarians believe that we transform sentences intuitively, by adding to, deleting from, or rearranging *kernel* sentences. Kernel sentences are sentences that make one proposition, such as *Judy did her homework*. In his book *Syntactic Structures*, Noam Chomsky theorizes that as language develops we build on simple declarative sentences through a variety of transformations. When transformations are formed on a single kernel sentence, they are called single-based transformations. When they embed one kernel sentence in another, they are called double-base transformations. Chomsky classifies the variety of transformations that he thinks takes place. For example, the declarative sentence, *Judy did her homework*, will be transformed into the following sentences with these single- and double-base transformations:

Single-Base Transformation

Judy did not do her homework.   (negative transformation)

The homework was done by Judy.   (passive transformation)

What homework was Judy doing?   (question transformation)

Double-Base Transformations

Judy, who did her homework, received good grades. (relative clause transformation) This sentence includes two kernel sentences: *Judy did her homework* and *Judy received good grades*.

The homework that Judy did was excellent. (relative clause transformation)

This sentence includes the two kernel sentences: *Judy did her homework. It was excellent. Judy's homework took time.* (gerund transformation)

Sentence combining exercises simulate single- and double-base transformations. For example, the last sentence is produced by combining these two sentences: *Judy did her homework* and *Her homework took time* (Lindemann 112).

Cued and Open-Ended Exercises

Sentence combining exercises can take the form of *cued* or *open-ended* exercises. In cued exercises, the cues tell students how to combine the sentences, giving them the opportunity to use structures they may not normally use. Cued exercises can be assigned without using grammatical terminology. For example, the following exercise encourages students to use subordinate clauses to indicate location:

Specifying Location

We use the subordinators *where* and *whenever* almost automatically to specify location. You can review this process by combining these two sentences into one:

> *She saw charm and security. He saw advanced dilapidation and imprisonment.*

If you choose to make the second sentence the base clause, your version probably looks like this:

> *Where she saw charm and security, he saw advanced dilapidation and imprisonment.*

Try writing two more versions of the combination.

Here's another example. In the following cued exercise, the word to be used to combine the sentences is indicated in parentheses:

Combine the following sentences:

> *I like ice cream.*
>
> *Ice cream is very good.* (because)

The student completing the exercise writes:

> *I like ice cream because it is very good.*

Another type of cued exercise, somewhat more advanced, requires students to change the form of a word.

Instructions: Use the *ing* form of a word to construct effective sentences.

    A. *Joe burst through the line.* (ING)

    B. *Joe forced the quarterback to catch the ball on the fourth down.*

(Possible combination) *Bursting through the line, Joe forced the quarterback to catch the ball on the fourth down.*

    A. *The angry crowd fell on the assassin.* (ING)

    B. *The angry crowd tore him limb from limb.*

(Possible combination) *Falling on the assassin, the angry crowd tore him limb from limb.*

Frank O'Hare, who created this exercise, demonstrated that students can perform sentence combining exercises without knowing grammatical terminology. In his research, published in *Sentence Combining: Improving Student Writing without Formal Grammar Instruction,* O'Hare eliminated grammar labels from sentence combining instruction and substituted a series of "little helps."

Here is another sentence combining exercise without grammatical cues (O'Hare Appendix A 94):

In the following example you'll be given signals to help you decide which words to delete and where to put commas.

    "She" means delete "She."

    The comma signal (,) means put a comma at the beginning of the base sentence.

    (AND,) means put a comma followed by an *and* at the beginning of this base sentence.

    Given the following three base sentences

    Helen raised her pistol.

    She took careful aim.

    She squeezed off five rapid shots to the center of the target. (, and)

you would write them out like this:

    Helen raised her pistol, took careful aim, and squeezed off five rapid shots to the center of the target.

O'Hare concluded that the seventh grade students who were exposed to grammar-free written and oral sentence combining practice showed evidence of a level of syntactic maturity well beyond that typical of eighth graders and in many respects similar to twelfth graders (66).

Open-Ended Exercises

William Strong, another leader in the development of sentence combining instruction, advocates open-ended combining exercises, especially when students first try sentence combining. He says, "At first it is probably not wise to impose your prejudices upon your students as to which transformation is best" (27). He favors sentence combining exercises within the context of paragraphs or short essays. He wants students to learn that the construction of sentences depends on the purpose, audience, and context of the writing. He believes that, after students have had practice in sentence combining, they should have the opportunity to examine the effect of using sentences other than the ones they originally constructed. Here is a typical open-ended sentence combining exercise in *Sentence Combining: A Composing Book* (Strong 40). He presents a list of short sentences that can be combined to form complex sentences and a paragraph.

Rock Concert

1. The singer was young.
2. The singer was swarthy.
3. He stepped into the spotlight.
4. The spotlight was red.
5. His shirt was unbuttoned.
6. The unbuttoning bared his chest.
7. Sounds ballooned around him.
8. The sounds were guitars.
9. The sounds were drums.
10. The sounds were of girls.
11. The girls were screaming.
12. He nodded.
13. He winked.
14. The wink was to his guitarist.
15. The drummer responded with the beat.
16. The singer became animated.
17. His legs were like rubber.
18. His body jerked.
19. His head was thrown back.
20. He wailed a shout.
21. The shout was into the microphone.
22. The microphone was at his lips.
23. His movements were twisting.
24. His movements were strobed.
25. The strobing was with floodlights.
26. His voice was a garble.
27. The garble was loud.
28. The auditorium was swirled.
29. The swirling was rock.
30. The rock was heavy.

Students can combine these sentences using their own choice of constructions. For example, here are two options for combining the first six sentences:

The singer, who was young and swarthy, stepped into the red spotlight and unbuttoned his shirt, baring his chest.

The young, swarthy singer stepped into the red spotlight, his unbuttoned shirt baring his chest.

The first sentence places more emphasis on the action of unbuttoning the singer's shirt, whereas the second sentence, in which there is only one verb (*stepped*), emphasizes his appearance. Students can discuss both options as they decide how best to convey the intended meaning.

Why Sentence Combining Works

The results of some studies on the effects of sentence combining instruction are more positive than others, but few have produced the dramatic results that O'Hare reports. However, when viewed as a whole, much of the research on sentence combining suggests that from the fourth grade through the college years sentence combining seems to improve students' repertoire of sentence options. Not only do these exercises help students develop a better eye and ear for prose rhythms, but they help to teach punctuation as well. When learning a new construction, such as a prepositional phrase used to introduce a sentence, students learn that introductory phrases are set off from the main part of the sentence with a comma.

The success of sentence combining must be due in some measure to the fact that when students are combining sentences, they are not concerned with error. They are not repairing sentences, but composing new ones. Sentence combining is a positive activity. It permits students to use their imaginations. Especially when they are completing open-ended exercises, they often find it challenging to come up with as many new constructions as possible. When these exercises are performed as a class, students often stimulate one another to develop innovative sentence constructions.

One note of caution: Sentence combining exercises should never be graded. If they are to serve the purpose of inviting students to experiment with new sentence constructions, students must feel that they can do so without the risk of being penalized.

Generative Rhetoric

Generative rhetoric offers students some of the same benefits as sentence combining. Francis Christensen developed generative rhetoric as a result of studying the writing of skilled writers and his personal attempts to use the sentence to generate ideas. In the 1960s, when composition experts were preoccupied with the problem of invention—how to help students produce information and ideas—Christensen said that the sentence could play an important role in invention: "We need a rhetoric of the sentence that will do more than combine the ideas of primer sentences. We need one that will generate ideas" (26). Once he noticed that the writing of skilled writers is characterized by an abundance of free modifiers, nonrestrictive and nonessential clauses and phrases set off by punctuation and modifying constructions, he concluded that a pedagogy that encouraged students to think about modification would motivate them to examine the ideas in sentences as they first write them and to expand these ideas through modification. As a result, they would write more complex, interesting sentences. For example, if I were to write: *Teaching writing is a challenging task* and then examined the ideas in the sentence with the possibility of adding modifiers, I might write, *Teaching writing is a challenging task, made even more demanding by students' distaste for writing by the time they reach high school.* In Christensen's terms I would have generated a new idea by adding a modifier to the original sentence (*made even more demanding by students' distaste for writing by the time they reach high school*) and written a more interesting sentence in the process. By adding the modifier, I changed the idea in the original sentence.

Christensen observed that in skilled writing modifiers can appear before the main clause (*when arriving at school, Mary . . .*) in the middle of the sentence (*Mary, who arrived at school late, . . .*), and after the main clause (*Mary arrived at school, her clothes in disarray and her hair uncombed.*). He developed the following four principles to describe the process and characteristics of sentence modification and their effect on emphasis and style.

1. *The principle of addition.* Nouns, verbs, or main clauses serve as a foundation or base to which we add details, qualifications, or new meanings.

2. *The principle of direction.* We can add these new meanings before or after the noun, verb, or base clause. The direction or movement of the sentence changes depending on where we have added modifiers or new meanings. When modifiers appear before the noun, verb, or base clause (which Christensen calls the "head" of the construction), the sentence moves forward. Modifiers placed after the noun, verb, or base clause move the sentence backward because they require readers to relate the new details, qualifications, and meanings back to the head appearing earlier in the sentence.

3. *The principle of the concrete.* Depending on the meanings of the words we add, the head becomes either more or less concrete. The base word or clause together with one or more of the modifying additions expresses several levels of generality or abstraction.

4. *The principle of texture.* This principle describes the writer's style. Christensen characterizes style as relatively dense or plain on the basis of the number and variety of additions writers make to nouns, verbs, and base clauses.

Students can perform generative rhetorical exercises without knowing the principles on which they are based and without knowing grammatical terminology. As with sentence combining exercises, generative rhetorical exercises can be cued or open ended. The value of Christensen's work is that it offers yet another method for students to enlarge their repertoire of sentence forming strategies. Here is how generative rhetorical exercises work.

Students are asked to write a simple sentence, such as *My family lives in the city.* They will be asked to add as many words as possible to both the front end and the back end of the sentence, and as many words as they wish in the middle. The sentence they write may not be stylistically effective, but it will give them an opportunity to experiment with sentence elements and to try to punctuate them. For example, if students were to write the following (overloaded) sentence, they can discuss the punctuation this sentence requires as well as the reasons it fails as an effective sentence.

> Because my family, which includes my two brothers and my parents and a dog, lives in the exciting, but often dangerous city, where we go to school and work, we have a greater understanding of the problems of the poor, though we also appreciate the many opportunities which the city offers.

Discussion can eventually lead to an analysis of the sentences that appear in students' own essays. They can seek out sentences in their essays that are either overburdened by modifiers or seem undernourished because of lack of modification.

The preceding exercise is an example of an open-ended exercise, whereas a cued exercise would tell students where to add the new construction, at the beginning, the middle, or the end of the sentence, and what kind of construction to add.

For example, the following exercise requires students to add an adverbial clause at the beginning of the sentence, and a verb cluster at the end of the sentence.

> John did his homework.

> <u>Because John was home early,</u> he did his homework. (*adverbial clause*)

> Because John was home early, he did his homework, <u>surprising his mother when she arrived.</u> (*verb cluster*)

The new sentence illustrates the value of placing modifiers both before and after the base clause.

You can experiment with generative rhetorical exercises in your own classes as early as the fifth grade. In *Three Strategies for Revising Sentences,* Bernarr Folta explains how she uses the Christensen method in a fifth grade class. She describes the lesson she taught after discussing a paragraph written by one of the students:

It was midnight. <u>I drifted down the river</u>. I was alone and awfully scared. There was a rushing sound ahead. I grabbed for a rock and held on for a few seconds. Suddenly I lost my grip and slipped down.

Folta says,

> *Before raising any question about "addition" I complimented the pupil on the creation of suspense with the first sentence. I then asked: Is there any one sentence in this paragraph which needs more words to tell where, when, why, how, what color, how many, or for what reason? Most of the class cited the second sentence. With the overhead, I projected the sentence and the possible slots for modifiers.*
>
> *I   drifted   down   the   river.* (18)

She says that the class cited gaps in the sentence and eventually revised the sentence to read as follows:

I <u>carelessly</u> drifted <u>on my home-made raft</u> down the <u>swollen</u> Nile River.

(The underlined words and phrases are the new modifiers.)

Folta concludes that she witnessed no "miraculous changes" in the writing habits of the students, but she did see some improvements in their style. Perhaps what is even more important is that Folta

> *encountered no pupil resentment about having to rewrite an assignment and no embarrassment about my discussing their writing in front of the class; but I did find pupils enjoying the discovery approaches to language. I hope their enjoyment with words and sentences leads them to more conscious and creative acts of ordering, selecting, and describing. I also hope that working on their own sentences has given them a heightened awareness, even an appreciation of sentences they encounter in their reading.* (19)

Assorted Exercises in Sentence Composing

In a series of texts on sentence composing for grades 10, 11, and 12, Don Kilgallon provides exercises in *sentence scrambling* and *sentence imitating,* as well as exercises in sentence combining and what he calls *sentence expanding,* a variation of Christensen's generative rhetoric. He defines sentence scrambling as "mixing up the parts of a sentence and then putting them back together to make a meaningful, well-written sentence" (4). For example, the sentence *Until I left for my mother's house, I was very impatient* could be reversed to read *I was very impatient, until I left for my mother's house.* These exercises demonstrate that by changing the order of parts in the sentence, the meaning is changed as well.

Sentence imitating requires students to carefully examine a sentence, especially noticing its punctuation pattern. Students copy the sentence as it is, and then create their own sentences using the same pattern. This technique works more effectively with mature writers, but it can be effective with beginning writers if the sentences are not overly complex. For example, the grammatical elements in the sentence, *I was very impatient, until I left my mother's house,* can be imitated as follows: *I was very angry, until my friend explained why he was late.*

Once you have learned about sentence combining, generative rhetoric, and other sentence manipulating techniques, you can develop your own exercises, or use the exercises in such texts as those by Strong and Kilgallon. Students should then be encouraged to use sentence combining and sentence generating techniques to improve the sentences in their own work.

Teaching Style

Style is another one of those words we use when we talk about writing that has many definitions. Whenever we teach students how to write for a particular purpose and audience, we are teaching them about style, about the most appropriate combination of words for the message they are creating. However, when we talk about helping students to develop style, we mean more than that. I like Allan Glatthorn's definition of style: "To write with style is to write in a way that seems effective in a given communication context, that conveys a sense of the unique voice of the writer, and that seems euphonious to the trained reader" (18). In other words, writing that has style is not only appropriate for the purpose and audience for which it is written, but it conveys a special sense of the writer's voice, and sounds pleasing to the ear.

Any writer who has tried to improve his or her style knows that it is not easy. Glatthorn believes that many high school students may not be ready to work on style, on economy of expression and gracefulness. Beverly Clark, in *Talking about Writing,* says that you should wait to discuss style until students have eliminated most errors. I am not sure I agree. My experience teaching writing suggests that even students who are not yet completely in control of sentence conventions can benefit from discussions about style. All students can be made aware of the sounds of written language. They can read their own writing aloud to listen for its distinctive rhythms, though they may not be able to develop their own voice. However, the more advanced the student, the more emphasis can be placed on instruction in style. Perhaps you were the kind of student who received an A– and wondered how you could turn that paper into an A paper. Instructors are often not sure how to help students with their writing after they have achieved correctness and a reasonable knowledge of sentence structure.

Allan Glatthorn's recommendations for teaching style apply to all secondary-level grades:

1. Stress the sound of language. *Since the sound of language is an important aspect of style, use activities that emphasize the sound of written language. Ask students to read aloud to each other what they have written. Have them try alternative phrasings so that they become more sensitive to the sound of language. Read aloud to them from the works of great stylists of the past and present, stressing the sounds and cadences.*

2. Give them good models to read and imitate. *While all experts do not agree about the desirability of using models, many great writers have attested to the value of reading and imitating authors they admired. The analysis of style is one obvious place where the study of literature and the teaching of writing can be usually related. As students read* Walden *they can analyze the distinctive features of Thoreau's style. As they study the presidency of John F. Kennedy, they can analyze the special stylistic features of his inaugural address.*

3. Emphasize the importance of the communication context. *All teachers should emphasize how the communication context affects the language used—the extent to which the language is subjective or objective, the extent to which words are literal or figurative, the way in which sentence and paragraph forms vary. Contrast, for example, a scientific description of a snake with Emily Dickinson's image of one; contrast a police bulletin's description of a woman with a portrait in the* Song of Songs. *Ask students to frame essentially the same message for two different contexts: write a persuasive message to be read over the public address system and then write the same message as a letter to the editor of the local newspaper.*

4. Let students try out different voices. *Since much student writing seems almost voiceless, lacking an individual tone, teachers should use methods that develop the sense of voice. Ask students to write about an emotion laden experience, trying their best to catch the nuances of the same experience assuming different voices: the newspaper reporter, the disapproving adult, the psychologist. Here again is where literature, history, and writing can connect. One activity that should be interesting, for example, would be to present students with excerpts illustrating the*

different voices of a candidate for political office. Have them read a speech on the same subject to different groups.

5. Teach them useful strategies for achieving clarity and grace. *All writing handbooks offer abundant advice about these matters, but much of it is of limited value. Too many of these handbooks include outdated rules ("don't split the infinitive") and vague admonitions ("avoid awkwardness"). An important exception is Joseph William's* Style: Ten Lessons in Clarity and Grace. *Its approach is sound; its content is useful and specific; and its style exemplifies what the author advocates. Regardless of which handbooks the teacher turns to for advice, students will learn more by applying the techniques to their own writing, not by doing contrived exercises. (18)*

Glatthorn ends by saying that "none of these approaches, obviously, will turn an inept writer into a master, but they can bring about small gains in appropriateness, individuality, and euphony" (18). His specific suggestions for improving style can apply to almost all kinds of writing:

1. *Put the main actor or agent in the subject of the sentence and the important action in the verb.*

   Poor: The final assessment is the responsibility of the teacher.
   Better: The teacher should make the final assessment.

2. *Watch for the excessive and inappropriate use of nominalizations. A nominalization is a noun made from a verb (accusation, reference, disturbance). A heavily nominalized style sounds pedantic and bureaucratic.*

   Poor: Make a determination of the effectiveness of the installation of the equipment.
   Better: Determine if the equipment was installed effectively.

3. *Avoid using long noun phrases in which two or more nouns are used as modifiers.*

   Poor: The school's learning disability assessment policy needs to be modified.
   Better: The school should modify its policy for assessing learning disabilities.

4. *In general, use the active instead of the passive voice; use the passive only when you wish to emphasize the receiver, not the doer of the action.*

   Poor Passive: A new homework policy was instituted by the superintendent.
   Better Active: The superintendent instituted a new homework policy.
   Effective Passive: The child was injured by a speeding car.

5. *Avoid stringing one long clause after another; break them up into shorter pieces or simpler structures.*

   Poor: *Because it was apparent that the students had failed to do what they had been assigned, the teacher changed her plan for that day.*
   Better: *Since the students had not done their assignment, the teacher changed her plan for that day.*

6. *Avoid putting long modifiers between the subject and the verb.*

   Poor: *The President, since he had made a commitment to reduce the deficit, found himself in an awkward predicament.*
   Better: *Because the President had promised to reduce the deficit, he found himself in an awkward predicament.*

7. *Express parallel ideas in parallel grammatical structures.*

   Poor: *We have to find a way to reduce pupil truancy, and the curriculum needs to be made more standard, while at the same time doing a better job with inservice.*
   Better: *There are three tasks that confront us: reducing pupil truancy, standardizing the curriculum, and improving inservice programs.*

8. *In general use the simplest grammatical structure that will convey your meaning: use a clause instead of a sentence, a phrase instead of a clause, a word instead of a phrase.*

   Poor: *Principals should be sure that they have sent in to the district office the forms they have completed.*
   Better: *Principals should send the completed forms to the district office.*
   (19–20)

Sentence Instruction: Nonstandard Dialect and ESL Students

The United States has the most heterogeneous population of any nation in the world. Large numbers of children in U.S. schools either speak a dialect defined by region or ethnic group or a native language other than English. In this section we will examine some of the issues relevant to working on the sentence level with these students. Standard American English is the dialect of the U.S. academic world and other institutions and businesses that require formal written English. Some composition specialists reserve the term *Standard American English* (SAE) for the spoken language and use the term *Edited American English* (EAE) to refer to writing. As Neman puts it, "Even a white Scarsdale banker's everyday speech differs somewhat from the language the banker would write in a business or academic setting" (208).

No one speaks pure Standard American English all of the time. During the last thirty years we have become particularly sensitive to the problems related to teaching Standard American English to children who speak a different dialect of English, without implying that the dialect they speak outside of school is inferior to it. Research shows that Black English Vernacular is not a "degenerative or ungrammatical version . . . of the standard dialect," but a "fully grammatical syntactically rigid language in [its] own right" with different grammatical rules than Standard American English. "Black English Vernacular still maintains some of the features of West African languages which shaped its development" (Neman 274). For example, Black English Vernacular includes the

> *habitual tense of the African languages which is not characteristic of Standard English but is expressed in Black English Vernacular by "be" ("He be coming," "Mama be working"). Black English Vernacular also shares the West African avoidance of a double signification of plurality ("two dog"), a feature also of Chinese American English derived from many of the Chinese languages. Black English Vernacular, like the Appalachian dialect, also retains features of the 16th and 17th century English spoken in Colonial America and immortalized in the King James Bible. Among these features are the repeated subject ("The boy, he . . ." as in "Thy rod and thy staff, they . . .") and the reinforced negative ("Nobody don't . . ."), commonplace in Shakespeare's plays. (Neman 275)*

Standard American English is not superior to Black Vernacular Dialect. Both serve the communication needs of their speakers and both have a rich vocabulary and systematic grammar. However, because Standard American English is the language used in government, business, and education, and is very similar to Edited American English, its written counterpart, students need to know it. We must teach SAE without insisting that students give up the dialect that they speak at home, which is their link to their families and friends. Our goal is to introduce students to the idea of code-switching, which is the ability to use the appropriate dialect for their communication needs in a given context.

The sentence instruction methods described earlier in this chapter can be used to help students become bidialectical. In addition, we can use various exercises or drills to make students aware of the differences between EAE and the dialect they speak. In "Fostering Dialect Shift in African-American Students," Susan Horn observes that as writers mature and begin to recognize the differences between dialects, they will make spontaneous shifts from their spoken dialect to EAE, if given enough time to write successive drafts. She quotes from an early draft of a paper, where the student wrote, "Mom, those kids alway [crossed out] just be trying to fake you out. They're not that nice." The final draft reads, "Mom, those kids are trying to fake you out; they're not nice." Horn says that at times students may have no choice but to rely on their native dialect to express certain ideas. She concludes, "As teachers and tutors, we must not gag the natural, outer manifestation of the students 'inner speech' before they have a chance to figure out what they want to say. We can always work on the fine points of Standard English later, after meaning has been established . . ." (108).

Regardless of the methods you choose to make students aware of dialect interference in their writing, always remain aware of their feelings. Avoid words such as *wrong* or *incorrect* and instead use words such as *appropriate*. One technique for emphasizing the value of nonstandard dialects is to give students the opportunity to describe their dialects to the class. All students can increase their understanding of the nature of language by learning about dialect difference.

The Student for Whom English Is a Second Language

Students for whom English is a second language (ESL) share some of the problems of students who speak nonstandard dialects. However, nonstandard dialect speakers already know the fundamental rules of sentence forms in English. In contrast, ESL speakers must make the transfer from languages based on grammatical features atypical of English. This example from the *Bedford Guide for Writing Tutors** illustrates the differences between a Korean sentence and English sentence:

English: *Last night, I ate rice instead of bread.*

Korean: *Yesterday evening in rice instead of bread ate. (L. Ryan 43)*

However, despite the difficulties of learning a new language, the ESL student is not hampered by the psychological barriers encountered by students who speak nonstandard dialects. Foreign-born students usually do not have feelings of inferiority about their language but may face other psychological barriers resulting from being unaccustomed to experiencing difficulty in school. Furthermore, the ESL instructor must be aware of cultural differences, especially as they pertain to schooling. In *The Bedford Guide,* Leigh Ryan offers

---

*All Ryan extracts adapted from *The Bedford Guide for Writing Tutors,* 2nd ed. Copyright © 8/97 by St. Martin's Press, Inc. Reprinted with permission of St. Martin's Press, Inc.

some suggestions that apply to both classroom instruction and one-on-one tutoring of ESL students:

> *When you tutor someone from a similar background to yours, you will both think and behave in similar ways; however, differences, especially in the areas of interpersonal and written communication may become apparent when you tutor someone from a different culture or subculture. For example, in some cultures questioning authority is frowned upon, and you may find students who are reluctant to ask you questions or admit they don't understand something. The amount of personal space people desire differs among cultures, and you may tutor students who make you feel uncomfortably crowded as you work together. Whatever differences you encounter, it is important to treat each student with respect and sensitivity.*
>
> *Likewise, acceptable ways of presenting information differ among cultures. Americans tend to value the direct approach, but some cultures believe that meaning should be implied rather than spelled out directly. Still others approach a problem by giving its detailed history first, information that we might find unnecessary. We need to recognize such differences as cultural and explain appropriate rhetorical patterns in English. (44)*

Ryan offers some suggestions for working with ESL students, which take into account cultural differences.

1. *Give directions plainly. Watch students' expressions and ask questions to see if they comprehend explanations. If you are not sure whether a student understands something you've said, ask him or her to explain what you have said or to give you an example.*
2. *If a student doesn't understand a comment or explanation, rephrase it. Don't raise your voice or simply repeat the same words.*
3. *If you have difficulty understanding an ESL student, watch for facial expressions as he or she speaks. The combination of saying and hearing can help you to follow what the student is saying.*
4. *Many ESL students write better than they speak. Don't assume that because you have trouble understanding a student's speech, he or she will have problems with their writing.*
5. *Do not feel compelled to give the grammatical explanation of constructions you are teaching the student. Many foreign students are accustomed to imitation as a form of instruction. You can help students rephrase a sentence and produce other sentences of the same kind. Producing such examples establishes patterns that students can begin to incorporate into their writing and their speaking. (44–45)*

We can also look to our native-speaking students to help our ESL students with their speaking and their writing. I grew up in New York City in the late 1940s and early 1950s during the large wave of immigration from Puerto Rico and China. The population of New York City schools changed rapidly during those years. To cope with this large influx of nonnative speakers, we were assigned "buddies," that is, students who could not speak or write English. We were given fifteen-minute breaks during the day to help them. At those times we would answer questions and review our buddy's written work. This was an enormously rewarding experience for both the native and nonnative speakers. The native speakers got to learn about another culture and language as our new classmates improved their English speaking and writing skills.

The Computer and Sentence Instruction

Whether your goal is to teach correctness, sentence variety, or style, the computer can help. When students switch to computers, their attitude toward writing and homework seems to improve (Griffin and others). Therefore, if computers are available, it makes sense for us to incorporate their use in sentence-level instruction. To edit for correct mechanics, students can learn to use the spell check and grammar check programs that come with most word processing programs. Spell check is especially useful for students who have extreme difficulty with spelling. My son is one such person. His seventh grade teacher, who vowed she would teach Josh to spell, is probably still recovering. Of course, students must be warned that spell check does not eliminate the need for editing by reading over the hard copy. Homophones (words that sound alike but are spelled differently, e.g., *bow* and *bough*) are one among several problems that spell check will not identify. There is no way for spell check to evaluate the context in which the word is being used. Therefore, it will not flag *bow* in the following sentence as an incorrect spelling: *The bow on the tree is about to break.* Grammar check also has its pitfalls. For example, when I used grammar check to review this chapter, it informed me that *Conclusion* is a sentence fragment, not being able to recognize it as a heading. Furthermore, grammar check highlighted all of the sentences that use the passive voice such as, *Students benefit from a language environment in which they are encouraged to recognize the need for writing more mature, correct sentences.* I chose the passive voice for this verb because it seemed more appropriate than the active voice when discussing the impact of environment. Like spell check, grammar check must be used critically. As a side benefit, grammar check may help students learn the terms used for parts of sentences because the program highlights the offending term in the isolated sentence while the suggested revision appears on the screen.

When students are ready to analyze the style of one of their essays, they can be introduced to software programs such as HOMER and Writers Workbench. HOMER will tell you the total number of words in a text, the number of sentences, and the number of *to be* forms. The Writers Workbench gives you information about the type and length of sentences, the kinds of sentence openers, and the percentages of abstract words, nominalizations (nouns made from verbs such as *recognition* instead of *recognize*) of passive verb forms and *to be* forms. Both of these programs and others like them favor a simpler style, so once again, students should learn that the software program is only a tool; it cannot be expected to provide the best answer. Only the writer can do that.

The computer can also be used for sentence-level exercises of all kinds. A software package accompanies every new handbook or sentence exercise book. For example, *Writing a Concise Handbook* (Heffernan and Lincoln) comes with Grammar Workouts: Interactive Exercises, which contains ninety sets of multiple-choice grammar and punctuation exercises. The exercises are free to anyone who uses the dial-up number (see References).

Conclusion

In this chapter I have introduced you to contemporary ideas about sentence-level instruction, the most neglected area in the teaching of writing. I urge you not to forget the sentence. Sentence-level instruction is compatible with a process approach to teaching writing and modern ideas about the development of writing ability.

To summarize:

1. We must understand how sentence ability develops, especially how it is related to language development outside of school, and we must then try to develop teaching practices that reflect those understandings. Students benefit from a rich language environment in which they are encouraged to recognize the need for writing more mature, correct sentences.

2. We should realize that making errors is a natural part of language learning and that it is our job to understand and help our students locate the origin of error.

3. We should understand the benefits and limitations of teaching students grammatical terminology.

4. For sentence exercises of any kind to be effective, they must be integrated into the writing process. They cannot be done in isolation. All of the exercises described previously can be scheduled during the drafting or revision stage

of writing a paper, whether they are textbook based or constructed by the teacher. You can develop mini-lessons on sentence-related issues any time during the writing process. During the revision stage, students can be urged to use their sentence combining skills for combining short, choppy sentences. When students apply the skills they learn through exercises to their own writing, the chances of their retaining these skills is much greater.

5. Encourage your students to develop an effective style of writing and provide direct instruction in style.

6. If your school has them, use computers to aid sentence-level instruction.

7. Be sensitive to the needs of students who speak a nonstandard dialect and students whose native language is not English. Language problems for these students may be compounded by feelings of inferiority and embarrassment.

Questions for Discussion and Writing

1. What role did grammar play in your development as a writer? Do you feel confident about your ability to use grammatical terminology to identify sentence constructions? Explain.

2. List three rules about writing sentences that you no longer believe to be accurate. When did you begin to believe in these rules? What kind of instruction has made you reconsider them?

3. Develop an open-ended sentence combining exercise for the seventh grade on a topic of interest to seventh graders. Write three sentences in each cluster.

4. Describe the sentences in the following two letters. Identify their punctuation problems. Develop a sentence combining exercise for the students who wrote these letters. Revise the letters using sentence combining.

Letter 1

Dear Melissa,

How are you? I am doing fine. I can't believe that we have a whole week off for Easter. What are you going to do next week? I am probably going to go shopping most of the week. Do you want to come?

Did you hear about Dina? She broke her arm by riding her bike, she crashed into a wall. She was at the hospital for two hours. Do you want to go to her house with me tomorrow? If you do, call me.

Do you have soccer practice today, if you do I will go with you to watch you play.

See you later, do not forget to call me.

Your friend

Letter 2

Dear Jeovanny,

Hi! I can't wait to go over to your house on Easter. I missed you yesterday. I hope you are feeling better than when I saw you on Sunday. I got my new Easter dress yesterday, it's the one you liked when you said "It does not look right on Samantha." I think she got really upset.

Your mother came over to my house last Wednesday to help my Mom start the decorations for Easter dinner. I asked her where you were. She said you were sleeping. That's why I came over. You looked like you were awake, that's why I started talking to you. When you woke you still acted like you were sleeping and I was talking to myself.

See you later

Joanne.

5. Write a letter to a friend who is a new teacher. Your friend has asked for some suggestions for teaching sentence skills. Explain the difference between the following three approaches to helping students improve their sentences.
   a. the traditional approach.
   b. the sentence combining approach.
   c. the generative rhetorical approach.

6. Interview a student who is not a native speaker. Ask the student to describe his or her experience learning English.

7. How did you achieve your present style of writing? Daniel File's paper (Appendix 2b) can serve as a model for your discussion. Cite important influences on your writing style, such as authors you have tried to imitate.

8. Analyze your writing style using Glatthorn's "Suggestions for Improving Clarity and Style" as a guide. How can you improve your writing style?

9. Analyze the writing style in Rosemary's paper. (See Appendix 4c.) How does this student's writing style compare to yours?

References

Bartholomae, David. "The Study of Error." *Rhetoric and Composition*. 2nd ed. Ed. Richard L. Graves. Upper Montclair, NJ: Boynton/Cook Publishers, 1984.

Chomsky, Noam. *Syntactic Structures*. NY: Mouton de Gruyter, 1978.

Christensen, Francis, and Bonniejean Christensen. *A New Rhetoric*. New York: Harper & Row, 1976.

Clark, Beverly. *Talking about Writing: A Guide for Tutor and Teacher Conferences*. Ann Arbor, MI: The University of Michigan Press, 1992.

Cooper, Charles R. "An Outline for Writing Sentence Combining Problems." *The Writing Teachers Sourcebook*. Eds. Gary Tate and Edward P. J. Corbett. New York: Oxford University Press, 1981.

Folta, Bernarr. *Three Strategies for Revising Sentences*. Terre Haute, IN: Indiana Council of Teachers of English, n.d.

Glatthorn, Allan. *The Teaching of Writing, A Review of Theory, Research and Practice*. Philadelphia: University of Pennsylvania, 1983.

Griffin, Jack. "The Effect of Computers on Secondary Remedial Writing." ERIC, ED340018, 1991.

Heffernan, James, and John Lincoln. *Writing: A Concise Handbook*. New York: W. W. Norton and Company, 1997. E-mail address for software: Grammar Workouts: Interactive Exercises, http://www.wwnorton.com/college/english/wacon.htm

Horn, Susan. "Fostering Spontaneous Dialect Shift in the Writing of African American Students." *Dynamics of the Writing Conference: Social and Cognitive Interaction*. Eds. Thomas Lynn and Mary King. Urbana, IL: NCTE, 1993.

Kilgallon, Don. *Sentence Composing 11 and the Complete Course*. 2 vols. Portsmouth, NH: Heineman-Boynton/Cook, 1984.

Lindemann, Erika. *A Rhetoric for Writing Teachers*. 2nd ed. New York: Oxford University Press, 1987.

Loban, Walter D. *Language Development: Kindergarten through Grade Twelve*. NCTE Research Report No. 18, Urbana, IL: NCTE, 1976.

Mapp, Larry. *Harbrace College Handbook: Form 12A*. Fort Worth, TX: Harcourt Brace College Publishers, 1994.

Mitzel, Harold, Ed. *Encyclopedia of Educational Research*. New York: Macmillan, 1982.

Neman, Beth. *Teaching Students to Write*. Columbus, OH: Charles E. Merrill Publishing Co., 1980.

O'Hare, Frank. *Sentence Combining: Improving Student Writing without Formal Grammar Instruction*. NCTE Research Report No. 15, Urbana, IL: NCTE, 1971.

Renwick, Mitzi. "Real Research into Real Problems of Grammar and Usage Instruction." *English Journal* 83 Oct. 1994: 29–33.

Ryan, Elizabeth. *How to Make Grammar Fun—and Easy!* Mahwah, NJ: Troll Associates, 1992.

Ryan, Leigh. *The Bedford Guide for Writing Tutors*. Boston: Bedford Books of St. Martins Press, 1994.

Strong, William. *Creative Approaches to Sentence Combining*. Urbana, IL: NCTE, 1986.

———. *Sentence Combining: A Composing Book*. 3rd ed. New York: McGraw Hill, 1994.

Walvoord, Barbara. *Helping Students Write Well*. New York: Modern Language Association, 1986.

Weaver, Constance. *Grammar for Teachers: Perspectives and Definitions*. Urbana, IL: NCTE, 1979.

White, Edward M. *Assigning, Responding, Evaluating: A Writing Teacher's Guide*. 2nd ed. New York: St. Martins Press, 1992.

Williams, Joseph. *Style: Ten Lessons in Clarity and Grace*. New York: Scott, Foresman, 1984.

APPENDIX

Appendix 4a: Sentence Revision Exercise

Sarah Schatzinger
Dr. Soven
College Writing 108
Final Exam

1. Old: This is because he finds meaning in what he does.
   Revised: Bryan Stevenson finds meaning in what he does.
   Explanation: clarity; reference not clear

2. Old: Not once did he base this meaning on annual
   income, unlike those friends, who now work for large
   corporate law firms, but hate what they're doing.
   Revised: Not once did he base this meaning on annual
   income, unlike those friends, who now work for large
   corporate law firms, but who hate what they are doing.
   Explanation: parallelism; avoid contractions in
   formal writing

3. Old: Despite his parents' separate beliefs and
   values, Bryan based his life on his own value system.
   Revised: Despite his parents' beliefs and values,
   Bryan based his life on his own value system.
   Explanation: wordy

4. Old: Norma later found herself also fighting to
   contribute much protection to Huntley Meadows Park.
   Revised: Norma later found herself fighting to
   protect Huntley Meadows Park.
   Explanation: wordy

5. Old: Each person's ideas and opinions on how to go
   about making changes in the environment are shared.
   Revised: Each person's ideas and opinions about
   making changes in the environment is shared.
   Explanation: wordy, subject/verb agreement

6. Old: Susan is the president of Friends of Huntley Meadows, and has recently become a board member of the Fairfax Audubon Society.
   Revised: Susan is the president of Friends of Huntley Meadows and has recently become a board member of the Fairfax Audubon Society.
   Explanation: superfluous comma

7. Old: "Never doubt that a small group of thoughtful, committed citizens can change the world. Indeed, it's the only thing that ever has," (Margaret Mead).
   Revised: Margaret Mead states, "Never doubt that a small group of thoughtful, committed citizens can change the world. Indeed, it's the only thing that ever has."
   Explanation: always lead into quotes

8. Old: This view is shared with the reader through extraordinary and extremely descriptive language.
   Revised: She shares this view with the reader through extraordinary and extremely descriptive language.
   Explanation: take out of passive (tense agreement)

9. Old: "My Life for the Poor" and "The Great Divide" both clearly demonstrate how important these factors truly are.
   Revised: "My Life for the Poor" and "The Great Divide" both demonstrate the importance of these factors.
   Explanation: wordy; clarity; for greater impact

10. Old: These people have all worked on their own personal levels to make a difference.
    Revised: These people have all worked in their own way to make a difference.
    Explanation: wordy; clarity

Cristina Andrade

Writing 108

Part II of the Final Exam

1. Old: They were trying to get contribution by protesting
   but instead they were disturbing the public.
   Revised: They attempted to obtain contributions by
   protesting, but instead they were disturbing the
   public.
   Explanation: <u>Contributions</u> should be plural because
   <u>they</u> is plural. In addition, there needs to be a
   comma before the <u>but</u> because it acts as a
   coordinating conjunction.

2. Old: Roaring lions, hissing snakes, croaking frogs,
   all harmless animals that peacefully inhabit the
   earth along with the human race.
   Revised: Roaring lions, hissing snakes, and croaking
   frogs are all harmless animals that peacefully
   inhabit the earth along with the human race.
   Explanation: The old sentence is a fragment because
   it does not contain a verb that describes an action,
   occurrence, or state of being.

3. Old: The island contains wild beaches, but because
   of the Exxon <u>Valdez</u> oil spill the sand is now
   covered with petroleum.
   Revised: The island contains wild beaches, but
   because of the Exxon <u>Valdez</u> oil spill, the sand is
   now covered with petroleum.
   Explanation: A comma is needed after <u>spill</u> to
   prevent misreading.

4. Old: Dillard mentions different instances in her
   life that demonstrate her appreciation of wildlife.
   Revised: Although Dillard never confronts the
   dangers of wildlife personally, like Gwinn does,

she has felt a sensitivity toward wild creatures throughout her life.

Explanation: Because this sentence is the beginning of a paragraph, there needs to be a transitional phrase or word that connects the old paragraph with the new paragraph.

5. Old: "Nature is very much a now-you-see it, now you don't affair."

   Revised: For this reason Annie Dillard says, "Nature is very much a now-you-see it, now you don't affair."

   Explanation: Because this sentence is a direct quote from a text, the sentence needs a lead-in phrase.

6. Old: She hosts those who crossed the border while they searched for a place to settle.

   Revised: She hosts those who cross the border while they search for a place to settle.

   Explanation: The old sentence does not use the same verb tense. For this reason, the revised sentence uses consistent verb tenses.

7. Old: Because unjust actions exist, legal or illegal actions are taken to achieve legality.

   Revised: Seeking justice in the world today demands determination from the people because unjust actions are taken to achieve legality.

   Explanation: The old sentence is not logical.

8. Old: Because of the serious consequences that the project can cause legal actions are performed by the neighborhood led by Maria Elena.

   Revised: Because of the serious consequences that the project can cause, the neighborhood that is led by Maria Elena performs legal actions.

Explanation: The verbs in the sentence need to be active. In addition, a comma is needed after <u>cause</u> to prevent misreading, and to separate the introductory phrase from the rest of the sentence.

9. Old: To confront the situation, the class elected a spokesperson who explained their concern on the problem.
   Revised: To confront the situation, the class elected a spokesperson who explained its concern about the problem.
   Explanation: The wrong preposition is used in the old sentence. You explain your concern about a certain topic, not on a certain topic.

10. Old: Competition among people of every age exists in the fields of work, sports, studying, and many other areas.
    Revised: Competition among people of every age exists in all fields such as work, sports, and school.
    Explanation: The sentence needs parallelism.

Adapted and reprinted by permission of Sarah Schatzinger and Christina Andrade.

Appendix 4b: Discussing Style

Daniel File
ENG 300
March 27, 1995
Dr. Soven

Discussing Style

As a future teacher and a developing writer, I believe it is important to examine my own style, in order to improve my overall knowledge of the writing process. Discussing style is highly analytical but bears importance because I need to examine and to reflect upon my writing. By becoming knowledgeable about what I am actually doing, various improvements and changes can be made. As a student and teacher of writing, I believe that various modes of style should be utilized, in order to experience different types of writing.

From the day I began reading until today, I have been influenced by the style of various authors. When I initially encountered the writing of Oscar Wilde, my view of literature and writing changed. Wilde's style was similar to nothing I had previously read. On a surface level, there was probably a strong attraction due to the level of formality of style in his works. Wilde keeps a great distance from his stories, while simultaneously involving himself with the characters. Like Wilde, I strive to be a detached participant, remaining in complete control of my writing.

Wilde's sentences exhibit a great deal of variety. He utilizes sentences that are short and to the point. Other sentences are long, flowery, and poetic. His choices seem to fit each particular situation perfectly. As a reader and writer, I could potentially become nervous about such variety, but Wilde's ability and style exist on a level of exceptional maturity. In my own writing, I attempt to use variety in my sentences. I am not close to Wilde's sophistication, but my exposure to writers like Wilde aids my development. In comparing our writing, both Wilde and I frequently use parallel structures. I "unknowingly" create this structure in my writing, while he consciously uses parallelisms in his narration, as well as in the dialogue of his characters. My knowledge of parallelism has enabled me to ensure correct usage in my sentences.

The level of writing proficiency that Wilde was able to attain was not a result of luck. His proficiency is possibly a result of his exposure and experimentation in reading and writing. I firmly believe that I need to continue with my own exposure to literature and also to experiment with style. In the past and present I have not done much experimentation with my style, which I feel has held back my growth as a writer. Although I possess a style of writing, I believe my writing will be enriched if I write in ways other than formal.

Recently, because of my own reflection on my writing, I have tried different informal styles of writing. By "informal" I mean more colloquial, everyday language. This style of writing allows for the expression of feelings, signaled by the pronoun "I." I realized that utilizing various styles allows a writer to undertake different subjects more easily. As a student, I plan to use my education as a means for further experimentation, and I plan to enroll in courses that will allow and encourage a deviation from a formal style of writing.

As a teacher, I plan to assign traditional writing assignments, in addition to more creative ones. Students should understand that there is more than one way to write an essay. Essentially, I hope to demonstrate various styles and their appropriateness to my students, using their own experience as writers to truly instruct. By possessing numerous writing styles, students will be more prepared to handle various written tasks. Also, because of their practice and knowledge of themselves as writers, they will improve their style.

As a student and teacher of writing, I will approach literature with an open mind and experiment with style. I hope that neither my students nor I will ever be forced to suppress an urge to write "nonacademically" because only formal, academic language is "permitted." I will utilize my present knowledge, as well as my soon to be acquired knowledge, to provide a foundation for my students' writing, remembering that developing a student's ability to write is greatly enhanced through experience and practice.

Adapted and reprinted by permission of Daniel File.

Appendix 4c: Summary

Rosemarie McConomy

ENG 300

Dr. Margot Soven

Summary
Speaker: Dr. Marjorie Allan

Dr. Allan was a very interesting speaker who gave great advice for future teachers of English. Her lesson addressed three main points that teachers need to deal with when teaching grammar: 1) correction of errors, 2) syntactic maturity, and 3) dealing with dialect interference. What she stressed most was that for progress with grammar to truly occur, students need to work with their own writing rather than sample sentences in a textbook exercise. Another point she stressed was the unimportance of grammatical terminology to students. The important part of grammar is not the memorization of terms, but rather being able to recognize errors and apply rules to correct them.

The idea I found most interesting in Dr. Allan's discussion was the distribution of responsibility upon the students. Her method of having each student be responsible for a different grammatical error seems excellent. The student becomes an expert on the error he or she was assigned and is called upon to help other students who come in contact with that error. This places responsibility on the students and gives them confidence in being called on for help as teachers. It also gives the teacher a break from the monotony of teaching grammar exercises and allows the students to become more active in the classroom. The students learn through helping others, as well as being helped by others. It seemed surprising to me that collaborative learning is not used as much in grammar as it is in writing.

In conclusion, Dr. Allan mentioned the importance of consistency in grading. As a future teacher, I would not want to give mixed messages to my students by only correcting a few errors on their drafts, but deducting for every error on their good copy. Dr. Allen's talk was very enlightening and I hope to learn a lot more about grammar when I take her class.

Adapted and reprinted by permission of Rosemarie McConomy.

5

Evaluating and Responding to Student Writing

Classroom A. Jennifer is in the ninth grade. She is ready to submit her completed essay but is pretty nervous. All she can think about at this moment is the anticipated grade. Will she get an A this time? She tried very hard on her last paper, but received only a C. A conscientious student, she had tried to remedy the problems her teacher cited in her last paper but somehow had missed the mark again.

Matthew, in the same class, is not nearly as nervous as Jennifer as he submits his paper. He is discouraged and has given up. His last three papers have received C's. Although he always tried to follow his teacher's suggestions, all he got for his efforts on his last paper was another C. Why bother? He thinks that this teacher has him pegged as a C student.

Classroom B. Tanya is in ninth grade. She is submitting a completed essay. However, her main concern is not her grade, which she knows she will have an opportunity to improve. Her instructor uses portfolios. Though she will receive a grade on her paper, she will be permitted to revise her paper to incorporate her teacher's suggestions and place the revised version in her portfolio.

Evaluation plays a powerful role when we teach students how to write, even in classes where instructors use a process approach to composition. The way we evaluate students' writing strongly influences the way they will approach their writing assignments. Teachers can construct the most ingenious assignments, they can teach students how to manage the writing process, but when it comes to sitting down to write, many students will be most influenced by their expectations regarding evaluation. These expectations are communicated in our direct comments on student papers and by our overall approach to teaching.

A study on college students' attitudes toward writing assignments, which I conducted several years ago, supports this general view. The students I interviewed were eager to write because they knew that criticism was not the instructor's main interest (Soven, "Designing Writing Assignments" 18). Other studies have shown that in classes in which students believe that the teacher is preoccupied with evaluation they may develop writer's block—they often are not able to even begin the task of writing because of their fear of criticism (Bechtel 152). The task for us as teachers is to avoid such extreme situations while simultaneously providing meaningful feedback to our students.

This chapter will help you to consider issues related to evaluation by raising and discussing several questions:

1. What role should evaluation play in the teaching of writing?
2. Does overgrading or overcorrecting prevent students from doing their best work?
3. What explains the overgrading syndrome?
4. What is the difference between evaluating and responding to student writing?
5. Which are more useful, written comments or individual conferences?
6. How can the use of portfolios help in the evaluation process?

Too Much Evaluation, Too Much Grading

In classes where the teacher evaluates only the final paper, writing becomes a matter of trial and error. If teachers do not also respond to students' prewriting exercises and multiple drafts, the burden falls on response to the final paper as the instructor's primary instructional tool. In the past, the red pencil became famous, perhaps one should say infamous, as frustrated teachers attempted to eliminate error, and teach students all there was to know about writing *after* the fact, after the student had written the paper. The rationale for this approach is not hard to understand. The assumption was, and often still is, that students would conscientiously study the little red marks, some of which were difficult to read or interpret, such as the ever present "awk," and automatically avoid the identified errors in the next paper. For some students this approach works. But we know from research, and our own experience as students, that for many it is ineffective. Many students rarely look at those squiggly little marks, or even at the comments, and instead, when a set of papers is returned, focus their attention on the grade and spend their time computing their grade average. When it comes time to write the next paper, the process of trial and error begins all over again.

What is grading? In *The Writing Process in Action: A Handbook for Teachers* Proett and Gill define grading as "the act of assigning a letter or a number to represent the performance of a writer" (25). In a writing program where final text evaluation is the primary method of teaching writing, grading is all important. Unfortunately, when a student receives a grade on a paper, it often has the effect of interrupting the learning process rather than furthering it, especially for students who receive a discouraging grade. The grade gives a report to the learner about what has been learned, and only secondarily provides stimulus for new learning, because the opportunity to improve is not immediate. The next opportunity to write may not arrive for another few weeks. This kind of evaluation is called *summative* evaluation, in contrast to *formative* evaluation, which is a response to a draft that allows the student to improve the paper. Summative evaluation often serves administrative purposes rather than students' needs. To fulfill school requirements, the instructor needs a certain number of grades to provide the basis and justification for the final grade at the end of the semester.

Graded papers are often marked intensively, every error underlined or checked, in part to justify the grade itself. But intensive correction can destroy the writer's morale. My own reaction to having my doctoral dissertation proposal returned with a blinding amount of green ink is a good example of an extreme case of morale injury. Somewhat horrified, I stashed the proposal away in a file draw, unable to look at it for several months; it took that long to get up the courage to read my dissertation advisor's criticism. And even then, I was incapable of revising it. The experience was a major setback. I had great difficulty returning to my research project and began to seriously doubt my ability to complete my doctoral dissertation. Secondary school students, just beginning to write formal papers, are even more vulnerable to criticism than graduate students, although no one likes negative criticism in heavy doses.

The overcorrecting syndrome has been the subject of much research. The most important and saddest part of this story is that there seems to be no significant difference between the improvement in the writing abilities of students whose teachers marked their papers intensively compared to those students whose teachers noted a moderate number of corrections. Data from the National Association for Educational Progress and studies by George Hillocks and others support this finding: "Correcting involves pointing out the student mistakes; if it is done by the teacher with no further response from the student, it is probably a *useless* [emphasis added] activity" (Proett and Gill 25).

Students are not the only ones who suffer from overcorrecting. Excessive correcting is burdensome to instructors and is probably the main reason that many teachers dislike teaching writing. It simply takes too much time. Zemel-man and Daniels have done the mathematics:

> With a student load of 125, a teacher who makes a single writing assignment and then spends ten minutes on each paper, has committed more than 20 hours to out-of-class time. Ironically such marking takes so much time that it tends to limit the amount of writing one assigns—after all a teacher cannot assign more writing than he can responsibly evaluate in the waking hours of his life. But if "responsibly evaluate" means to correct intensively every word that every student ever writes, the teacher-evaluator becomes a bottle-neck in the process; you begin to constrain the amount of writing practice students get. And since research says that students grow more from practice than from correction, this becomes an insidious professional trap. (212)

Sometimes teachers overcorrect because of their blind adherence to the "rules of good writing." For example, using the passive voice is generally a bad idea—it often produces weak sentences. But in a laboratory report, in which the subject doing the action is not as important as the action itself, the passive voice is appropriate. For example, it is reasonable to say, "The experiment was performed by Tom, Sally, and Don," if the experiment, rather than the students who performed it, is the subject of interest. Another example of correcting students for the wrong reasons is faulting them for using the first person pronoun, *I*. In personal essays, where students are writing about themselves, using *one* instead of *I* is awkward and weakens the effect of the paper. In *On Writing Well*, William Zinnser says, "Writers are obviously at their most natural when they write in the first person. Writing is a personal transaction between two people, conducted on paper, and the transaction will go well to the extent that it retains its humanity. Therefore, I urge people to write in the first person: to use 'I' and 'me' and 'we' and 'us'" (22). No doubt Zinnser was responding to the writing practices of students in his classes who had previously been taught a rule of "good writing" that does not have universal applicability.

One of my favorite examples of an inappropriate "correction" is a teacher's response to a fifth grade paper written by Andy Soven.

Animals

Animals in the park are numerios. Here are some commen except for the bob-cat. The bobcat is about 15 inchs high and weighs about 15–20 pounds. They are mostly pale colored and live in the busy ravines in Bryce. Another ani-mal is the chipmunk. which stands about 8 in. long, including the tail and if they don't get killed it shoud be about 2–3 years in age. The mountain lion is about 4–5 feet long and have a 2½ foot tail. Their color is either gray or tawny. The live to 10–12 years old. The coyote of Bryce is about 16–21 inches at the sholder. The coyote also has a long bushy tail. Some other animals are muledeer, porcupines an gray foxes.

The teacher's sole comment: "Make separate paragraphs for each topic."

What is it about paragraphing that this instructor tried to convey? If Andy were to take her advice, his essay would consist of one-sentence paragraphs, a very atypical construction. What does *new topic* mean? The definition of the paragraph as a block of prose needed every time the reader begins a new topic does not begin to describe all of the reasons writers begin new paragraphs. For example, a major reason for paragraphing is to give the reader a rest. Paragraphs in modern prose are approximately a hundred words in length. And *new topic* is a relative term, depending on how the writer plans to divide his or her subject. Andy would need to add a lot more information about each animal for the instructor's suggestion to be meaningful.

The teacher's comment also illustrates a lack of awareness about the development of writing ability. Most students in the fifth grade have a very hazy view of the paragraph as an element of discourse. But Andy's teacher's high expectations are not surprising. English teachers' expectations for novice writers are often unrealistic. We know that because writing is a complex activity and, because writing skills take considerable time to develop, it is unreasonable to expect that students will develop skills in all areas of writing simultaneously.

What Is the Value of Not Grading?

In real life we don't believe that we must be constantly monitored and corrected every time we learn. On the contrary, when we consciously structure optimal learning situations outside of school, we tend to provide a rather low ratio of evaluative feedback to unmonitored practice. Think of the way we teach piano. The customary arrangement is that the pupil practices perhaps five or ten hours per week and then sees the teacher for a single hour. And during that session the teacher does not just evaluate, or criticize, and give feedback; she also listens, plays the instrument a bit, talks about feelings and attitudes, plans the practice schedule for the following week, and attends to a variety of other matters. Even when she the teacher is evaluating, she does not stop the student to point out and criticize every single misplayed note or passage. Instead, the effective music teacher is selective—she skillfully focuses the pupil on a few problems at a time, ones that are within the student's reach to attend to and correct (Zemelman and Daniels 209). I would add that the piano teacher also listens to her student when he explains why he is having trouble playing the music. Or the student may ask questions. He may even question her criticism: "I thought that was the way you wanted me to do it," or he may say, "I can't seem to get that right this week."

Anyone who has studied music knows that unless coerced by a well-meaning parent to keep at it, many students only continue their lessons because they develop a significant relationship with their teacher. This is in spite of the fact that a large part of learning how to play an instrument consists of criticism. The teacher not only models a love of music but listens sympathetically as the beginner tries to develop the language of music, a language more difficult to learn than the one we use for writing.

I can still see my son, whose legs were too short to reach the pedals of the piano, proudly playing a very short piece at his first recital. His instructor smiled encouragingly, even as he made one or two mistakes. Her approach to teaching combined criticism and compliments in just the right amounts to keep a very active seven-year-old boy interested in playing the piano and even practicing at home. After she died, we tried several other instructors, who turned out to be either too demanding or overly positive. Andrew gave up the piano.

The analogy to teaching writing is obvious. If unmonitored practice with limited feedback works very nicely in learning the piano and other pursuits in life, we have no reason to think it won't work in writing too (Zemelman and Daniels 210). Students will tolerate criticism when they believe that they are writing for a teacher who cares about them, who is interested in what they have to say, and cheers them on as they experiment with new kinds of writing.

Like the music teacher, the writing instructor begins a dialogue with each student in the class through the spoken and written comments related to the student's work. If successful, it is an ongoing dialogue that establishes a relationship between the student and instructor in which the instructor convinces the student that she is interested in what he has to say. Furthermore, this dialogue stresses the continuity between each of the student's efforts. The instructor keeps reminding the student that the development of writing skills is an ongoing process, that each paper is related to those that came before it and to the assignments that will come after it. How to develop that dialogue is what the rest of this chapter is all about.

Evaluation and Response: How Do They Differ?

The fundamental principle that informs the following suggestions is that for evaluation to be effective, instructors must distinguish between *evaluating* and *responding* to student writing. Evaluation is your assessment of the writing. Your knowledge of the characteristics of various kinds of writing and of the developmental writing norms for your class or school will help you to judge the quality of your students' writing. Responding is what you say to your students. You must decide what to say and how to convey your appraisal of their writing. Rarely will you give your students a comprehensive report of your evaluation because you recognize that they cannot possibly attend to everything at once. Once you have decided what to say, the words you use in your comments must be carefully chosen both to give students an honest judgment about their writing and to motivate them to try again, to keep on writing.

Evaluation and response are part of a process that begins long before the finished paper is submitted. It starts when you first communicate expectations for the assignment, and it does not end until you grade the last paper of the semester or have reviewed the student's portfolio.

Five steps are necessary in developing successful evaluations for student writing. Each of these steps requires you to make important decisions that will affect not only your students' writing but their attitudes toward writing.

The Evaluation Process

1. Begin by developing an explicit set of criteria, which reflects the skills you have taught, developmental norms, the special characteristics of the assignment, and the general qualities required of all assignments regardless of content or form.
2. If a grade is to be assigned to the paper, develop a grading scale, a description of the qualities a paper must demonstrate to receive each grade.
3. Distribute the evaluation criteria to your students at the same time you give the assignment.
4. Choose a form of response. Do you plan to write comments on the papers or set up student conferences, or both?
5. Choose a method for reviewing the students' progress during and at the end of the semester.

Step 1: Developing Explicit Criteria for Evaluating
Papers and Assigning Grades

To develop criteria and grading scales, ask "What are my criteria for judgment and what are my standards for quality?" Some instructors believe that evaluation should be limited to skills taught for the specific paper. A more balanced approach would place more emphasis on the skill that has been taught recently and less on other features of the paper. But it is important that the students understand your grading criteria.

For example, when I teach the summary, I explain that I will grade students' work using the following criteria:

1. Are the main ideas of the reading clearly stated?
2. Are the relationships between the ideas clearly indicated?
3. Are important examples and explanations included?

4. Is all essential information (names, costs, places, dates, etc.) included?
5. Is the length of the summary appropriate in view of the purpose of the summary and the nature of the material being summarized?
6. Has the writer avoided including his or her own opinion in the summary?
7. Are spelling, punctuation, and sentence structure correct?

Regardless of the skill you're teaching, your standards should be developmentally appropriate to your students. In "A District Wide Plan for Evaluation of Student Writing,"* Roger McCaig describes how one school district developed such standards:

> The evaluation model was not developed and validated by traditional techniques. The source for the evaluation criteria was not defined as the content of five of the eight most commonly used English textbooks, a procedure often used in validating the content of standard tests. And it was not the opinion of a group of experts sitting around a big table deciding what student writing ought to be like. The data base for development of the model was the actual writing of the students. This decision about the process for developing the model is probably the primary reason for the remarkable applicability of the criteria as a way of looking at student writing and the even more remarkable improvement of student writing in the Grosse Pointe Schools. The model is based upon the reality of what students can do, not a conception of what adults think students ought to be able to do. (82)

For example, these standards were established for ninth and tenth grade students:

Level 1—Not competent: Content is inadequate for the topic selected, or deficiencies in the conventions of written expression are so great that they interfere with communication.

Level 2—Not competent: The student can express a message that can be readily understood, contains adequate content for the selected topic, and at least a marginal command of sentence sense. The writing, however, is greatly deficient in one or more of these skills, judged by the standards appropriate for the high school: spelling, usage, and punctuation and capitalization.

Level 3—Marginally competent: The student can compose a completed series of ideas about a topic with a minimum of deficiencies in spelling, usage, or punctuation, judged by the standards of the high school. The writing, however, does not contain at least one competent paragraph or is not competent in one of more of the following skills: sentence sense, spelling, usage, and punctuation, or capitalization.

Level 4—Competent: The student can compose a completed series of ideas about a topic with basic skills at a level appropriate for high school with at least one competent paragraph. The writing, however, does not demonstrate all the characteristics of highly competent writing: good overall organization, good sentence structure, competent paragraphing, good vocabulary, regular use of transitions, appropriate use of subordination, interpretive meaning, (as opposed to literal writing).

Level 5—Highly Competent: The student can compose a completed series of ideas about a topic with basic skills at a level appropriate for high school with the characteristics of highly competent writing listed above. The writing does not, however, demonstrate thesis development and does not contain critical or creative thinking.

Level 6—Superior: The student can compose a completed series of ideas about a topic with excellent basic skills, with the characteristics of highly competent writing, with adequate thesis development, and with at least one passage demonstrating critical or creative thinking. The passage of superior writing, however, tends to be an isolated example.

Level 7—Superior: The student can compose a completed series of ideas about a topic with excellent basic skills, with critical and creative thinking, and with a sustained vitality and richness of expression. (79)

Notice that Level 5, Highly Competent, does not assume that students in ninth or tenth grade can typically develop effective thesis statements, which is one of the skills teachers often incorrectly assume students have mastered by ninth grade.

When you are developing the criteria for a particular assignment, you should be aware of the reasonable levels of attainment for students in your school. If your school or district has not gone through a process similar to the one in the Grosse Point Schools, perhaps you can work with a group of your colleagues to develop descriptions of levels of attainment for each grade that reflect the writing of the students in your school or school district. You should not assume that the Grosse Pointe descriptions are appropriate for your students.

Start the year off in your own classroom with several writing samples, representing different kinds of writing to get a sense of how your students write. Remember that

One sample is not enough; research suggests that different topics elicit different levels of performance. Take all the samples for a given student and read them for several important general qualities. These four qualities have

been found to be significant for assessment purposes: relevance to the topic, coherence between paragraphs, concreteness and specificity; and mechanics and form. Recording all your individual assessments will give you a general picture of class achievement. (Glatthorn, "Teaching of Writing" 27)

Step 2: Developing Grading Scales

Although it is impossible to develop a mechanical formula for assigning grades, it is possible to describe a range of characteristics typical of papers that will receive specific grades. Developing such descriptions has the added advantage of helping instructors avoid the eccentricity of judgment that can occur if they focus too heavily on one element in the paper when assigning a grade.

Here are two examples of grading scales, one an example of *primary trait scoring,* which uses criteria specific to an individual assignment; the second is an example of *rubric scoring,* which uses general criteria that can be applied to a variety of assignments. The primary trait scale is presented with the specific assignment to which it refers; the rubric scoring scale is general and is presented without reference to a particular assignment.

Expository Essay Assignment

Assignment: You are an expert about many things—how to play a certain sport, how to do some craft or hobby, how to make something, how to achieve some school or personal goal. Identify some process that you know especially well. Choose an audience for whom you would like to write. Then write an essay explaining that process. If you have trouble thinking of a topic, complete this statement: "I know how to. . . ." The essay should contain four to six paragraphs.

Objectives: Your essay should demonstrate that you know how to achieve the following writing objectives:

1. Selection of an appropriate topic for the essay and identification of the audience.
2. Development of a useful plan for the essay, using a chronological order.
3. Beginning the essay effectively so that it arouses interest and makes clear the main idea.
4. Identification of the skills, materials, equipment, or special preparations required for the process.
5. Providing a clear explanation of the steps in the order in which they are done.
6. Defining and illustrating any terms not likely to be clear to the audience.
7. Providing enough detail in terms of the audience's knowledge and interest.
8. Concluding the essay effectively.

Standards: Your essay will be read with the following objectives in mind. In addition you will be expected to show that you can write an essay reasonably free of major errors. You will be given three grades:

A: This paper is an excellent paper. It demonstrates that all of the objectives have been met; that the writing has a personal style; and the paper is free of major errors.
B: This paper is a good paper. It demonstrates the most important writing objectives have been met; that the writing has a personal style; and that the paper has no more than four major errors.
I: This paper is considered incomplete. It does not demonstrate the mastery of the writing objectives and/or contains more than four major errors. Do the necessary corrective activities and resubmit a revised paper.

Major errors: For the purpose of this assignment, a major error is one of the following, indicated by the symbol noted.

S = a word misspelled.
Fr = a fragment or piece of sentence has been written as a sentence.
R = two sentences have been run together with incorrect punctuation.
¶ = an error in paragraphing has been made, or a paragraph has not been fully developed. (Glatthorn, *A Guide* 131)

The following descriptions, based on more general criteria, were designed for a freshman composition course but can be modified for the secondary grades.

General Scoring Scale: The Expository Essay

The A Paper

The grade of A ought to represent a range of accomplishment. Although we do not want to give out A's capriciously, we should not give them out begrudgingly either. Perhaps the following description will help us all to recognize an A paper with greater confidence. An A paper is inviting to read because it says something; it looks beyond the surface of things because it demonstrates the writer's ability to observe and reflect. It draws upon reading and personal experience for examples and has an organization that is rhetorically effective in advancing the writer's purpose. A strong sense of coherence often distinguishes the A from the B paper; the student who gets the A is clearly in command of strategies such as the repetition of key phrases, the use of accurate transitional expressions and of parallel structures. Sentence structure is fluent and for the most part free of errors in usage, punctuation and spelling. However, because A papers are often written by students who are willing to take risks with language, they may be characterized by slightly awkward or pretentious vocabulary or sentence structure. The A paper is not necessarily a perfect paper.

The B Paper

In a B paper the writer has actively engaged the topic, although the essay lacks the provocative quality and the sense of coherence that characterize an A paper. The essay is unified around a thesis and all of the supporting material is relevant; however, some ideas may not be as well developed as others. A plan of organization is obvious, but transitions between ideas are less fluid than the A paper. The introduction and the conclusion are satisfactory, and sentence structure, usage, spelling, and punctuation are for the most part correct. In some cases a teacher will give an essay a B (rather than a C) if the content is particularly strong even though the paper is weak in another area such as punctuation.

The C Paper

The most common characteristic of the C paper is simplicity of thought and expression. The writing seems "thin" because ideas are not sufficiently developed. The paper contains generalizations supported with one sentence reasons. The paper definitely contains a thesis statement, although one that is possibly in need of clarification. Organization is discernible, but may be difficult to follow because of poor transitions. ("Today I will discuss three points.") The diction in a C paper reveals lack of range and the mechanics are often inconsistent. On the other hand, as a consequence of the C paper's general simplicity, there may be few problems in spelling, punctuation, and sentence structure.

The D Paper

The D paper is difficult to read. It contains a thesis, although not clearly stated or supported with reasons or examples. There may be a discernible but illogical plan of organization. The paper may contain serious errors in syntax, usage, and punctuation, although a paper which is woefully thin in meaning but free from these errors can still receive a grade of D. Nevertheless a paper which contains good ideas and demonstrates competent development and organization should receive a D if it is riddled with major errors.

The F Paper

The F paper has demonstrable and serious weaknesses in both content and mechanics. It fails to state a thesis. The substance is thin, often because the writer has not come to grips with the topic. The organization shows no sense of purpose. The diction is either simplistic or inaccurate. There are fragments or comma splices. The rate of mechanical error is high enough to call attention to itself and seriously interferes with the reader's expectations. However, a paper may be given an F even if it does not contain a vast number of errors but is missing a thesis. In papers of this type, every sentence seems to introduce a new topic. (Soven, "A Guide" 39–41)

Notice that these descriptions acknowledge the difficulty of devising a mechanical formula for assigning grades. Each description tries to account for a range of writing that can receive the same grade.

Step 3: Informing Students about Your Criteria for Evaluating Writing

Distribute your criteria for evaluation and grading scales at the same time you give an assignment, as in the expository essay assignment described earlier. Include a section on evaluation in each assignment handout. Unfortunately, after many years of schooling, students often assume that instructors intend to be vague about their standards of evaluation. Many believe it is useless to question a grade. You should attempt to dissuade them of that. Both their writing and their attitudes toward writing are bound to improve when grading standards are made explicit. When students talk about their worst writing experiences, they rank murky grading standards with vague, misleading assignments as a major cause of dissatisfaction. Another advantage of distributing criteria is that students can use the evaluation criteria or grade descriptions as checklists during peer review sessions before revising their final copies, as discussed in Chapter 3.

Step 4: Responding to Student Writing

The following suggestions for writing comments on student papers should help you avoid many of the problems discussed earlier in the chapter. Keep in mind that the content and form of your remarks depend on the goal of evaluation and on the stage of the student's writing. If the goal is for your students to revise a draft, your comments should be more extensive than on the finished paper, when comments simply justify the grade. However, you may not wish to comment extensively about sentence-level errors in early drafts because these errors may not be present in later drafts.

1. *Give reader-based feedback as well as criterion-based feedback.* Reader-based feedback (a term coined by Peter Elbow) tells the writer what is happening to you while you are reading the paper and summarizes your general impression of the paper, in contrast to criterion-based feedback, which explains how the writing measures up to preestablished criteria, such as quality of ideas, organization, and so on. Comments such as "I got lost in paragraph three," "What happened to juvenile crime?" or "Until page two on the bottom, I was able to follow your argument; then I got sidetracked by too many quotes from the story," and "The many spelling and sentence errors kept me from paying full attention to what you were saying in this paper" show that you are trying to understand your student's ideas, not simply reading to correct the paper. Then sum up by describing how the student's essay impressed you: Did you learn something new? Were you surprised, saddened, or amazed by the information? Keep in mind that the most important question we can ask about any piece of writing is how it affects the audience.

2. *Use marginal comments to respond to content issues as well as sentence-level matters such as style, usage, mechanics, and spelling.* Marginal comments have the advantage of appearing adjacent to the sections that are the subjects of the comments. However, if not written intelligibly, they can be too difficult to read. Keep them brief.

3. *Comments should be clearly stated in a vocabulary familiar to the student.* Try to avoid terse comments such as "awkward" and "unclear." For example, the sentence "I do not have enough information to understand your point. You need at least one more example" is more explicit than the phrase "lacks development."

4. *Comments should encourage self-sufficiency.* There are three kinds of comments. At the first level you point out that you have a problem understanding the writing, but you do not say why: (e.g., "I do not understand the main point of your paper"). This comment assumes that the student is capable of identifying the problem and correcting it. At the second level, you point out the problem and explain why it is a problem, but you stop short of explaining how to solve the problem: (e.g., "I do not understand the point of your paper because your introduction does not seem to state a main idea"). At the third level, you explain how to correct the problem. You might say, "State the main idea of your paper in the last sentence of your first paragraph."

5. *Comments should not be discouraging.* When possible, stress the positive. Paul Diederich, in his landmark essay, "In Praise of Praise," says, "Find in each paper at least one thing that the student has done well, or better than before. Then, if you must, find one thing, and preferably not more than one thing he should try to improve in his next paper. Whenever possible make this a suggestion, not a prescription." Diederich continues, "If a student concentrates on one error at a time, progress is possible; if he tries to overcome all his weaknesses at once, he will only be overwhelmed. I do not know where the scientific truth lies, but I have more faith in the value of a few appreciative comments than in any amount or kind of correction" (40). Diederich's comments on the essay shown in Figure 5.1 demonstrate his approach.

Although not everyone would agree with Diederich, most instructors acknowledge that a positive comment such as "good point" or "well expressed"

One day, I descended the stairs in my longest skirt, knee high

socks, loafers, and my red, bulky turtle-neck sweater. My paternal

grandmother was <u>sitting primly on our pink flowered chair</u>, sipping a   *Lovely choice of details*

cup of tea. As I walked into the room, I thought she was going to

spit the tea all over the wall.   *Shattering contrast!*

"Beverly!" she screamed to my mother. "Beverly, you must do   *well-chosen word*

something about this child. Why, the way she dresses is <u>obscene!</u>   *In character.*

Just look at the length of her skirt."

Her face was red and purple-striped, and since I had never seen

her in such a rage, I became rather frightened.

Splendid!
Sounds just   "Why, when I was a girl, if I had worn that outfit, people would
like her.   have suspected that I was of questionable morals., Why don't you buy

that girl some high-button shoes and black stockings?"

My mother tried to calm her by saying, "Now, now, mother, that

is the fashion of the times, you know."

"Pshaw!" answered my grandmother and <u>tottered grandly</u> out of

the room.   *Some would say that one cannot totter grandly; but*
I think grandma could. Like Charles De Gaulle.

I think the trouble with families is that they are not up with

the times, but I have no time to prove it. It takes me too long to

button up those high-button shoes.

A snapper of an ending! Very effective to
leave it like this — without putting in the
intervening steps.

You make grandma come to life. A few bold
strokes, and everything in character.
                    PB Diederich   A!

FIGURE 5.1   Diederich—Example Paper

Source: Paul B. Diederich, "In Praise of Praise." *A Guide for Evaluating Composition.* (Urbana, IL: NCTE, 1965). Copyright 1965 by the National Council of Teachers of English. Reprinted with permission.

can often inspire greater effort than many negative comments. When it is impossible to give unqualified praise, a comment such as "the beginning of a good idea" may be appropriate for a paper that reflects hard work but requires substantial revision.

Do not get discouraged as you try to develop an effective style of commenting. It does take time. Here is an essay about Philadelphia, written by my daughter when she was in the eighth grade. In commenting on the essay, I have tried to model my views on comments.

Philadelphia

omit capital "T"
—add colon

Independence Hall, Boat House Row, the statue of Ben Franklin on the top of City Hall, Society Hill, and the Gallery. These places are all connected to Philadelphia, my hometown and the place which I like best. Lots of people joke about Philadelphia, but I like it. It is a very pretty city with a lots of things to do and places to go.

Even if you live in the suburbs you can have fun in Philadelphia. You can get into Philadelphia in 20–25 minutes and do many things. You can go shopping or to the Art Museum.

Perhaps you can combine these sentences

Philadelphia's colonial heritage also makes it special. It has interesting places such as the Liberty Bell and Ben Franklin's house. You have a sense of American history by living in Philadelphia that you would not get in another city. After all, the declaration of independence was signed here! and you can see where that happened if you visit Independence Hall.

The suburbs around Philadelphia are nice too, such as where I live. I do not think there are many other cities as beautiful as this one. I have seen many artists painting a street in this area. Also, when you ride along the West River Drive, the lights of boat house row are quite a sight.

Philadelphia is a great city. I certainly feel lucky to be living here. My family has taken many summer trips, so I have seen a lot of other places. They were nice and it is always great to be on vacation, but Philadelphia is a wonderful place to return to.

You need a
comma here

My Comment:

Ruthy,

Your good feelings about Philadelphia really came through to me. You use good examples of the kinds of things you like about Philadelphia. I especially liked your description of Boat House Row at night. I would like to know even more about the places you like to visit in Philadelphia and other places which remind you of Philadelphia's colonial heritage. Your last sentence is very effective. It sums up your positive attitude about Philadelphia.

I noted several sentences which you can combine to achieve a more fluent style, and two others with punctuation errors. Let me know if you have trouble understanding these suggestions.

Notice that I did not choose to comment on the lack of a comprehensive thesis statement, nor did I comment on all of the sentences that could be improved. I decided that Ruthy should concentrate on developing ideas in her next essay or in a revision of this essay, although she still needs to work on sentence elaboration and punctuation. Of course, you may need to limit your comments when you are confronted with a huge stack of papers.

   6. *Give students a chance to comment on* your *writing.* This opportunity will help them to understand the problems you face when you try to offer helpful comments to them. Melanie's comment on a poem by her teacher Leif Gustavson, an eighth grade teacher at Friends' Central School in Wynnewood, Pennsylvania, illustrates several of the qualities of a good comment (see Figure 5.2): It is personal; it sounds honest. Melanie takes the writer into account, when she says, "It fits your personality to a tee. I can see it being read in a smoke filled coffeehouse somewhere perhaps with a background of drums." But she is also specific and concrete in her criticism: "The last two lines are trying too hard, or so it seems."

Zoe and the leaves

In a late afternoon winter walk,
my dog listens to the
dead leaves,
tugging the lead
taut as a guitar string.
Only she can hear their sad song,
straining to breathe the melody of the
lazy summer
whispered between brittle, brown lips.
I'm whistling my own tune,
watching others
walk through the cold
when it occurs to me:

You can't go back

I kiss the air   *–stronger*
and my dog heels.

> Mr G.,
> Good work. It fits your personality to a tee. I can see it being read in a smoke-filled coffeehouse somewhere perhaps accompanied in the background w/ a rythmic banging of drums.
>   Here's my one criticism: The last 2 lines are trying too hard, or so it seems. Ever see on Saturday Night Live? -- that skit series called Deep Thoughts? That's what it reminds me of. You are trying too hard to be non-chalant and avant-garde. It's a good poem. Give it the ending it deserves.
>   –Melanie

FIGURE 5.2   Leif Gustavson's Poem and Student Response

Adapted and reprinted by permission of Leif Gustavson and Melanie Allen.

Conferencing

Most students enjoy one-on-one writing conferences, but junior and senior high school teachers, who teach four or five classes a day, may think it's impossible to schedule conferences for all but their weakest students. Some teachers attempt to see students before or after scheduled classes, during preparation periods, or during their lunch hours. However, conferencing during class may be the most practical approach to one-on-one writing conferences. Teachers can see students individually while the other students in the class are writing or working in groups. Several years ago, I observed in-class conferencing at Girls High School in Philadelphia. Dr. Morton Maimon, chairman of the English department at that time, would hold short conferences in class with individual students while the other students were working on their drafts. The chairs in the class faced the side of the room rather than the front, to give teacher and student more private space for the conference. Dr. Maimon would read the draft quickly, asking questions and offering suggestions. Each conference lasted five to ten minutes. Although the classroom may not be the ideal place for a student conference, Dr. Maimon's conferences seem to have several benefits—students received immediate feedback and encouragement as they continued to write their papers. They returned to their seats eager to keep working.

You may want to try longer conferences (twenty to thirty minutes) if your class is structured so that students are accustomed to group work or to working independently. A longer conference permits students to play a more active role during the conference. Research on writing conferences (Harris, and others) suggests that conferences are most effective when students help to set the agenda for the conference and play an active role in the conference. The following suggestions, from *The Bedford Guide for Writing Tutors* by Leigh Ryan, can help teachers, as well as peer tutors, conduct successful conferences.

1. Arrange the conference situation so that you sit side by side with your student, rather than across the desk. This arrangement makes you seem less authoritarian and permits you and the student to look at the work together.
2. The paper should be in front of the student. Ryan says, "If you are working at a computer, let the student sit in front of it and let him control the keyboard. This placement reinforces the idea that the paper is the student's work not yours."
3. Ask the student to read the essay or a section of the essay aloud. When students read their writing aloud, they often catch mistakes they have missed during their previous silent reading of the paper.
4. Be sure to have a pencil, scrap paper, a handbook, and a dictionary nearby. The student should do most of the writing; however, you may occasionally want to demonstrate a point, but it would be best if you limited your

writing to the scrap paper. By writing down suggestions and making revisions, the student remains in charge of his or her paper. A handbook and a dictionary can be very helpful for clarifying a rule of grammar or punctuation, or checking an ambiguous spelling.

5. Tell your students to come prepared to conferences with questions or problems. For example, a student might begin the conference by admitting, "I had trouble writing the conclusion. I don't know how to write good conclusions." Students are more likely to pay attention at conferences when they initiate or help to control the conference discussion.

6. Try *not* to do most of the talking. Ask questions which will invite writers to elaborate their ideas. Open-ended questions can work well to start the conversation, such as "Do I have the right idea?" "Is that what you meant?" "Can you tell me more about . . . ?"

7. End the conference by reviewing the student's plans for revision. If the student has taken notes during the conference, he or she should be able to leave the conference with some concrete ideas for revising. (15–16)

I conclude this section on conferences with just one warning: Do not reserve conferences for weak writers. All students can benefit from reviewing their writing, and all students need the encouragement and personal attention that are the benefits of the writing conference. Furthermore, any time you single out weak writers, you run the risk of increasing the negative feelings about writing that students may harbor as a result of their lack of success with former assignments.

The Computer and Responding to Writing

In schools where both instructors and students are connected through e-mail hookups, students can submit their drafts or final papers electronically and receive comments on the screen. Some instructors seem pleased with this method. The pile of paper has been reduced, and they can type their comments. Not many secondary schools have this much computer equipment. Although I am in favor of responding via electronic mail to drafts or journals, I believe that the students should print their final copies and teacher comments should appear in print as well. "Publication" is appropriate for the finished product.

Portfolios

Portfolios are an alternative way to evaluate writing, which places the emphasis on a student's progress rather than on an accumulation of grades on individual papers. Portfolios are not to be confused with writing folders.

Peggy Raines makes the point that for years teachers have asked their students to keep their papers in writing folders, but the objective of these folders was primarily practical. She says,

> *Basically these folders did little more than simply "house" the students' work in progress. Then, however, from the perspective of a junior high school teacher keeping students' work within the confines of my classroom was an important matter of practicality. I might never see their work again if, in fact, it walked out the door. Student assignments were often reported as being eaten by the family pet, or in some other equally creative way meeting an untimely demise. (41)*

Raines goes on to say that keeping their papers in folders usually had no direct benefit to the students, but served as a collection device for the instructor, who might need to review them to either corroborate grades or review a student's progress.

However, when we talk about portfolios today, we mean a collection of the student's work that enables both the teacher and student to collect and make periodic and cumulative evaluations of a variety of written products. The portfolio is a working document collection, similar to the portfolios of professional artists and writers. Some teachers permit students to withdraw papers that are not their best work. As Lytle and Botel suggest, "From time to time these portfolios might be pruned and the best work of the student retained. Grading of these portfolios can be periodic, with students selecting pieces they want to revise for a grade" (147).

Portfolios can be scored using the variety of methods suggested by Lytle and Botel:

> Selected samples from the portfolio could be scored using holistic, primary trait, analytic or some combination of these. A holistic score is a general impression score based on comparison (ranking) with anchor papers or a set of quality descriptors. Students can learn to score papers holistically as well. A primary trait score is based on stated qualities described for a specific writing sample (with particular audience and purpose). An analytic score is a profile of subscores based upon a number specific features of a composition (such as organization, coherence, spelling etc.)
>
> Rather than adapt a ready-made system of holistic or analytic scoring, teachers can generate their own system. For example, in Philadelphia recently, teachers in grade level groups from across the city came together to generate writing assignments which fit with their curriculum. Meeting again in these groups, they compared their experiences using the assignment and then evaluated their students' writing, using criteria they developed collaboratively, The same process could be used to evaluate portfolios.

The portfolio itself may be evaluated holistically and analytically using adaptations of the assessment of the single sample. Educational Testing Service has been working with several school systems to develop a portfolio approach to assessment.

A system for holistic scoring and analyzing portfolios can be devised by teachers using a process similar to that discussed in the previous section for single writing samples. In general, the procedure is for teachers to take a group of portfolios for a given subject and negotiate their ranking in four to six piles. By studying each pile for its qualities, a set of criteria are available for the ranking of other portfolios. Or a group of ranked anchor portfolios might serve as the basis for judging other portfolios. (148)

Also, portfolios give you the opportunity to reward your students for a comprehensiveness and effective presentation as well as for the quality of their writing. For example, when I recently used portfolios in a freshman composition class, I used the following criteria to evaluate them.

An A portfolio, is comprehensive and inviting to read.

A B portfolio is missing some ungraded writing and notes, but must include all final papers and revisions, and be inviting to read.

A C portfolio includes all of the qualities of a B portfolio but will be less inviting to read.

As part of writing instruction students should learn that a professional-looking presentation adds to the readability of any document. Although there is no need for students to get carried away by creating elaborate covers using medieval fonts, they should include aids for the reader, such as a table of contents and index separators.

Not all portfolios need to be graded. Instead, teachers can write summary comments about the students' developing writing process and writing skills, or the students themselves can evaluate their portfolios. Some instructors permit students to improve their portfolios. Leif Gustavson uses the checklist in Figure 5.3 for evaluating portfolios; note his final comment: "If you wish to work further on your portfolio, in the hopes of raising the score, please do." Gustavson's students know that grades are not cast in stone. They can continue to improve their portfolios after he has evaluated them.

Lytle and Botel explain how one teacher uses portfolios. They say, "She asked her students to (1) put their work in order, and (2) read and take notes on their own writing." This teacher suggested that students notice changes in growth, any surprises, the piece that gave them the most trouble, and the piece about which they are most proud. Finally, the students were asked to

FIGURE 5.3 Checkpoint for Portfolio–Leif Gustavson

Portfolio owner

Your portfolio was rated using the following criteria. If you wish to work further on your portfolio in hopes of raising the score, please do.

ORGANIZATION AND MARKETING

1	2	3	4	5	X2

AMOUNT OF WRITING (DRAFTS, EXPERIMENTS, YELLOW STICKIES)

1	2	3	4	5	X6

QUALITY OF WORK

1	2	3	4	5	X2

LOG RESPONSES

1	2	3	4	5	X6

INQUIRY AND RESEARCH EFFORT

1	2	3	4	5	X2

OVERALL IMPRESSION

1	2	3	4	5	X2

TOTAL SCORE _____

COMMENTS: _____

_____

_____

_____

_____

Reprinted by permission of Leif Gustavson.

write down how they see themselves as writers. This self-evaluation can lead to teacher–student or student–student discussions and further analysis and interpretation of how writers and writing develops (148).

Students' self-reviews of their portfolios can be guided by asking them to become thoughtful about a number of issues. The following list is adapted from "Writing Portfolios: Turning the House into a Home" by Peggy Raines.*

Portfolio Survey 1

What are your writing goals?

In what ways have you achieved those goals?

What still needs to be done?

What is your best work?

Why do you believe that is your best work?

What changes do you see in your work over time?

What would you like a reader to consider when looking at your portfolio?

What have you learned about yourself as a writer?

Many kinds of surveys can be developed. Some surveys consist of more detailed questions about the composing process than Portfolio Survey 1. For example,

Portfolio Survey 2

After reviewing your notes, drafts, and final papers, place an (A) or a (B) next to each item and explain.

(A) means you are able to apply this strategy or skill to most papers.

(B) means you need more practice applying this strategy or skill.

_____ 1. Starting a paper. Using prewriting strategies such as making lists and freewriting.

_____ 2. Organizing your ideas.

_____ 3. Developing your ideas with enough detail.

_____ 4. Writing correct sentences.

_____ 5. Finding the right word.

_____ 6. Using correct punctuation.

_____ 7. Using correct spelling.

_____ 8. Using revision strategies such as reading your papers aloud.

*In *English Journal* (Jan. 1996). Copyright 1996 by the National Council of Teachers of English. Reprinted with permission.

Raines suggests that students will be motivated to examine and discuss their portfolios by arranging parent conferences. She explains, "Students sent letters home to their parents explaining that they had been keeping a writing portfolio and inviting them to attend a viewing of the contents that the student would be conducting. They role played the actual conference the week before to become more eloquent in their presentation of their material" (43).

The use of portfolios encourages students to view writing ability in developmental terms. Portfolios help students recognize that the growth of writing ability is not one dimensional. Their progress in one area, such as the ability to develop ideas, may be more obvious during some semesters than their progress in other areas, such as the ability to use varied sentence structure. They also begin to realize that the nature of their writing assignments strongly influences their success on a particular paper, thereby preventing the disappointment or surprise they might experience when their third paper is not better than the first paper. When they review their papers, they realize that some kinds of assignments, such as the personal essay, elicit their best writing. Because instructors often give students an opportunity to revise papers before placing them in the portfolio, keeping a portfolio also encourages revision. Perhaps most important, by taking some of the responsibility for evaluating their work, students come to feel a greater sense of ownership of their writing. The portfolio symbolizes ownership. Gustavson makes it a point not to keep his students' portfolios. By returning them as quickly as possible, he sends his students a message: "These are yours, not mine." His list of the portfolios' benefits for both students and teachers includes these items:

For Learners:

- a sense of how work is ordered, organized, and displayed.
- a sense of freedom of process and strategy through choices and decisions.
- a sense of how to talk about, reflect upon, and understand their work and themselves as learners.
- a sense of growth and progress over time.
- a growing sense of good work and satisfactory performance and an inclination toward self-assessment and excellence.
- a sense of accountability and responsibility.
- a sense of completeness and pride of accomplishment.

For Teachers:

- a sense of how students are progressing, and how they are developing over time.
- a sense of student thought processes and problem-solving strategies and a more informed sense of the meanings each student is making.
- a sense of students' ability to verbalize about their work and what they are learning.

- a sense that the students are more in charge of their own learning and are developing feelings of ownership over their work.
- a sense of finding new roles in our classrooms as model, mentor, coach, and learning partner.
- a sense of grading less and valuing more, a more authentic way of knowing what students know.

Conclusion

We have come full circle in this chapter. We began with an anecdote about a student who had an opportunity to revise her work for her portfolio. Because all evaluation should lead to positive attitudes toward revision and toward improving writing skills, portfolios are a fitting technique with which to end this chapter. As a new teacher, you should experiment with the forms of response discussed in this chapter and try to develop a system for evaluating student writing that is effective, efficient, and humane. If you have been teaching, but never have used portfolios, give them a try. You will be pleasantly surprised!

Questions for Discussion and Writing

1. Analyze your instructor's comments on three papers you have written recently. Review the comments in the margin and the end comment, if there is one. Use Walvoord's three levels of response to classify the comments. How many of the comments are first-level responses, second-level responses, and third-level responses?

2. Review several other papers you have written recently. Analyze your instructor's comments using the following questions:
   a. Are they clear?
   b. How many comments are positive?
   c. How many comments refer to the reader's interest in the content?
   d. How many comments refer to sentence-level issues?

3. How would you change the comments on the following paper to conform to the principles of evaluation discussed in this chapter, if this letter was written by a student in the sixth grade?

Dear Rita,

I was kind of wondering why I didn't get a letter this week. Is there something wrong? Well since you didn't write to me this week I guess I have to pick a topic.

How about music? Well I like music a lot. I mostly like hip-hop and some of your old folk music. My favorite rap artist are Craig Mack, WeeTang Clan, and the riotous BIG. What kind of music do you like? Who are your favorite artists?

How is your family? Mine is fine. I really don't know what to say, because I'm not use to writing letters to people. I guess that's all.

Your friend, Shameka.

P.S. don't forget to write this week.

Revise this end comment.

Shameka,

Your letter is not about one subject. You switch from music to family. It also has many punctuation and spelling errors, which I have noted. Your ending is weak.

References

Bechtel, Judith. *Improving Writing and Learning in Every Class.* Boston: Allyn and Bacon, 1985.

Diederich, Paul B. "In Praise of Praise." *A Guide for Evaluating Composition.* Ed. Sister H. Judine, IHM. Urbana, IL: NCTE, 1965.

Elbow, Peter. *Writing with Power.* New York: Oxford University Press, 1981.

Glatthorn, Allan. *The Teaching of Writing, A Review of Theory, Research, and Practice.* Philadelphia: University of Pennsylvania, 1983.

———. *A Guide for Developing an English Curriculum for the Eighties.* Urbana, IL: NCTE, 1980.

Gustavson, Leif. Unpublished Teaching Materials. Friends' Central School, Wynnewood, PA: 1996.

Harris, Muriel. *Teaching One to One. The Writing Conference.* Urbana, IL: NCTE, 1986.

Lytle, Susan, and Morton Botel. *The Pennsylvania Framework for Reading, Writing, and Talking across the Curriculum.* Harrisburg, PA: The Pennsylvania Department of Education, 1990.

McCaig, Roger. "A District Wide Plan for Evaluation of Student Writing." *Perspectives on Writing in Grades 1–8.* Ed. Shirley Haley James. Urbana, IL: NCTE, 1983.

Proett, Jackie, and Kent Gill. *The Writing Process in Action: A Handbook for Teachers.* Urbana, IL: NCTE, 1986.

Raines, Peggy. "Writing Portfolios: Turning the House into a Home." *English Journal* 85 Jan. 1996: 41–46.

Ryan, Leigh. *The Bedford Guide for Writing Tutors.* Boston: Bedford Books of St. Martins Press, 1998.

Soven, Margot. "A Guide to Freshman Composition" (unpublished). La Salle University, 1984.

———. "Designing Writing Assignments: Some New Considerations." *Kansas English* 76 Fall 1990: 10–19.

Walvoord, Barbara. *Helping Students Write Well.* New York: Modern Language Association, 1986.

Zemelman, Steven, and Harvey Daniels. *A Community of Writers: Teaching Writing in the Junior and Senior High School.* Portsmouth, NH: Heinemann-Boynton/Cook, 1988.

Zinnser, William. *On Writing Well: An Informal Guide to Writing Non-Fiction.* 2nd ed. New York: Harper and Row, 1980.

6

Designing Writing
Assignments

Two very different but related incidents illustrate what happens when students receive poorly designed writing assignments. You will remember the first incident from the preface.

Incident 1: "Snow—What Is It?"

When my son, Josh, was in the eleventh grade, he was asked to write a paper about snow. That was all the information he was given. Josh had the whole family in an uproar that night. "What do I say about snow? What does she want?" We all joined in the conversation and tried to "psyche" out what the instructor was after. We decided that because she spent far more time teaching literature than teaching writing she probably would prefer something literary sounding, maybe with some metaphors about snow or even an allusion to Robert Frost's poem entitled "Snow." After much grouching and grumbling, Josh set to work, and in an hour he had completed his essay. It was returned the following week with a C and no comments. Several sentences were corrected. Needless to say, Josh was baffled. The teacher deserved the C, or perhaps an F, not Josh.

Incident 2: "The Contract of Vagueness: How Can We Destroy It?"

The Scene: a seminar on the teaching of writing at Beaver College in the summer of 1977. *The Speaker:* Rexford Brown, from the National Assessment for Educational Progress. Brown used the term *contract of vagueness* to describe the relationship between teachers and students when teachers give writing assignments. The teachers are often rather vague about what they expect, but *students expect* English teachers to be vague, so they complete their part of the contract by not complaining.

Although I cannot remember Brown's exact words, I do remember feeling somewhat uncomfortable. As a young high school teacher, who had had very little instruction about teaching writing, I unwittingly established my own "contract of vagueness" with my students. I was vague about my assignments, but my students did not complain, nor, I might add, did they produce very good papers. I could have avoided the "contract of vagueness" if I had paid more attention to developing writing assignments. Like many novice English teachers, I did not have the skills to design clear, appropriate assignments. "Devising writing assignments for students in writing courses is one of the most taxing and least understood parts of the teacher's job," according to Ed White, who has studied the relationship between writing cues, assignments, and assessment. He continues, "There is no escaping this task [designing assignments], not even if we believe that students should select their own topics. That just shifts the job of selecting assignments to the students, who need much help in figuring out what to write about and how to write it" (75).

Experience tells us that students appreciate assignments that are well thought out. Writing assignments that succeed include clear explanations of the teacher's expectations and provide cues for how the assignment should be accomplished. This chapter explores some of the problems involved in designing writing assignments and offers some suggestions for solving them. The first half of the chapter deals with general principles that apply to all kinds of writing assignments, including those written for an immediate grade and those that are part of an ongoing project. The second half of the chapter focuses on techniques for evaluating ongoing writing, such as journal writing.

Research on writing assignments has not completely resolved the question Lee Odell asked almost twenty years ago: "Is it in fact true that different kinds of writing tasks make different demands on writers and elicit different kinds of writing performances from students?" (41). However, we are fairly certain that the variables listed in Figure 6.1 affect students' writing.

Although current research on writing assignments does not tell us how each of these variables influences students' approaches to assignments, many writing problems are related to assignments that fail in one or more of these areas.

1. Students have insufficient time for completing the assignment (the context).
2. Students have too little or too much choice (the format).
3. The directions are unclear (directions).
4. The purpose and audience for writing are unclear (directions).
5. The task is too difficult or not sufficiently challenging (cognitive demands, affective demands, linguistic demands).

FIGURE 6.1   Assignment Variables

The Context
Encompassing situation (i.e., text, in-class assignment, out-of-class assignment)
Importance (i.e., graded assignment, nongraded assignment, test)

The Format
Number of topics or questions from which to choose
Type of topic (word, phrase, sentence, paragraph, poem, picture, cartoon)

The Directions
Reader/audience (actual versus imaginary)
Purpose (actual versus imaginary)
Time limit and/or suggested use of time
Number of pages
Number of drafts or revisions called for
Clues about appropriate form (i.e., letters, essays, reports, personal essays)
Clues about appropriate organization (i.e., comparison/contrast, chronological order)
Criteria that will be used to evaluate the writing

Cognitive Demands
Amount of information presented
Specificity of information presented
Rhetorical skills call for (i.e., ability to write introductions, conclusions)

Affective Demands
Amount of assumed knowledge
Degree of personal experience called for
Biases of subject matter (sexual, racial, political, religious, socioeconomic)

Linguistic Demands
Syntactic complexity (sentence variety)
Semantic complexity (vocabulary)

We can tackle these problems by making careful decisions about the degree of structure students require to complete a writing assignment, the terms we use to describe it, the kinds of thinking tasks we ask students to perform, the purpose of the assignment, the audience for whom the student is to write, and the amount of time students are given to complete the assignment. How can we make intelligent decisions about each of these elements in the assignment?

How Much Structure? How Much Freedom?

We would all agree that students cannot complete a writing task successfully without clear instructions. However, the number of instructions and the degree of structure necessary for completing an assignment successfully are hotly

FIGURE 6.2   Writing about Your School

Write an essay about your school. Explain which aspect of school is most important to you. Your audience is composed of new students.

1. Introduce your essay by describing your school.

   a. Discuss your favorite subject.

   b. Discuss your least favorite subject.

   c. Describe two important school events.

2. In your conclusion comment on the value of going to your school.

debated. Some teachers believe that assignments should be tightly structured, whereas others fear that too much structure will limit students' thinking. Those who favor unstructured assignments that give students many choices believe that structured assignments leave little room for interpretation or creativity. A very general assignment, such as "write about your family," may be too general for many students, but the assignment on that topic in Figure 6.2 may rob the student of important decision-making activity.

Instructors who are concerned about too much structure in assignments fear that students will follow instructions in a lockstep fashion, thereby avoiding some of the thinking tasks the teacher was hoping to encourage through the assignment. For example, in the assignment in Figure 6.2, students do not choose their thesis statement. The thesis statement is already dictated by the command: "Explain which aspect of school is most important to you."

My research on the effect of assignment instructions on student writing revealed that some students show a preference for writing assignments framed in the form of questions that include cues for formulating the thesis statement and organizing their information, but still permit them to choose their own thesis statements and organizational plan (Soven 14). Figure 6.3 provides an example.

To accomplish this assignment, some students will begin their essays by explaining the drug prevention program initiated by the president and stating their opinions about it. They then can choose to discuss the develop-

FIGURE 6.3   The President's War against Drugs

The president has declared a "war" on drugs. What does the president mean by a war on drugs? Give your own opinion about the possible effect of such a war, using examples from the newspaper to support your opinion.

ment of the "war against drugs" chronologically or by citing examples of the "war" in order of their importance. The questions provide a structure for the essay but leave room within that structure for the students to make decisions about content.

Open-ended assignments give students many choices, sometimes too many. For example, the assignment "write about snow," referred to earlier, required Josh to make the following choices:

1. What is the purpose for writing about snow? Should I try to persuade the teacher that a snowy day is a fun day?
2. What does the teacher as the audience want to know about snow?
3. How should I approach the task? Should I write a scientific explanation about the composition of snow, or should I write a descriptive essay about a snowy day, or should I write about my attitude toward snow— do I like to play in it, do I resent being obligated to shovel the driveway, and so on?
4. How should I organize this essay? Would it be effective to compare snow to rain? Would it be better to simply write a story about snow?

It is obvious that the more choices a student has, the more difficult the assignment. However, some choice is necessary for students to feel that they own the assignment, that the paper is theirs, and that their paper will not be like all the rest. Students want to be unique. They want to stand out. Often students have said to me, "I chose that topic because I did not think anyone else would choose it." Students can be given a choice related to any element in the assignment design: the topic, the purpose for writing, the audience, the form, or the style. When instructors are confident that students are aware of the options for choice and have the skills to make the choice, they can be confident that giving their students choices will induce better writing. Students are more motivated to write effectively when they believe they have some choice.

For example, the following assignment allows students to select materials from the class readings to fulfill the assignment requirements, although the subject of the essay is defined by the teacher:

> *We have read several stories that deal with the problems of young teenagers. What do these stories say about the subject of friendship? Why are some teenagers more popular than others? Use at least two of the works we read to discuss this issue in your essay.*

On the other hand, students in my classes have done very well creating their own assignments. For example, I will often give students a list of novels at the beginning of the semester. They can read any one of these novels and write a paper from a variety of perspectives. Most students welcome this freedom, but there are always some who haunt me until I give them a question about which to write.

Some instructors strongly believe that writing assignments should grow out of collaborative discussion among the students themselves and self-initiated questions. Ken Bruffee, in "Collaborative Learning: Some Practical Models," demonstrates how teachers can serve as facilitators when students are given this kind of authority over their writing assignments.

Assignment Terminology: What Is the Difference between Explain and Discuss?

You can help your students understand assignments by providing definitions of the terms frequently used in assignment instructions. For example, several of these terms are often used interchangeably, such as *discuss* and *explain* (see Figure 6.4).

Finally, be sure to give instructions for assignments in writing. Written assignment directions will not only help your students remember them, but the act of writing out your assignment instructions will help you clarify your assignments and perhaps revise them.

FIGURE 6.4   Terms Used in Assignment Instructions

Analyze: give main divisions or elements, emphasizing essential parts.

Classify: arrange into main classes of division.

Compare: point out similarities and differences. Sometimes *compare* means to identify only the similarities.

Contrast: point out differences.

Define: identify or state the important characteristics of a thing or a term that distinguishes it from other similar things or terms.

Defend: show to be right.

Discuss: examine in detail.

Evaluate: judge the value of something.

Explain: make clear; give reasons for.

Illustrate: give one or more examples of something.

Interpret: give the meaning or significance.

Review: examine on a broad scale.

Summarize: go over essentials briefly.

Choosing the Assignment: What Should Students Write About?

The assignment task makes demands on the students' cognitive, affective, and linguistic facilities. By cognitive demands, we mean: How will the student be required to think about the topic? Will the student need to use analysis skills, for example? How will the student be required to write about the topic? What kinds of writing will the student need to know how to do? For example, will the student need to be familiar with the conventions of the report or the research essay? By affective demands, we mean: How will the student feel about the topic? Is the material to be written about familiar or unfamiliar? Will the subject matter be easy or difficult to write about because of the student's feelings about the subject matter? Students who must write about emotionally charged issues, such as abortion, may either be inspired to do their best, or they may have difficulty writing with clarity because of feelings of anger or sadness. By linguistic demands, we mean: Does the student have the necessary vocabulary and sentence skills to write about the topic? For example, students who have not been trained to use the vocabulary common to argumentative writing may run into trouble if they use phrases such as "I think" or "I feel," which are more appropriate for a personal essay rather than a formal argument. How can we avoid assigning writing that makes too many cognitive demands? Assignments are often too difficult because the thinking skills needed for completing the assignment have not yet been taught or sufficiently reinforced. When the task is too difficult, students will often simply ignore part of the task or reinterpret the task in a way that makes it doable. The following book review assignment is a good example. Students will often write a summary rather than a review because they are not familiar with the questions underlying book reviews.*

The Book Review

Has the author accomplished her purpose?
Do I agree with the author's ideas?
Is the information useful?

To respond to the first question, "Has the author accomplished her purpose?", the writer needs to ask:

   a) What authority or credentials does the author bring to the subject?
   b) Is the date of publication or copyright significant for my interpreting the author's words?
   c) What does the author state?
   d) What does the author imply? Assume?

*Adapted from N. Kahn, *More Learning in Less Time.* Reprinted by permission of the author.

e) Is the argument valid (internally consistent, logical, the conclusions following from the premises)?

f) Is the argument reliable (supported by evidence, authentic)?

g) Does the form strengthen or support the content (by being clear, concise, coherent)?

The second question, "Do I agree with the author's ideas?", can be approached by comparing the text to other texts or personal experience:

a) How does the material relate to:
   1) my own experience, opinion, or knowledge?
   2) other sources (oral or written) on a similar subject from other schools or fields?/based on other paradigms or models, or theories/ by other authors in the same school or field?

b) What additions can I think of (improvements, more evidence, additional arguments, new questions)?

The third question, "Is the information useful?", can be answered by assessing the usefulness of the information for various audiences:

a) What applications can I think of?

b) For whom might this be of value?

c) How can this book change me? (65–66)

Assignments about literature make many demands on our students and, therefore, require much preparation. The character analysis paper is a popular assignment for writing about fiction, but this assignment will surely fail if students have not learned both the elements of character analysis through class discussion and how to think about character from a literary perspective. The Literary Characters' Value Profile Activity Sheet (Kahn, Walter, and Johannessen)* can be used to teach students some of the elements of character analysis and how to write about character (31). It can serve as an outline for a short theme on character.

Literary Characters' Value Profile Activity Sheet

Character: _____

A. Thesis: Explain what the character values most.

   or

   Explain the character's change in values.

B. What are the character's top three values? (If a change occurs, also list the top three after the change.)

C. Give evidence for the top value. (If there is a change, give evidence separately for the top value, both before and after.)

D. In a sentence or two explain how the evidence in C supports your thesis.

E. Give evidence to show that 2 and 3 are less important than 1. (31)

Sequencing Assignments: How Do We Increase Assignment Difficulty?

The kind and number of thinking tasks and the kind and amount of data required for the assignment contribute to the difficulty of the assignment. Writing about one text requires summary skills, but writing about several texts requires that students be able to summarize and synthesize the ideas from different texts. Students can learn to compare texts from several perspectives. For example, an important question is: "Do books differ on ideas or the examples they use to support them, or both?" If students are then asked to evaluate the book, this adds yet another series of thinking tasks to the assignment, as we noticed in the questions related to writing the book review. The thinking task variable increases the difficulty of assignments by increasing the number of thinking tasks, by increasing the complexity of the thinking tasks, or by having the students apply the same thinking tasks to increasingly more challenging subjects.

Writing about personal experiences is usually less difficult for students than writing about an unfamiliar text. In my writing classes, students summarizing the essay entitled "What It Means to Be an American" found this assignment more difficult than simply writing a personal essay entitled "How Does My Family Demonstrate What It Means to Be an American?" Although students must always interpret whatever they are writing about to demonstrate its significance, writing about texts is usually more difficult than writing about personal experience.

Yet, assignments that offer too few challenges are just as poor as those that offer too many. Some writing assignments in your classes should require that students engage in original thinking about significant issues. At all secondary grade levels students are capable of thinking about problems that affect their lives and the lives of those around them. These assignments may require more preparation, but students rise to the challenge if the topic or question is an engaging one. Richard Larson put it well: ". . . a theme assignment ought not to be given simply to evoke an essay to be judged. Its purpose should be to teach, to give students an experience in composing, selecting, arranging, and expressing thoughts from which they can learn as much as from the reaction of his [her] teacher to the essay. The very act of writing the assignment should help students think a little more incisively, reason a little more soundly, and write a little more effectively than before encountering it" (22).

The Purpose and Audience for the Assignment: Why Are We Writing? For Whom Are We Writing?

Although there is debate about how the choice of purpose and audience affects students' writing, most teachers agree that students write better when they write for purposes other than to receive a grade and for audiences other than the teacher. A peer group can serve as an excellent audience for writing, even when students are aware that their teacher will eventually read and grade their papers. As we discussed in Chapter 3, peer groups can be excellent sounding boards during the revision process.

Teachers often report that the most successful assignments are those written about real problems for real audiences. For example, Stephanie Yearwood from Beaumont, Texas, designed a proposal assignment. She asked her students to write a proposal "which is realistic" to a "real, specific" audience proposing a solution to a local problem, such as

- to impose fines on late library books.
- to change the layout of the school parking lot.
- to improve security at the local agricultural barn.
- to be allowed to take the family car out of town.

She says that "her students welcomed the opportunity to prepare carefully a piece of writing in school, and put it in the hands of a parent or boss, or principal, knowing that they had made their best, most logical shot at affecting the world they inhabit" (11).

Assuming fictional roles and writing for fictional audiences can also lead to lively papers. Students enjoy putting themselves in the shoes of someone else and experimenting with different voices. For example, one assignment I have used successfully in a freshman composition class, which can easily be adapted for secondary school students, asks students to pretend they are recent immigrants to America, describing the trials and tribulations of their early days in their new country.

For students who have recently immigrated to the United States, alternative assignments might be "How did you feel when you first came to this country?" or "Pretend that you were born in the United States. How would your life be different than it is today?"

A teacher can be an effective audience, if students view the teacher as a reader with a sincere interest in what they have to say and they understand how the teacher plans to "read" the paper. Will the teacher read it as an informed reader or as a reader who simulates ignorance of the topic? For example, when assigning an analysis paper about a short story, the teacher can tell students to omit a plot summary due to his or her familiarity with the work.

Theories about sequencing assignments in terms of purpose and audience, discussed in Chapter 7 on curriculum, especially the theories of James Moffett and James Britton, suggest that the less familiar the purpose and audience, the more difficult the assignment. For example, writing a letter to a relative about your summer vacation is probably easier than writing a letter to the editor of the city newspaper arguing for more trash collection in your community. The student already knows the answer to several questions about the audience in the case of the relative, such as: "How can I appeal to my audience's interests? What will my audience want to know about this subject? What kind of style of writing should I use for writing to this audience?" A letter to the editor requires an understanding of the interests of the newspaper's typical readership and of the editorial staff that must be convinced to publish the letter. A letter to relatives is usually informative and will make liberal use of narration and storytelling, whereas a letter to an editor is usually persuasive and requires a more complex organizational structure than simple narration.

Assignment Deadlines: When Is the Paper Due?

All writing assignments, no matter how short, require that students have time to go through the steps of the writing process—to generate ideas, to draft, and to revise. As Janet Emig discovered in her landmark study, *The Composing Process of Twelfth Graders,* teachers often undermine the composing process by setting deadlines that do not give their students enough time to plan and revise their papers. However, assignments given out too far in advance of the due date may be forgotten and put off until the last minute, unless the instructor guides the students through the stages of the writing process. For long-range assignments, such as research papers, instructors should create intermediate deadlines, which help students develop a schedule for completing the assignment. For example, the instructor can identify the tasks necessary for writing a research paper and evaluate the students' progress after each section is due. Figure 6.5 shows a sample schedule for a research paper assigned in January and due in March.

FIGURE 6.5   Research Paper Due Dates: January 28–March 12

Topic Sheet Due: February 1

Preliminary Bibliography Cards Due: February 11

Preliminary Outline Due: February 16

Sample Note Cards Due: February 25

Draft of Paper Due: March 5

Final Paper Due: March 12

Developing Evaluation Criteria: "How Can I Get an A?"

Developing the criteria that will be used to evaluate the assignment is an important part of developing the assignment, even for assignments that will not receive a letter grade. It is only fair that students know what to expect. Spelling out the evaluation criteria can help to decrease students' anxiety about writing and provide them with guidelines for reviewing their papers before they submit them. This is yet another strategy for breaking the "contract of vagueness." (Review Chapter 5 for more information on evaluation.) In the following assignment, the mastery objectives and the standards section detail the criteria for completing the assignment successfully (Glatthorn, class handout, reprinted with permission).

Persuasive Essay Assignment

The Assignment: Choose a current issue that interests you and about which you have formed an opinion. Investigate the issue to gather more information and to sharpen your thinking. Identify an audience you wish to persuade and write a persuasive essay that advances your arguments and attacks the arguments of those likely to oppose your position.

Mastery Objectives: Your persuasive essay should demonstrate that you know how to achieve the following writing objectives:

1. Develop a coherent plan for the essay, arranging your arguments and your attack on the other arguments in a manner that will be most persuasive.
2. Begin the essay in a way that will interest your audience and make clear your position.
3. Advance logical and convincing arguments supported by evidence designed to persuade your audience.

4. Attack the arguments and evidence likely to be advanced by those opposing your position.
5. Use a tone of language which will seem acceptable and persuasive by your audience.

Standards: Your essay will be read with the above objectives in mind. In addition you will be expected to show that you can write an essay reasonably free of major errors. You will be given one of three grades:

A—This paper is an excellent paper. It demonstrates that the objectives have been met; that the writing has a personal style; that the paper is free of major errors.

B—This paper is a good paper. It demonstrates that the most important writing objectives have been met; that the style is clear; and that there are no more than four major errors.

I—This paper is considered incomplete. It does not demonstrate the mastery writing objectives and/or contains more than four major errors. Do the necessary revising and resubmit your new paper.

Assigning and Evaluating Ungraded Writing: "Teacher, How Will You Grade My Journal?"

The practice of assigning ungraded writing has grown increasingly popular as we have come to recognize its value as a learning tool and the role that ungraded writing plays in increasing fluency and developing ideas. Joan Didion says, "Had I been blessed with even limited access to my own mind, there would be no reason to write. I write entirely to find out what I'm thinking, what I'm looking at, what I see and what it means" (335). For Didion, as well as many other writers, keeping journals helps them clarify their thoughts and find their significance. This is just one of the many purposes for which you can assign ungraded writing in your classroom.

Ungraded writing gives students the opportunity to write far more material than the instructor can read, without worrying about grades. As many teachers agree, ungraded writing assignments play an important role in the development of writing ability. Tom Romano, in *Clearing the Way: Working with Teen-Age Writers*, says,

> *In any writing class, then, the first and constant order of business is to enable students to establish their own voices. Teachers must cut loose the first day. Let them write in the form they choose. But make sure they write and sustain that writing long enough to rev up their own voices. . . . Call it whatever you like. Just be sure to cut students loose. Let them write rapidly*

*and frequently for a set amount of time—say ten minutes in the beginning
of a course—without regard to error, expectation, or self. Let them and you
find out what they sound like when they know their words will not be
marked wrong, when adhering to a particular form is not the prime requirement, when failure is an impossibility. Such free or nonstop writing should
be the staple in every English class. Its objective, its goal is the development
of fluency and self-confidence, the parents of voice. Plenty of honest language production—fluency—is the sole criterion for successful free writing. Quality of language production is not. But even so, frequent language
engagement in rapid writing will improve the quality of writing. . . . Although the main goal of journal writing, of any kind of free writing, is not
the production of high-quality prose, it often happens. When cut loose from
premature concerns about correctness and proper forms, when freed to use
the language they've been able to write for years teenagers will strike phrases,
lines, paragraphs, and sometimes whole pages that are nothing short of good
writing. (13)*

Ungraded writing takes various forms—the ongoing journals that Romano describes, and exercises and responses to questions at home or in class.
Regardless of what I am teaching, my students write before every class session. Since I have begun this practice, class discussions have become more
lively. Even those students who are naturally shy have something to say. As I
tell my students, journal writing reduces their dependence on me and the rest
of the class. No longer can they come to class to retrieve the "right" answer
either from me or the five or so students who typically dominate class discussion. Ungraded, ongoing writing encourages students to think about the
topic, whether it be a short story or the subject of an essay, before class and
motivates them to become active participants in class discussion.

To summarize, according to Anson and Beach (22), informal ungraded
writing can be assigned for these purposes:

Enhancing formal writing
- developing material for essay writing
- generating categories for organizing drafts

Enhancing the social context of the classroom
- enhancing classroom discussion
- constructing social identities and relationships

Improving thinking
- develop fluency
- learning to concentrate

- attending to intuitions
- discovering alternative modes of learning
- expressing emotional reactions
- recording, summarizing, and organizing perceptions
- exploring and extending thinking
- formulating and testing beliefs

Developing writing assignments that will not be graded requires the same care as developing assignments that will be graded. Assignments must stipulate a purpose and audience, even if the audience is the students themselves. Instructions must be clear and the procedure for evaluating the writing must be stated. Even when teachers assign writing that will not be graded, students assume that the teacher is in fact evaluating their writing, and they are right. There are successful journals and unsuccessful journals, just as there are well-written research papers and poorly written research papers. Whenever teachers read student papers, they are evaluating writing, although they may not be assigning letter grades.

Journals

Some teachers have students write in their journals every day. Students use their journals to store ideas for future papers or as personal diaries. In Romano's classes journals account for a fifth of the total course grade. Students can say anything they like in their journals; he doesn't grade them, or even read them, unless they ask him to. He collects the journals and thumbs through the number of pages. Grades for the journals are earned by the quantity of writing produced. Three pages per week earn a C, four a B, and five an A. "What if we write more than five pages?" asked one student. Romano claims ". . . I said with a magnanimous wave of my hand, that you will receive an A+" (12). Peter Elbow assigns "think pieces" in literature and writing across the curriculum courses. He uses the criteria listed in Figure 6.6 to evaluate them.

To be acceptable, the piece must be at least 750 words. You don't have to have a unified essay with a single thesis or point. And you don't have to be right in everything you say about the course material. I invite you to speculate and pursue hunches. But you must seriously wrestle with or engage the academic material in the week's reading and the topic or issue that I specify. Informal, colloquial writing is fine, but it must be clear to me as a reader. Handwriting is acceptable—even a few scratch-outs and write-ins are fine as long as the piece is neat enough to make it genuinely easy to read.

FIGURE 6.6   Criteria for "Think Pieces"

A variation on the journal is the dialogue journal. The dialogue journal is written in the form of letters between the student and the teacher. Janine Pierpont's fifth graders write dialogue journals about literature instead of book reports. Pierpont was curious to know what students thought and would say about literature without the teacher's questions. She and her students wrote letters back and forth about their recent reading selections.

Dear Mrs. Pierpont:

I am reading a book called The Iceberg Hermit. It's about a man who lived on an iceberg. It's a good book.

> from Marc

Dear Marc,

I'm glad you found a book you like. Who's the author? I'm curious—why do you like the book? Does it have lots of adventure?

> Mrs. Pierpont

Dear Mrs. Pierpont,

The author is Arthur Roth. It's about a guy on a whaling ship that crashes into an iceberg, and he lives on the iceberg, I don't know why I liked it. I just did.

> From Marc

As Pierpont explains, Marc's letters were typical of the letters she received at the beginning of the school year. However, the letters got longer as the year progressed, and students began to summarize the reading selections as part of their dialogue journal. In November she began giving open-ended prompts at the beginning of class, such as "How do you think the story will end?" These prompts became more like the kinds of questions teachers ask to encourage literary analysis, such as "Who is the main character in this book?" By alternating the prompts with the literary dialogue journal, Pierpont found that gradually students began to "delve deeper into their thoughts and feelings as they read and use the vocabulary of literary analysis to discuss their books" (1–4).

Journals come in all varieties. Some are more structured than others, but regardless of their form, they are rarely evaluated with grades. For example, I use the following journal assignment in a freshman literature course, but grade it *check-plus, check-minus,* and *check-needs improvement* to satisfy those students who are compulsive about grades; I prefer to just write comments. When a student presents a carelessly written journal entry, I refuse to read it and, instead, write back that it does not meet the requirements for the journal assignment. I urge the student to take the journal assignment more seriously when writing the next entry. In my literature classes, journal writing is worth 30 percent to 40 percent of the grade. The following assignment is an example of the kind of journal assignment I use in literature classes.

Assignment: Structured Ungraded Writing about Literature

To encourage you to respond independently to the reading selection I will ask you to write briefly about each selection before coming to class. These brief writings will change as the semester progresses.

For the first group of entries choose a passage from the reading. Jot down the first and last phrases in the passage. Discuss your reasons for choosing the passage by completing one of the following sentences:

1. This passage reveals the main character's problem. (Explain the nature of the problem.)
2. This passage reveals the main character's personality or values.
3. This passage reveals a very important insight about life.
4. I find this passage confusing because . . .

Each entry should be about a half to a whole page in length. Evaluation: I will collect your journals periodically and respond with comments, not grades. Good journals will respond to at least one of the questions with supporting detail from the reading.

The Computer and Ungraded Writing

In schools where students have access to computers and the instructor has one at home, students can send their journal comments to their teachers and to each other via e-mail. One of my colleagues who tried this approach last semester said that e-mail encouraged spontaneity and fluency (students wrote longer journal entries on the computer than in their notebooks) and enabled her to know the students' reactions to a reading selection prior to the next class session. The downside was that there were too many messages to read because she felt obliged to read them all before the next class session.

E-mail correspondence to other students, sometimes in other schools or even in other countries, is another kind of ungraded writing made possible by the computer. The notion of computer pen pals has become very popular. Jeffrey Schwartz describes three-way exchanges between students at Sewickly Academy, Sewickly, Pennsylvania, and students at Wilsall High School in Wilsall, Montana, and Little Wound High School on the Pine Reservation in Kyle, South Dakota. Students exchanged over 500 messages including letters, interviews, drafts, revisions, questions, and local histories. He believes that the students not only wrote better after the project but learned a great deal about communities considerably different than their own.

Several services for obtaining "electronic pen pals" are listed in the Bread Loaf School of English/Educational Resources. For example, "E-Mail Classroom Exchange" provides students with an opportunity to meet and correspond with other students from around the world. The class submits a classroom profile and then has access to other classrooms around the world.

We have yet to assess the impact of e-mail on the development of writing skills, nor do we know how it will affect the way students write. However, e-mail may become the most important site for ungraded writing. The possibilities it offers for real communication through writing are very exciting.

In-Class Ungraded Writing

Ungraded writing can be used in class to encourage learning of the course material. Starting class by having students write a response to a question on the blackboard helps them to connect the new lesson to the lesson of the previous day. During class, writing can be used to record small group discussions, often an effective way to encourage quiet students to speak in class. The class is divided into small groups, each having the same or a different list of questions. Each group can report their written responses to the class.

For example, in a literature class discussing *The Great Gatsby* students might be asked to paraphrase significant lines in the novel in small groups (see Figure 6.7).

Ungraded writing can be used as a vehicle for summarizing the discussion of the day. As the lesson comes to a close, the instructor can ask students to once again open their journals or learning logs and jot down an important fact or idea from the class discussion. All of these ungraded writing assignments can be adapted to other subjects. The writing across the curriculum movement has played an important role in promoting the use of ungraded writing. Teachers in all disciplines have found the following guidelines useful for designing ungraded writing (adapted from a document drafted by Toby Fulwiler, with considerable help from members of the NCTE Commission on Composition, including Glenda Bissex, Lynn Galbraith, Ron Goba, Audrey Roth, Charles Schuster, Marilyn Sternglass, and Tilly Warnock).

Guidelines for Assigning Ungraded Writing

1. *Explain that journals are neither diaries or class notebooks, but borrow features from each: like diaries, journals are written in first person about issues the writer cares about; like class notebooks, journals are concerned with the content of a particular course.*

Paraphrase the following lines:

1. "It was an extraordinary gift for hope, a romantic readiness such as I have never found in another person . . ." (2)

2. "Almost any exhibition of complete self-sufficiency draws a stunned tribute from me . . ." (9)

3. "They knew that presently dinner would be over and a little later the evening too, would be over and casually put away." (cont. to end of paragraph) (13)

4. "There was something pathetic in his concentration, as if his complacency was more acute than of old, was not enough for him anymore." (14)

5. "To a certain temperament the situation might have seemed intriguing— my own instinct was to telephone immediately for the police." (16)

6. "When I looked once more for Gatsby he had vanished. I was alone again in the unquiet darkness." (22)

FIGURE 6.7 *Gatsby* **Discussion Sheet 1**

2. *Ask students to buy loose-leaf note books. They can hand in to you only those pages which pertain directly to your class, if you are collecting journals periodically.*

3. *Suggest that students divide their journals into several sections, if they are keeping them for more than one course.*

4. *Every time you ask students to write in class, do something active and deliberate with what they have written. For example, students can read written comments aloud, or share their writing with one another in small groups.*

5. *Count, but do not grade journals. While it's important not to qualitatively evaluate specific journal entries (for here students must be allowed to take risks), good journals should count in some quantitative way: a certain number of points, a plus added to a grade, or an in-class resource for taking tests.*

6. *Do not write back to every entry; it will burn you out. Instead, skim journals and write responses to entries that especially concern you.*

7. *At the end of the term ask students to put in (a) page numbers, (b) title each entry (c) a table of contents and (d) an evaluative conclusion. This synthesizing activity requires journal writers to treat their documents seriously and to review what they have written during the whole term of study. (Newkirk 277)*

Conclusion

By now you should realize that there are no hard-and-fast rules for constructing and presenting assignments. However, by asking yourself the following questions, you will design assignments that will give your students a chance to write well (adapted from Lytel and Botel, *The Pennsylvania Framework for Reading, Writing, and Talking Across the Curriculum*).

1. The teacher's purpose in making the assignment: What will students learn? How does the assignment relate to the ongoing work in the class? How will the rationale and purpose of the assignment be communicated to the students? How can I make this assignment authentic to the students?

2. The audience for the assignment: Who will be the audience for the writing? The teacher as collaborator or evaluator? The writer's peers or another audience appropriate for the assignment? Several audiences or readers, perhaps peers followed by teachers followed by some distant audience (as in the case of a letter to the editor)? Will there be some choice on the part of the writer with regard to purpose and audience?

3. The topic: Will one or several possibilities be suggested? How will the teacher know if the students understand what is meant by these topics? If students select and develop their own topics, what resources (print, people) will they need?

4. The type of writing: What function will the writing serve—expressive, informational, or poetic? Can the student choose the most appropriate function and type of writing, or is that predetermined by the assignment?

5. The assignment-related processes: What suggestions can the teacher (or peers) make about the processes of writing that would be helpful in completing this assignment? That is, does the assignment seem to require extensive research and/or planning, or can the writer begin with brainstorming or drafting? Are several drafts necessary? Desirable? Does the piece require careful editing? Can the writer anticipate an opportunity to publish this piece, perhaps for a wider audience? Does the assignment require several steps, and, if so, how much time is required? Will students work alone or together? In what ways will the teacher guide or respond to the work? Will conferences—peer and/or teacher—be part of the process?

6. The assignment-related skills: Do the students have the skills to complete this assignment? Will they need to learn new skills? (For example, if the assignment requires conducting interviews, students will need to learn interviewing skills.)

7. Length of the paper and time required to complete the assignment: What is an appropriate length for this assignment? Will the students choose the length of the paper? How much time do students have to complete the assignment?

8. The criteria for evaluation: What is especially important in completing this assignment? How will it be evaluated? By whom? The teacher? By other students? By another audience (e.g., readers of the school newspaper)? Will it also be graded? (69)

Even after taking all of these issues into account when you are assigning writing, you may still be disappointed in your students' work. A good assignment can encourage students to engage in stages of the writing process once they have practiced writing process strategies. But even a good assignment cannot succeed if students refuse to spend "time on the line." Students must realize that writing well takes time. A good assignment cannot succeed if students have a poor understanding of the course material that is the subject for writing. Often reading problems, which can lead to deficiencies in students' content knowledge, are mislabeled as writing problems. But even the best students will not write well without a carefully designed invitation to write. It is your role to develop writing assignments that will get the best from your students.

Questions for Discussing and Writing

1. Describe your favorite writing assignment. Were the directions clear? Did it leave some room for choice? What were the benefits of completing it? Did you like the topic? Please explain.

2. Describe your least favorite writing assignment. Answer the questions that appear in question 1.

3. Rank the following assignment tasks in terms of difficulty and explain your choices:

    ___ Write about any topic.

    ___ Write about your friend.

    ___ Write about the role your friend plays in your life.

    ___ Summarize the short story.

    ___ Write a thank-you note to your aunt for a present you received from her.

    ___ You have been out late. Write the explanation you will give for being late.

4. Revise the following assignment to be a complete assignment. Be sure to include purpose, audience, assignment task, and evaluation criteria. Be sure to leave some room for choice.

    Write an essay describing your favorite friend.

5. Construct a comprehensive writing assignment to be written for a grade. Include the same elements as in Question 4.

6. Write the instructions for a learning log. Include the same elements as in Question 4.

References

Anson, Chris M., and Richard Beach. *Journals in the Classroom: Writing to Learn.* Norwood, MA: Christorpher-Gordon Publishers, 1995.

Bread Loaf School of English/Educational Resources. Online posting. http://tigger. clemson.edu/bnet/resources/comp.html. Internet. 18 Dec. 1997.

Bruffee, Kenneth. "Collaborative Learning: Some Practical Models." *College English* 37 Feb. 1973: 634–643.

Didion, Joan. "Why I Write." *Eight Modern Essays.* Ed. William Smart. New York: St. Martins Press, 1980.

Elbow, Peter. Unpublished Paper. Annual Conference on College Composition and Communication, Milwaukee, WI: 1996.

Emig, Janet. *The Composing Process of Twelfth Graders.* NCTE Report No. 13. Urbana, IL: NCTE, 1971.

Fitzgerald, F. Scott. *The Great Gatsby.* New York: Scribner's, 1953.

Glatthorn, Allan. *The Teaching of Writing, A Review of Theory, Research and Practice.* Philadelphia: University of Pennsylvania, 1983.

Kahn, Elizabeth A., Carolyn Calhoun Walter, and Larry R. Johannessen. *Writing about Literature.* Urbana, IL: NCTE, 1984.

Kahn, Norma. *More Learning in Less Time.* 5th ed. Gwynedd Valley, PA: Ways-to-Books, Inc., 1998.

Larson, Richard. "Teaching Before We Judge: Planning Assignments in Composition." *The Writing Teacher's Sourcebook.* Eds. Gary Tate and Edward P. J. Corbett. New York: Oxford University Press, 1981.

Lytle, Susan, and Morton Botel. *The Pennsylvania Framework for Reading, Writing, and Talking across the Curriculum.* Harrisburg, PA: The Pennsylvania Department of Education, 1990.

Nelson, Jenny. *"This Was an Easy Assignment": Examining How Students Interpret Writing Tasks.* Technical Report No. 43. Berkeley, CA: Center for the Study of Writing, 1990.

Newkirk, Thomas, ed. *To Compose: Teaching Writing in High School and College.* 2nd ed. Portsmouth, NH: Heinemann-Boynton/Cook, 1990.

Odell, Lee. "The Process of Writing and the Process of Learning." *The Writing Teacher's Sourcebook.* 2nd ed. Eds. Gary Tate and Edward Corbett. New York: Oxford University Press, 1988, 103–110.

Pierpont, Janine. "Dialogue Journals," in "Ideas from the Classroom." *Notes Plus.* Urbana, IL: NCTE, Mar. 1996: 1–4.

Romano, Tom. *Clearing the Way: Working with Teen-Age Writers.* Portsmouth, NH: Heinemann-Boynton/Cook, 1987.

Schwartz, Jeffrey. "Writing Exchanges on an Electronic Network." *The English Classroom in the Computer: Thirty Lesson Plans.* Ed. William Wresch. Urbana, IL: NCTE, 1991.

Soven, Margot. "Designing Writing Assignments: Some New Considerations." *Kansas English* 76 No. 1 (Fall, 1990): 110–119.

Yearwood, Stephanie. "The Proposal: Real World Writing and Research." *Notes Plus.* Urbana, IL: NCTE, Dec. 1995: 10–11.

White, Edward. *Assigning, Responding, Evaluating: A Writing Teacher's Guide.* 2nd ed. New York: St. Martins Press, 1992.

7

Writing about Literature

Write about your favorite character in *To Kill a Mockingbird*.

Summarize the plot of *To Kill a Mockingbird*.

Write a character analysis of the lawyer in *To Kill a Mockingbird*.

Write a short story in which a character experiences the effects of racism.

Pretend you are a newspaper reporter. You have been asked to write an article about the trial in *To Kill a Mockingbird*.

These are the kinds of assignments teachers use to encourage responses to literature. Good teachers want to motivate their students to enjoy literature and to see the connection between literature and their own lives. Teachers know that students' enjoyment of literature is enhanced when they feel comfortable reading literature and have some tools for interpreting it. They also want their students to be able to evaluate literature, to recognize that reading good literature offers greater rewards for the reader than reading the kind of literature that demands very little from the reader and gives little in return.

Teachers want their students to know what it feels like to be the author of a literary work, even one as simple as a haiku poem or a short fable. Writing fiction can help students become more aware of the elements of fiction. This chapter discusses a variety of approaches to writing about literature to help students read with greater appreciation and understanding.

Writing about Literature

There is general agreement about the instructional value of writing about literature. A comprehensive summary of research that demonstrates some of these benefits can be found in *Writing about Literature* by Kahn, Walter, and Johannessen. These teacher-authors and others stress the value of writing for helping students understand and interpret what they read and encourage frequent writing assignments to accomplish this aim. For example, Anthony Petrosky says, "our comprehension of texts, whether they are literary or not, is more an act of composition—for understanding *is* composing rather than information retrieval, and that the best possible representation of our understanding of texts begins with certain kinds of compositions, not multiple choice tests or written free responses" (19). Petrosky criticizes the use of short answer tests because they encourage memorizing the details of literature but discourage interpretation and evaluation.

Responding to Literature: Three Dimensions

The questions we use for writing assignments reflect the kinds of responses to literature we hope to encourage. George Hillocks classifies responses to literature in terms of three dimensions: the cognitive, the affective, and the aesthetic. The cognitive dimension includes understanding the explicit and implicit meanings in the text, drawn from the author's use of "words, images, characters, and events" in the work. What Hillocks calls the "cognitive response" will sound familiar to you because it describes what we think of as the traditional approach to interpreting literature, which has as its purpose the discovery of the author's intentions. The affective dimension describes the emotional impact of the work on the reader, how the reader is affected by the work. The aesthetic dimension describes the pleasure we feel in the art and artifice of the work; it involves the total artistic impact of the work, the unique blend of words, images, and characters, and events. Hillocks says that although the reader can respond on each of these dimensions of the work, ultimately they cannot be isolated from one another. According to Hillocks, it is the inseparability of these three dimensions that makes literature a distinct way of knowing (Kahn 3).

Teachers who use writing routinely in their literature lessons agree that both formal and informal writing assignments can help students respond in all three dimensions. Many instructors begin the study of a literary work by assigning informal writing, such as journal entries. Informal writing gives students the opportunity to respond to a text without worrying about the elements of the formal paper. Informal writing can help students clarify their responses to literature on the cognitive, the affective, and the aesthetic dimensions. Hillocks, in *The Dynamics of English Instruction: Grades 7–12*, and

Kahn, Walter, and Johannessen, in *Writing about Literature*, argue that we should begin with the cognitive response. Hillocks says that "if the cognitive response is inadequate, the emotional, and aesthetic response may be inappropriate" (168). Hillocks gives this example. Students reading the title "Brother Timothy" as a statement of kinship rather than as a clerical title can easily misinterpret James Hanley's story, "The Butterfly." He points out that one student who read the word this way came up with an emotional response not related to the story. Although he agrees that in some cases the affective response may simply be a result of the students' values or experiences, the cognitive response can help students judge whether their affective responses are justified. Furthermore, he argues, once students begin to explain their affective responses, how they feel about a work of literature, they draw on the cognitive or interpretive response. The two are almost inseparable. Hillocks says, "The two are so closely related, leading one to the other and back again, that they cannot be treated exclusively" (170).

The aesthetic response, in Hillocks's classification, comes last because it is based on a combination of both the cognitive and affective responses: ". . . we seem to appreciate what a writer has done with language as we respond with understanding and feeling" (171). Only a reader who can interpret a work and understand its impact on him or her can evaluate the effectiveness of the techniques the author uses to achieve these effects. Then questions that belong in the aesthetic dimension such as "Are the last three lines of the poem necessary, in achieving its impact?" can be addressed. However, instructors should not wait until students have read widely before urging them to respond to the aesthetic dimension of a particular work. If we want students to learn how to evaluate the quality of the literature they read, then we should have them write about the aesthetic dimension routinely. For example, students who read and love the works of Judy Blume can be asked to judge her ability to develop character, one of her major strengths as an author of popular books for teens.

Hillocks believes that the cognitive dimension can be elicited through sequencing questions and related writing assignments on the basis of increasingly abstract levels of thinking. He identifies seven levels of thinking, three of which stress the literal level of comprehension and four types that stress the inferential level of comprehension. For example, students could write responses to *The Pearl*, by John Steinbeck, to encourage them to respond on all seven levels in the following list. *The Pearl* is the story of a Mexican fisherman whose great wealth, suddenly acquired by finding a large pearl, brings unhappiness to his people.

Literal Level of Comprehension:

1. *Basic Stated Information: Identifying frequently stated information which presents some condition crucial to the story. Example: What happened to Coyitoto?*

2. *Key Detail: Identifying a detail which appears at some key juncture of the plot and which bears a causal relation to what happens. Example: Where did Coyitoto sleep?*
3. *Stated Relationship: Identifying a statement which explains the relationship between at least two pieces of information in the text. Example: What were the beggar's reasons for following Kino and Juana to the doctor's house?*

Inferential Level of Comprehension:

4. *Simple Implied Relationship: Inferring the relationship between two pieces of information usually closely juxtaposed in the text. Example: What were Kino's feelings about the pearls he offers the doctor?*
5. *Complex Implied Relationship: Inferring the relationship(s) among many pieces of information spread through large parts of the text. A question of this type, for example, would refer to the causes of character change. Example: What are the differences between the way Kino acts and feels at home and in town? Apart from what happened to Coyotito, explain the causes of the differences.*
6. *Author's Generalization: Inferring a generalization about the world outside the work from the fabric of the work as a whole. These questions demand a statement of what the work suggests about human nature or the human condition as it exists outside the text. Example: What comment or generalization does this chapter make on the way civilization influenced human behavior and attitudes? Give evidence from the story to support your answer.*
7. *Structural Generalization: Generalizing about how parts of the work operate together to achieve certain effects. To belong properly to this category, a question must first require the reader to generalize about the arrangement of certain parts of the work. Second, it must require an explanation of how those parts work in achieving certain effects. Example: Steinbeck presents a group of beggars in the story. a) Explain what purpose they serve in relationship to the first eleven paragraphs of the story. b) Present evidence from the story to support your answer. (Kahn 5)**

These questions can form the basis of ungraded writing in class or more formal essays. Students can be taught how to write formal essays about literature incorporating these responses by using Stephen Toulmin's framework for developing arguments. Kahn, Walter, and Johannessen create a series of structured exercises for proceeding from interpreting literature to writing formal essays about literature, using this scheme. They argue that although students may eventually be able to make insightful interpretations of literature using the Hillocks scheme, they will not necessarily be able to write successful essays if they are not taught the general rules of argument (7). They have found Toulmin's framework for developing arguments particularly useful for teaching students how to write essays about literature.

Toulmin identifies three basic parts of any effective argument: the claim, the data, and the warrant. The claim is the conclusion or the thesis statement, the data include the evidence for the claim, and the warrant is the explanation of why the data justify the claim, or, in other words, how you can make the connection between the data and the claim. For example, the thesis for a paper about *The Great Gatsby* might be, "Nick returns to the Midwest because of his disillusionment with New York society." The evidence in the essay would include Nick's comments about Gatsby "turning out all right" in the end, and his disgust with the behavior of other characters in the book, such as Tom and Daisy. The warrant would be a statement about disillusionment being related to recognizing the immorality of people whom you had previously admired.

Teachers can devise exercises and informal writing tasks for demonstrating the importance of claims, evidence, and warrants when writing about literature. The Evidence Abstract assignment, for example, teaches students how to accumulate and evaluate evidence to support their arguments:

Evidence Abstract

Students have been given the following assignment:

At several points in *The Great Gatsby*, Gatsby shows his love for Daisy. Do you believe that Daisy is in love with Gatsby? Write five specific examples or details from the novel that support your viewpoint.

A student might write the following Evidence Abstract to respond to this question:

Evidence Abstract: Student A

Thesis: Gatsby's love for Daisy is demonstrated through his actions and his words.

1. Gatsby buys a house near Daisy's house in order to be near her.
2. When he sees the green light at the end of the dock, Nick thinks about Gatsby's attraction for Daisy.
3. Gatsby invites many people to his parties in the hope that Daisy will come.
4. Gatsby asks Nick to arrange a meeting with Daisy.
5. Gatsby tries to protect Daisy after she has run down Myrtle with Gatsby's car.

After students have written their drafts, based on their Evidence Abstracts, they can review each other's drafts to evaluate the quality of evidence in the draft. The following questions help them make that assessment.

Draft Review

A. For each paper, identify any statements that you believe are incorrect or do not support the student's viewpoint. Explain the problems you find.
B. On each of the papers, which statements present specific evidence? Explain the reasons for your choices.
C. On each of the papers, which statements are not specific enough? Explain the reasons for your choices.
D. Write two additional examples that provide good, specific evidence to support your own conclusion.

Other prewriting assignments and revising assignments based on the Hillocks and Toulmin scheme for writing about poems, short stories, novels, and plays can be found in *Writing about Literature* (Kahn et al.).

Responding to Literature: The Reader-Response Approach

Many teachers agree with Louise Rosenblatt's theory of literary interpretation and have found it to be the most effective theory for developing a pedagogy for teaching literature at the secondary grade level. Rosenblatt says in *Literature as Exploration*:

> *Surely of all the arts, literature is the most immediately implicated with life itself. The very medium through which a writer shapes the text—language —is grounded in the shared lives of human beings. Language is the bloodstream of a common culture, a common history. What might otherwise be mere vibrations in the air or black marks on a page can point to all that has been thought or imagined—in Henry James' phrases to "all life, all feeling, all observation, all vision." (165)*

In contrast to Hillocks, Rosenblatt places greater emphasis on the reader in interpreting literature, which explains why this approach to interpreting literature is called the reader-response approach. She says, "the basis for intelligent productive reading is in the unique, individual, perhaps idiosyncratic connection between readers and the text. . . . Meaning is the product of active minds and the words on the page—it does not reside in the ink, to be ferreted out, unearthed, uncovered" (168). However, Rosenblatt does not believe that literary analysis should end with the spontaneous reaction of the reader to the work. The individual reader's response is only the beginning of the process of interpretation. Widely accepted interpretations of a particular work are the results of the sharing of many interpretations.

Rosenblatt's view of literature led her to formulate several principles for teaching literature, which have strong implications for designing writing assignments.

1. *Students must be free to deal with their own reactions.*
2. *There must be an opportunity for "an initial crystallization of a personal sense of the work."*
3. *The teacher should attempt to find points of contact among opinions of students.*
4. *The teacher's influence should be an elaboration of the vital influence inherent in the literature itself. (167)*

One method for applying Rosenblatt's principles to the classroom is to construct a set of questions such as those developed by Robert Probst. Probst recommends choosing approximately ten of these questions and placing each question to be used on a separate small page (4 × 5) stapled into a small book. This practice provides a place for students to jot down notes and encourages them to respond to each question fully. It also helps discussion later on, when students share their responses to the text. Probst says, "The questions suggest the possibility of moving from response to analysis without denying the validity of initial responses, of unique personal reactions and associations" (163). These general questions that follow can be used for reading various works (Newkirk). They permit students to focus initially on themselves and their own reactions to the work. Later questions encourage them to consider their classmates' views.

Focus	*Questions*
First reaction	What is your first reaction or response to the text? Describe or explain it briefly.
Feelings	What feelings did the text awaken in you? What emotions did you feel as you read the text?
Perceptions	What did you see happening in the text? Paraphrase it—retell the major events briefly.
Visual images	What image was called to mind by the text? Describe it briefly.

Associations	What memory does the text call to mind —of people, places, events, sights, smells, even of something more ambiguous, perhaps feelings or attitudes?
Thoughts, ideas	What idea or thought was suggested by the text? Explain it briefly.
Selection of textual elements	Upon what in the text did you focus most intently as you read—what word, phrase, image, or idea?
Judgments of importance	What is the most important word in the text? What is the most important phrase in the text? What is the most important aspect of the text?
Identification of problems	What is the most difficult word in the text? What is there in the text or in your reading that you have the most trouble understanding?
Author	What sort of person do you imagine the author of this text to be?
Patterns of response	How did you respond to the text— emotionally or intellectually? Did you feel involved with the text or distant from it?
Other readings	How did your reading of the text differ from that of your discussion partner (or the others in your group)? In what ways were they similar?
Evolution of your reading	How did your understanding of the text or your feelings about it change as you talked?
Evaluations	Do you think the text is a good one—why or why not?
Literary associations	Does this text call to mind any other literary work (poem, play, film, story—any genre)? If it does, what is the work and what is the connection between the two?
Writing	If you were asked to write about your reading of this text, upon what would you focus? Would you write about some asso-

ciation, some memory, some aspect of the
text itself, about the author, or about some
other matter?

Other readers   What did you observe about your discussion partner (or the others in your group
as the talk progressed)? (Newkirk 171)

As the last question indicates, Rosenblatt emphasizes the importance of
encouraging students to collaborate as they develop their interpretations.

Comparing Hillocks and Rosenblatt

When students in my course on teaching writing are introduced to Rosenblatt's reader-response approach, they are immediately enthusiastic. They
regret not having received writing assignments based on Probst's questions
in their own English classes. They recall writing many "dry" papers about literature in high school. After we use *Ethan Frome* as a test case, and write
responses to that text using these questions, students are even more convinced of the effectiveness of this approach.

My own experience teaching literature both on the high school and the
college levels leads me to agree with them. Moving from "response to analysis without denying the validity of initial responses" (Probst 63) seems to
engage students more successfully than starting off with an analysis paper.
They seem more eager to work on analysis once they have had a chance to
respond on a personal level. Hillocks's dimensional approach has much to
offer once the students are ready for the analytical stage of the process. Many
publications are available for implementing both the personal and the analytical stages of response. For example, Judith Langer's *Literature Instruction:
A Focus on Student Response* reviews current classroom practices of reader-
response theory and Michael Smith's *Understanding Unreliable Narrators:
Reading between the Lines in the Literature Classroom* presents techniques for
analyzing the role of the narrator in fictional works.

Both approaches to interpreting literature, George Hillocks's dimensions
and Louise Rosenblatt's reader-response approach, can employ writing to
help students record and clarify their responses to the text. In both cases,
questions can become the cues for short, ungraded assignments or for more
formal papers.

Teaching Literature and Critical Theory

The teaching of literature has typically reflected current trends in literary
criticism. However, although numerous theories are now routinely being applied to studying and explicating literature, most teachers still model the "new

criticism" perspective reflected in Hillocks's questions. More teachers are experimenting with reader-response strategies in their classrooms, but few teachers are applying the strategies of more recently developed critical theories, such as those underlying feminist criticism, new historical criticism, and deconstructionism, just to name a few. Although the limitations of this text do not permit an explanation of these theories, I do urge teachers to become familiar with them and to consider using them in the classroom. Some of these theories can be successfully applied at the secondary level, and, as one of the reviewers of this text commented, "[they] can open up literature in surprising ways to students." Texts such as Sharon Crowley's *A Teacher's Introduction to Deconstruction* and Steven Lynn's *Texts and Contexts: Writing about Literature with Critical Theory* can introduce you to these theories and their possible classroom applications.

Writing the Formal Essay about Literature

The formal essay about literature, often written for a grade, teaches the student how to convince an audience to agree with his or her interpretation of a text. Thus far, we have examined one approach for teaching students the characteristics of the academic essay by introducing them to the concept of claim, evidence, and warrant.

Throughout this text, I have stressed the importance of experimenting with a variety of approaches for teaching writing skills, and that different approaches work well with different students. The formal essay can also be taught using a variety of techniques. For some students the concept of claim, evidence, and warrant may be too abstract. They may benefit from an approach to the formal essay that offers a series of questions related specifically to the assignment question. Here are several examples of related assignments about theme and character, which incorporate the elements of assignment design discussed in Chapter 6 and which can be assigned after students have had considerable experience using informal writing for responding to literature. These formal essays offer students an opportunity for integrating the variety of responses discussed in this chapter.

The first assignment includes suggested prewriting activities as well as criteria for evaluation. This assignment is designed for students in the eleventh grade, who have completed reading "Paul's Case" by Willa Cather and have been introduced to the concept of claim, evidence, and warrant. The second assignment invites students to use their own experiences to develop ideas about the theme of the story. The third requires students to integrate their interpretations with the affective and aesthetic response to the story.

Assignment 1

The "Paul's Case" Assignment

Write a persuasive answer to the following question: Why does Paul leave home? Pretend that your audience is a group of teenagers who would like to help prevent teenagers from leaving home. Consider the following questions as you write the paper:

1. To what extent does Paul's father understand him?
2. To what extent do his teachers try to help him?
3. What does Paul want?
4. To what extent is Paul similar to the teenagers you know?

Suggested Prewriting Activities

List the qualities of a good parent.
List the qualities of a good teacher.
List the characteristic needs of teenagers.

Form
Write your paper in the form of an argument. Include a thesis statement (claim) in the introduction to your paper. In the body of the paper include evidence to support the claim, and the warrant, which will explain how the evidence is related to the claim. The warrant will be related to the fourth question, "Is Paul similar to the teenagers you know?" Conclude by suggesting how Paul's leaving home could have been prevented.

Length
3–4 pages.

Criteria for Grading
Papers that include a clear thesis statement (claim), sufficient evidence, and a warrant, and for the most part are correct, will receive an A. Papers that include all of these elements but contain minor errors in sentence structure and mechanics will receive a B. Papers that do not have a clear claim, sufficient evidence, or a clear warrant will receive a C. Because you will be permitted to revise, all students should eventually receive an A or a B.

Assignment 2

The Response Essay

Purpose
The purpose of this essay is to write about the relationship of a significant theme in one of the stories we read, to your experience, common sense,

or point of view. By "significant," I mean a theme that demonstrates that moral choices are difficult to make. You will need to decide if this theme or insight confirms your own experience, common sense, or point of view, or changes your point of view. In other words, does the story increase your understanding of how people behave or simply confirm what you already know to be true?

Developing the Essay
Develop the essay by explaining how you know the author is trying to express this theme. For example, you can discuss the consequences of the character's actions. Then explain your reasons for finding this theme significant.

Concluding the Essay
There are several possibilities for concluding the essay. You may reflect on other insights in the story you could not develop or you may compare the story to other stories that attempt to deal with the subject of the story in different ways.

Length
3–4 pages.

Assignment 3

The Character Analysis Essay

Purpose
The purpose of this paper is to examine the techniques by which an author creates a character through an in-depth study of a character in the story you wrote about in the first paper.

In your first paper you commented on a theme or insight you believed to be significant. This theme helped to explain how characters relate to one another. For example, some students writing about "Hills Like White Elephants" said that Ernest Hemingway shows that when people are selfish, they often hurt one another. Some students writing about "Death of a Traveling Salesman" commented that Eudora Welty says that people are insensitive to each other's needs.

In this paper I would like you to try to explain one of the character's motives for behaving the way he or she does in greater detail by:

a. identifying the character's values or character traits (at least three examples—self-respect, honesty, success, etc.).
b. indicating the techniques by which the author creates this character. Does the author use direct or indirect methods, for example, statements about the character, the character's actions and words, or what other characters say about the character?

Developing the Essay
Most of the essay will consist of examples from the story that demonstrate the author's methods of creating character.

Concluding the Essay
Conclude the essay by deciding if the author has been successful in creating the character. Does the author give you enough information for understanding the character, for liking or disliking the character?

Length
3–4 pages.

Literature Papers: Stylistic Conventions

When students are ready to write a formal essay about literature, they can learn the conventions of style described in the following list adapted from Barbarouse (40).*

Literary Essay Conventions

- Use the present tense when discussing works of literature and events within those works.
- Use the past tense only when discussing events that have happened in the past, whether in the author's life or in the story itself.
- Work quotations into your paper smoothly, conforming to correct sentence structure and grammatical form. Quotations should always have lead-ins.
- Incorrect: "I have been acquainted with the night" (543). This is an example of Robert Frost's metaphorical language in his poem, "Acquainted with the Night."
- Correct: Robert Frost uses metaphorical language in his poem "Acquainted with the Night," in which he describes his loneliness as his acquaintance with the night (543).
- Quotations should not be overly long; instead they should become a part of the text, acting as support for your points.
- Use parenthetical documentation for all quotes and include a Works Cited page, according to MLA (Modern Language Association) documentation style.
- Identify works of literature correctly. Titles of novels and plays should be underlined or italicized (e.g., a novel, *The Great Gatsby* by F. Scott Fitzgerald, and a play, *The Death of a Salesman* by Arthur Miller). Titles of short stories and poems should be enclosed within quotation marks (e.g., "The

---

*Barberousse, Deborah. *A Brief Guide to Writing about Literature*. Copyright © 1994 by Houghton Mifflin Company. Used with permission.

Fall of the House of Usher," a short story, and "The Raven," a poem, both by Edgar Allan Poe).

- Avoid contractions and colloquialisms.

Writing about Literature: Alternatives to the Essay

When students are not ready to learn how to write the formal essay about literature, they can write in forms that are less demanding to express their responses to literature. For example, in *Just Teach Me Mrs. Krogness*, Mary Mercer Krogness describes her experience teaching literature to students, who not only lacked previous experience writing about literature, but also had serious skill deficiencies and behavior problems.

Krogness tells about her years in Shaker Heights Middle School teaching adolescents who had failed in traditional classrooms. These students scored in the 70's, 80's, and 90's on the IQ test and they had scored at below the local third stanine in reading, comprehension, and vocabulary on the Standard Achievement Test. Nearly all of them were grouped in the lower tracks. She had heard about the low test scores, the negative teacher assessments, but nothing prepared her for the students she was to encounter—their recalcitrance, short attention spans, outlandish behavior, or worse, stony passivity and apparent lack of interest in learning. She says, "They were overage, underprepared, and weighted down with serious emotional baggage. But an occasional glimpse of their creativity and their fetching personalities captured my imagination, even though too many came to class ready to 'pick with' each other" (2).

Krogness's students had previously been taught through exercises and drills. Her aim was to "hook these students on talking, reading, and writing, to immerse them in language and give them plenty of practice doing what they'd learned not to like or feel good about" (18). She began by experimenting with unconventional kinds of assignments, assignments that were unlike the academic assignments they had already failed to master, and chose topics that might have personal interest for them. For example, she often had them write in the form of newspaper articles. She hoped that as they assumed the role of "reporters," they would leave behind their student personas, which they associated with failure. After reading *Julius Caesar*, they were given the following assignment.

You and your teammates are investigative reporters: You have just heard rumors that Julius Caesar, the prospective emperor of Rome, will be assassinated on the Ides of March, March 15. The five of you are to interview various people who might have feelings, opinions, knowledge, or concerns about his death or the threat to his life.

The class talked briefly about what it's like to be a reporter. Krogness helped them to formulate interview questions. She gave them a list of facts, which they developed into these questions:

Sample Interview:

1. Brutus, what is your relationship with Caesar?
2. Soothsayer, how do you know that Julius will be murdered tomorrow?
3. Man in the Street, do you know anything about a plot to kill Caesar?

The assignment was very successful. Students wrote lively accounts of the mock interviews.

When she assigned fairy tales, Krogness's students wrote their own fairy tales. In class they discussed fairy tale themes, "good struggling to overcome evil, generosity struggling to overcome greed, humility struggling to overcome arrogance, and so forth." Through brainstorming sessions they imagined the personalities of wizards, genies, and gremlins, and wrote some excellent fairy tales as a result (155).

At Thanksgiving Krogness assigned Martin Luther King's "I Have a Dream" speech. She says, "After we heard King's stirring speech, I asked the students to respond in writing." She gave two assignments: "broad enough to give each writer latitude, yet specific enough to help him or her focus:"

1. Write a paragraph about the dreams you have for yourself;
2. Write a second paragraph about the dreams you have for the world.

Krogness was constantly searching for topics and writing assignments that would "hook seventh and especially eighth graders on literature." She concludes by saying, "My students had begun the difficult transition from mostly working their way through packaged writing kits, filling in blanks, and writing short answers to questions to thinking independently. But the process would take time. Each experience that engaged them in real inquiry contributed to changing their perceptions of themselves as well" (145).

Emphasizing the Reciprocal Nature of Writing and Reading

Many teachers adopt methods that consistently emphasize the reciprocal nature between reading and writing. "Reading helps students write better and writing helps students read better," says Nancy Atwell. "I never asked my students to relate reading and writing—nor sponsor activities calling on kids to make reading-writing connections. It happens naturally, inevitably, in workshop settings. In writing workshop conferences and mini-lessons we talk about what authors do. In reading workshop conferences (the journals) and mini-lessons we talk about what authors do. It doesn't take very long for students to begin to bring knowledge and expertise from one area to the other—to view literacy as both considering and trying what authors do" (226).

For example, after a discussion about writing "leads" for essays in an eighth grade class, a student said that when she was trying to decide what book to read next, she looked at the leads in short stories they were reading. In a writing workshop, after a reading mini-lesson on leads in *One Fat Summer* by Robert Lipsyte, *A Ring of Endless Light* by Madeline L'Engle, and *That Was Then, This Is Now* by S. E. Hinton, another student said "I think my lead is all fouled up. It doesn't really attract my attention like the books you read to us. I'm trying to tell too much about the whole camp. Maybe I should just begin with the lecture by the Detroit Pistons' coach. That way people will get some good stuff right from the start like in *One Fat Summer*" (Atwell 227).

At the half point during the year, Atwell asked this question: "As a writer do you think you learn from other authors' writing—what you read?" The class response was a unanimous, "yes." Atwell posed two follow-up questions: "If so, who has influenced your writing? What kinds of things do you do differently in your own writing because of the author(s)?" Students named three kinds of literary influences: professional authors, other students, and Atwell herself. They were able to mention specific borrowings. These borrowings took three forms: Students borrowed genres, trying a new mode after reading another author's writing; students borrowed topics and themes; a student borrowed both the content and verse form from a teacher's poem, and students borrowed specific literary techniques from authors they had read.

Unfortunately, many students believe that all borrowing is plagiarism. Because of the heavy emphasis placed on originality in our schools, students are often very reluctant to imitate other authors. Atwell's lessons illustrate that when students are invited to borrow genres, topics, themes, and techniques, when they are told that all great authors are great borrowers, they become aware of the benefits of imitation. They are often surprised to learn that the devices used in fiction, such as imagery and metaphor, can enhance their style of writing in expository essays.

Writing Fiction, Poetry, and Plays

Teachers can also assign the writing of literature—poems, short stories, and plays—not only to help students appreciate the literature they read, but as a technique for teaching exposition.

Writing Fiction

Writing fiction, poetry, and plays helps students appreciate imaginative literature. Once they experience authorship, and sense their own imaginations at work, they are better able to engage the imagination of the authors whose works they read. Students do not need a great deal of instruction about form to write poems, short stories, and plays, though they will need some guidance. But teachers must inspire students to use their imagination by giving them a great deal of freedom. This is the time to let go, to let the student be. A supportive atmosphere and rich language experiences are the best preparation for writing imaginative literature.

Deborah Fedder, who teaches at the middle school at Friends' Central School in Wynnewood, Pennsylvania, briefly explains the genre assigned (in the following sample assignment it is a radio play) and then stages the assignment to help students construct their play.

Mystery Play/Radio Drama Requirements

The following is a list of elements essential to incorporate in the writing of your mystery radio play. Use the information as a checklist as you develop the piece.

1. A message or theme.
2. Characters who are believable, compelling, and fully characterized by their action, inactions, words spoken and unspoken.
3. A story line that rises to a climax and falls.
4. Murder mystery elements: alibi (placement of characters), believable clues (leading and misleading), suspects, suspense, believable endings (not too convenient).
5. Dialogue that tells all.
6. Stage directions, relevant information, and narration.
7. Language that is meant to be heard, not read.
8. Sound effects as cued by stage directions.

Tentative Due Dates

Feb. 21: You will have written the message of the play and planned the plot.

Feb. 27: You will have developed the characters and detailed the setting.

Mar. 1: You will have written the script (action: telling the story through dialogue and stage directions/effects; draft).

Mar. 6: You will have reviewed the script several times and polished its content (edit).

Mar. 8: You will have submitted the completed formal script to Mrs. Fedder.

Fedder's class had been reading mystery plays and students were familiar with the elements of a mystery play before this assignment. During the staging of the project, she used a series of worksheets to help students with each element of the play. For example, this is the worksheet she uses for character development.

Characterizing a Character*

To fully characterize something, you have to know enough about your character to believe he or she actually exists. You have to describe the character well enough that you could feel you've known this character for a very long time. Sometimes it helps to characterize someone you know before characterizing someone you have created. The questions below can help you fully characterize a well-known figure. Then use the same questions to characterize a fictional person.

1. Fully characterize an existing well-known fictional TV figure.

   A. Character's Name _____

   B. Give ten adjectives to describe his personality.

   C. Give ten adjectives to describe his physical attributes.

   D. What three foods would you think this character likes? dislikes?

   E. Place this character in the Art Museum. What does he or she say about what he sees and feels there?

   F. What five things can your character not do?

   G. What five things can your character not feel?

   H. Compare your character to three other well-known characters.

   I. What place in the world would your character most like to visit and why?

   J. Now make up three clever questions you could answer about your character. Then answer the questions.

Fedder knows that students write with greater motivation when they have an audience for their writing other than their teacher. In the case of the mystery play, she offered students bonus points if they volunteered to perform their play for the class. When her students completed a poetry unit, they produced booklets of their poems for students in other grades. The booklet assignment

*Both works reprinted by permission of Deborah P. Fedder.

was especially popular in her seventh grade class. (See Appendices 7a and 7b for Fedder's assignment and the booklet written by one of her students.)

Writing Imaginative Literature and Teaching the Essay

It may come as a surprise that writing fables can help students learn how to write expository essays. Marie Ponsot and Rosemary Deen (*Beat Not the Poor Desk*) argue that by writing in the basic forms of fiction students begin to internalize the structures of the essay, which is an abstract kind of writing that grows naturally by starting writing instruction in forms that closely resemble literature of the oral tradition.

They believe that this approach is more successful than the conventional one of teaching students how to write essays by describing the features of an essay and then teaching students the stages in the process of writing one. The two genres they find most useful for teaching students about form are the fable and the parable. They define the fable "as a two part structure of which each part is a literary structure. The first part is concrete, a dramatic dialogue; its other function is to demonstrate the second part. The second part is abstract, an aphorism; its other function is to sharpen the focus of the dialogue, making an analogy, a memorable statement about it" (14).

Ponsot and Deen begin instruction in fable writing with what they call a diversionary tactic. They give a lesson in punctuation—how to use quotation marks, commas, and paragraphing to punctuate dialogue. They then suggest that students practice using these punctuation marks by writing an imaginary dialogue using the following guidelines.

> *Imagine that in the world of the imagination, it is the middle of the night in the middle of a countryside through which a road runs. A horse is coming down the road and meets a bear. For your first paragraph, write what the horse says to the bear.*
>
> *Now for paragraph two, write what the bear says to the horse.*
>
> *In paragraph three write what the horse says to the bear.*
>
> *All of a sudden a storm breaks out—lightning, thunder, rain. Write a sentence or two about paragraph four.*
>
> *In paragraphs five and six write one more exchange between the horse and the bear.*
>
> *Now skip a few lines and write, "the moral of this fable is . . ." (15)*

When students have written the final sentence, they begin to experience a "sense of accomplished structure." After they read their fables aloud, they discuss what it was like to write them. Ponsot and Deen argue that this method helps students to gain a concept of form that carries over to their writing of exposition.

The Computer and Teaching Literature

The computer can be used in several ways to strengthen the teaching of literature. For those English teachers who view computers as unwelcome strangers when it comes to teaching the humanities, it is important to keep in mind that many students respond more positively to technology than to the printed word. Increasingly, our students are receiving more and more information from a screen rather than from a book. Software exists for all aspects of teaching literature: Many texts are on-line, there are exercises on-line, and there is the Internet for research related to authors and texts. Michael LoMonico, who teaches at Farmingdale High School in New York, believes that using computers to teach Shakespeare has improved his students attitudes' toward studying Shakespeare. One of his favorite assignments is to perform a word search through one of Shakespeare's plays using a program called Word-Cruncher. Students locate all references to the word and write a paper demonstrating the importance of the word in the play (59).

For students who want to write fiction on-line there are many web sites, including *The Endless Star Trek Episode* ("Just read the story so far and then answer the questions at the end, adding your thoughts about the story. The best writing of the week will be added to the episode, and a new set of questions will be created."). Another is *Wacky Web Tales* ("Remember those Mad Libs where you filled in words to complete the story? This is a good way to create a silly story and review parts of speech."). "Positively Poetry," a homepage created by a fourteen-year-old interested in writing and reading poetry, is made up of poems submitted by children around the world. Opportunities for publishing imaginative writing on-line are numerous. Some of these can be found at the end of Chapter 3.

Conclusion

The many resources available for integrating the teaching of writing and literature can help you develop your own assignments, perhaps similar to those in this chapter. Texts that I have found valuable for this purpose include *Getting From Here to There: Writing and Reading Poetry* by Florence Grossman (1981) and *Ways In: Analyzing and Responding to Literature* by Kahn, Walter, and Johannessen (1984). *Notes Plus, A Quarterly of Practical Teaching Ideas,* published quarterly by The National Council of Teaching English, is another valuable resource for writing assignments related to literature that should not be overlooked. For example, in the March 1997 issue, the "Writing Assignment of the Month" is entitled "Reading Through Writing about Rashomon: A Review Pointing Strategy." The kinds of assignments you construct for students to write about literature and to write literature are limited only by your own imagination. Your students' enjoyment and understanding of literature will be strengthened if you develop a repertoire of interesting assignments, among which the analytical essay will be only one alternative.

Questions for Discussion and Writing

Read a novel or short story frequently taught in middle school or high school, for example, the novel *Ethan Frome,* by Edith Wharton, or the short story "The Lottery," by Shirley Jackson, and use it as the basis for the next questions.

1. Develop a series of questions for the novel based on George Hillocks's literal level of comprehension category.

2. Develop an essay assignment and write a sample evidence abstract for the assignment.

3. Develop an assignment based on Louise Rosenblatt's reader-response approach to interpreting literature.

4. Develop an essay assignment related to "The Lottery" using the structure of the "Paul's Case" assignment (page 00) as a model.

5. Develop a letter writing assignment and a newspaper report assignment related to *Ethan Frome.*

6. Write a short story based on a theme from either "The Lottery" or *Ethan Frome.*

7. Write a poem based on a theme from either "The Lottery" or *Ethan Frome.* Choose your own subject for writing a fable using Ponsot and Deen's suggestions.

References

Atwell, Nancy. *In the Middle: Reading, Writing, and Learning with Adolescents.* Portsmouth, NH: Heinemann-Boynton/Cook, 1987.

Barberousse, Deborah. *A Brief Guide to Writing Literature.* Boston: Houghton Mifflin, 1994.

Cather, Willa. "Paul's Case." *Five Stories.* New York: Vintage Books, 1956.

Crowley, Sharon. *A Teacher's Introduction to Deconstruction.* Urbana, IL: NCTE, 1989.

The Endless Star Trek Episode and *Wacky Web Tales.* http://tigger.clemson.edu/bnet/resources/comp.html Internet. 18 Dec. 1997.

Fedder, Deborah. Teaching Materials (unpublished). Friends' Central School, Wynnewood, PA, 1995.

Fitzgerald, F. Scott. *The Great Gatsby.* San Diego, CA: Greenhaven Press, 1997.

Frost, Robert. "Acquainted with the Night." *An Introduction to Literature.* Eds. Sylvan Barnet, Morton Berman, & Willber Burto. New York: HarperCollins, 1993.

Grossman, Florence. *Getting from Here to There: Writing and Reading Poetry.* Urbana, IL: NCTE, 1981.

Hemingway, Ernest. "Hills Like White Elephants." *The Story and Its Writer.* 3rd ed. Ed. Ann Charters. Boston: St. Martins Press, 1991.

Hillocks, George Jr., Bernard J. McCabe, and J. E. Campbell. *The Dynamics of English Instruction.* New York: Random House, 1971.

Hinton, S. E. *That Was Then, This Is Now.* New York: Viking Child Books, 1971.

Jackson, Shirley. "The Lottery." *The Short Story and Its Writer.* 3rd ed. Ed. Ann Charters. New York: Bedford/St. Martins Press, 1991.

Kahn, Elizabeth A., Carolyn Calhoun Walter, and Larry R. Johannessen. *Writing about Literature.* Urbana, IL: NCTE, 1984.

King, Martin Luther Jr. *I Have a Dream: Writings and Speeches that Changed the World.* Ed. James Melvin Washington. San Francisco: Harper, 1992.

Krogness, Mary Mercer. *Just Teach Me Mrs. Krogness.* Portsmouth, NH: Heinemann-Boyton/Cook, 1995.

Langer, Judith, ed. *Literature Instruction: A Focus on Student Response.* Urbana, IL: 1992.

Lee, Harper. *To Kill a Mockingbird.* Troy, MO: Holt, Rhinehart, and Winston, 1989.

L'Engle, Madeline. *The Ring of Endless Light.* Des Plaines, IL: Bantam/Doubleday/Dell, 1981.

Lipsyte, Robert. *One Fat Summer.* Glenview, IL: Harper Collins, 1991.

LoMonico, Michael. "Using Computers to Teach Shakespeare." *English Journal* Oct. 1995: 58–62.

Lynn, Steven. *Texts and Contexts: Writing about Literature with Critical Theory.* New York: Longman, 1997.

Mandel, Dustin. "Sweet Poetry" unpublished student booklet. Friends' Central School. Wynnewood, PA.

Miller, Arthur. "Death of a Salesman" in *Eight Plays.* Garden City, New York: Nelson Doubleday, 1981.

Newkirk, Thomas, ed. *To Compose: Teaching Writing in High School and College.* Portsmouth, NH: Heinemann, 1990.

Petrosky, Anthony R. "From Story to Essay: Reading and Writing." *College Composition and Communication* 39 (1982): 19–36.

Poe, Edgar Allan. "The Fall of the House of Usher." "The Raven." *Great Short Works of Edgar Allen Poe.* Ed. G. R. Thomson. New York: Harper, 1970.

Ponsot, Marie, and Rosemarie Deen. *Beat Not the Poor Desk.* Portsmouth, NH: Heinemann-Boynton/Cook, 1982.

"Positively Poetry." http://advicom.net/~e-media/kv/poetry1.html. Internet. 18 Dec. 1997.

Probst, Robert. "Dialogue with Text." *To Compose: Teaching Writing in High School and College.* 2nd ed. Ed. Thomas Newkirk. Portsmouth, NH: Heinemann, 1990.

Rosenblatt, Louise. *Literature as Exploration.* 5th ed. New York: Modern Language Association, 1995.

Shakespeare, William. *Julius Caesar.* London: The Folio Society, 1962.

Smith, Michael. *Understanding Unreliable Narrators: Reading between the Lines in the Literature Classroom.* Urbana, IL: NCTE, 1991.

Steinbeck, John. *The Pearl of Lapaz.* In *The Portable Steinbeck.* Ed. Pascal Covici, Jr. New York: Penguin, 1978.

Wharton, Edith. *Ethan Frome.* New York: Scribner, 1911.

APPENDIX

7a • *Poetry Booklet Assignment*
   by Deborah Fedder

7b • *"Sweet Poetry"*
   by Dustin Mandel

Appendix 7a: Poetry Booklet Assignment

Friends' Central School
SIXTY-EIGHTH STREET AND CITY LINE • PHILADELPHIA, PENNSYLVANIA 19151
(215) 649-7440

THINGS EVERY BOOK MUST INCLUDE . . . . . .

1. Cover.   Special artwork, including title and author's name.

2. Title page.   Repeat of title and author.

3. Other side of title page.   Dedication (Can also be on its own page)
   Copyright date
   Publisher's name
   Place of publication

4. Dedication.   As mentioned above, this may be placed on its own page or
   on the back of the title page.

5. Text

6. Pictures

7. About the author.   Either bring in a picture of yourself or one will
   be taken in service project. Glue in at end of
   book. Write a five-line summary of yourself,
   in the third person. (Example: Seth is a student in
   the seventh grade at Friends' Central School. He
   enjoys . . .)

Spend about half the project on your "dummy." Then you will go to your final
copy. Some markers will bleed through to the reverse page, so we usually use
colored pencils or thin pen or pencil. Computer-printed text is fine. You can
use our Appleworks upstairs in the library or bring in your text from home or
the computer room.

It is best to decide an age for which your book is intended. Then we can
decide if your book will be mailed overseas to a third world country like
Ghana or Somalia or if it will go to a local agency like Early Intervention
Program or the Jefferson Rehabilitation Hospital.

Appendix 7b: "Sweet Poetry"

© 1996
SWEET TOOTH Co.

SWEET, California

Dedication:

I dedicate this book, to my teacher, Mrs. Fedder, and all of my friends, who aided me in times of need.

Contents:

The Candy Store

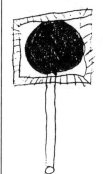

Lollipops, Jawbreakers, Gummy worms,
Sweets All Around.

'Can I have this?'
Words that come from every kid's mouth.

'No, No, No,'
That's all you'll hear, from a concerned Mom or Dad.

'Then, why am I here?' 'I love this stuff but I can't have it...I crave it...I
gotta have it...here go the tears...it's working...oh, yes, a lollipop for
me...they're giving in...

Filling the bags with tootsie rolls, lemon drops, bubble gum balls, Hershey's
kisses...I'm in heaven!

The Circus

Cotton candy, with peanuts,

Yum!

Clowns and Jugglers,

Lot's of Fun!

Lions, Tigers,

and Bears, Oh my.

Acrobats flying through the air,

Woah,

Tightrope walkers, watch them balance their bodies, Yeah,

What could be more fun, than a day at the Big Tent.

Red

Red is feeling angry,
Red tastes like sweet cherries or cinnamon chewing gum.
Blood, Draculas, and molten volcanic lava are red,
Red sounds like bombs and screams, with sirens blaring.
Red can scald you and bothers you when you seem like there is too much
weight upon your shoulder,
Red stings like a thorny rose bush and smells like the flowers from the same
bush, too.
When you see a firecracker exploding, and at the same time, you enjoy
munching from a bowl of strawberries, once again, you have red!

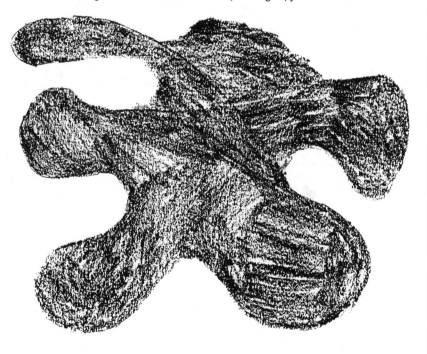

The Pool

Kids screaming, water splashing,
the young, brave boy on the diving board,
the seasoned woman, laying on a lounge chair, getting her really, unnecessary
tan,
Some more kids waiting in line at the canteen for water ices,
and a single, rainbow colored beach ball floating on a calm section of the
sweltering water.
Then a lone, determined seagull flies on by, overhead, and catches everyone's
eye, as the lifeguard beckons with her whistle,
for all to get out of the water.

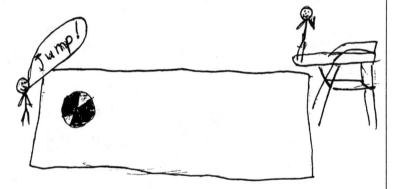

Ice Cream

Vanilla, chocolate, and strawberry malts,
floats, sundaes, and banana splits galore,
add a choice of 48 flavors, and everyone agrees on ice cream.
The sweet, gooey, sticky, cold, messy consistency....
-ice cream-
But every kid won't be denied a lick....slurp....ahhh.

The Rainbow

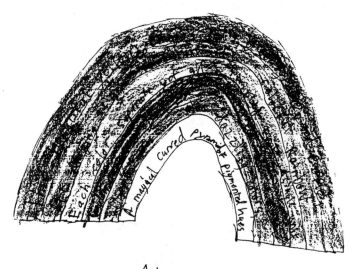

ALL
IS
GOOD.

The Sled

The sleek and whetted blades, running down the length of the wooden frame, greased and ready to go, down the hill, at signs of the first snow.

It snowed...

He stands ready, at the top of the mountain, gathering courage, to make the leap of an unscaredy cat, to fly down the hill at go-cart speeds.

He's off...

He skillfully dodges each dip and rock, and for icing on the cake, performs a 180° skid stop, to, finally, show off his new Red Flyer.

The Piano Recital

The much recognized notes of "Mary Had a Little Lamb" resound from the
heavy, large ebony instrument,
The little girl is diligently practicing for her upcoming recital,
She makes mistakes but persistently corrects them,
Minding her rests, staccatos, and repeats,
The little pianist, studiously, adjusts her hand positions.

In the background, her attentive parents discuss her cute appearance upon the
cushioned bench,
they project ahead to the day when their child would reach her musical
calling,
they are so proud and encouraging.

The following day, the little girl in an appropriately selected spectacled dress,
remembering her part well, and gives it her best version yet,
she finishes with a professional curtsy and earns a well deserved round of
applause,
from the captivated audience.

The Performance

Hey shang shi shang shuwap Heres

The auditorium doors closed to ward out any late stragglers,
Introductions to the performers were made and the lights disappeared to total
darkness,
The music began, as the curtains opened to a stage of gloriously costumed
dancers,
And the show began.....

The theme had been favorite movies and plays from Broadway,
the musical and dance pieces unfolded, as the performers with their high
energies, took the audience under their wing.

A whole bunch of selections, displayed the skilled dancers and the beautifully
artistic scenery,
when suddenly, the Flinstones popped out onto the stage, to thrill the kids in
the crowd.
They were followed by cast performers from the likes of <u>Phantom of the
Opera,</u> and <u>Grease,</u>
when, finally,
the combination of the concluding songs from <u>Grease,</u> 'Greased Lightning'
and 'We Go Together,'
gave you almost the desire to get up on stage and dance along.

A splendid evening of young talent....

We Go together *Hey*

The way it will Be waooo Yeah!

The End

The end....
Does this mean that it's over or is it just another beginning?
When something ends does something always follow?
Does "The End" at the finale of a movie mean that a sequel is but another six months in the future?
Or is it that things never end and humans just label their endings, as a means of convenience or as a momentary pause of time?
What is the **only** true end?
Maybe 'Death' isn't even it!

THE END

About the Author . . .

Dustin Mandel is a seventh grade student at Friend's Central School, in Wynnewood, Pennsylvania. When not involved with homework, he enjoys playing basketball, designing and building for fun, and reading good, long novels for pleasure. His favorite subjects in school, math and art, provide much of the inspiration for his many design projects. As a means of relaxation, Dustin hacks at his computer, usually immersed in some strategy game. Otherwise, you'll probably be sure to find him sleeping, for long lengths at a time, to make up for all the sleep lost because of late night school activities. For him, writing this book was a great deal of fun, as it combined much creativity in composing his poetry and providing the illustrations for them.

8

Composition Curricula: Four Approaches

Most composition experts would support a classroom writing program like this one adapted from "The Teaching of Writing: A Review of Research and Practice," by Allan Glatthorn, reprinted by permission (29–31).

- The teacher develops a balanced and comprehensive program, one which gives adequate attention to writing without crowding out other essential learning. In developing a program, the teacher uses curriculum guides as a general framework, but relies as well upon a diagnosis of the students' learning abilities and educational needs.
- There is sufficient time for personal writing. Students are encouraged to keep a writer's journal in which they record their experiences, their feelings, and their reactions, their questions and ideas. The teacher does not grade this writing—but encourages students to write often and write freely, using journal writing as a source for more structured writing assignments.
- The teacher routinely plans and implements composition units which teach specific writing and the organizational skills required for specific kinds of writing. The teacher provides appropriate units covering a variety of modes and purposes; expository writing, persuasive writing, writing about literature, writing for college and career, writing stories, plays and poems.
- Sentence level skills are taught in each writing unit.
- Whenever appropriate, the teacher integrates the teaching of writing with other components in the curriculum, so that students understand the importance of writing as a way of learning.
- The teacher continues to emphasize the composing process, and provides adequate class time for pre-writing, drafting, revising, editing, and publishing.

However, we do not design our classroom writing programs or writing units in a vacuum, but within the context of our school's curriculum for writing instruction. The writing program you design must be compatible with this curriculum but it should also reflect your own philosophy of teaching writing. If you are fortunate, you will be able to do both. This chapter presents four approaches to curriculum design. Although your school's curriculum guide will probably reflect a combination of these approaches, examining the characteristics of each should help you to analyze and evaluate your school's composition curriculum and recognize its underlying philosophy and its strengths and weaknesses.

A curriculum provides guidelines for a course of study. Composition curricula mandate the kinds of writing that should be taught, the skills students need to accomplish that writing, and in some cases, the methods for teaching those skills. These decisions are based on assumptions about the purpose of teaching writing, how students learn to write, and which techniques are most productive in fostering the development of writing skills. As a result of the substantial body of research supporting a process approach to teaching writing, many schools have adopted a curriculum that emphasizes prewriting, drafting, and revision. For example, the Tredyffrin/Easttown School District's curriculum guide for teaching writing stipulates that from fifth grade on students practice prewriting strategies such as freewriting and brainstorming (see Figure 8.1). However, there are still differences of opinion about which purposes for teaching writing are most important at various grade levels, such as learning how to write for correctness, writing for personal growth, writing to become a well-rounded person, or writing as preparation for writing on the job. These different views have a profound effect on curriculum design, especially when it comes to the kinds of writing that should be taught at different grade levels. For example, some high school curricula now include units on writing for business, which teach students how to write résumés, job application letters, and other documents associated with the world of commerce. And although a process approach to writing may predominate, some curricula include analysis of models and drill as part of the methodology suggested for composition instruction.

Most composition curricula are dominated by one of four approaches—the correctness approach, the personal growth approach, the rhetorical approach, or the sociocultural approach—though it is rare to find any of these approaches in a pure form. As one of my favorite professors has said, "All classifications leak." Categories are never found in their pure form, but they help us to understand important distinctions. Each approach contributes to composition instruction, but the rhetorical approach is the most comprehensive, and the correctness approach is the least comprehensive.

Curriculum rows are organized by grade level across the following columns: FIFTH GRADE, SIXTH GRADE, SEVENTH GRADE, EIGHTH GRADE, NINTH GRADE, AMERICAN LITERATURE/WESTERN LITERATURE.

Responsive/Exploratory/Strategic

FIFTH GRADE	SIXTH GRADE	SEVENTH GRADE	EIGHTH GRADE	NINTH GRADE	AMERICAN LITERATURE/WESTERN LITERATURE
• JOURNALS: FREQUENT NON-CORRECTED ENTRIES TO ENCOURAGE FLUENCY, RISK-TAKING, REFLECTION AND SEARCHING FOR MEANING • TOPICS: ASSIGNED AND/OR FREE CHOICE • POSSIBLE FORMATS: FREE FORM, DIALOGUE, POETRY, DRAWING • FREE WRITING/BRAINSTORMING • CLUSTERING • MAPPING	• Journals: Frequent non-corrected entries to encourage fluency, risk-taking, reflection and searching for meaning • Topics: Assigned and/or free choice • Possible formats: free form, dialogue, poetry, drawing • Free writing/brainstorming • CLUSTERING • MAPPING	• Journals: Frequent non-corrected entries to encourage fluency, risk-taking, reflection and searching for meaning • Topics: Assigned and/or free choice • Possible formats: free form, dialogue, poetry, drawing • Free writing/brainstorming • Clustering • Mapping	• Journals: Frequent non-corrected entries to encourage fluency, risk-taking, reflection and searching for meaning • Topics: Assigned and/or free choice • Possible formats: free form, dialogue, poetry, drawing • Free writing/brainstorming • Clustering • Mapping	• Journals: Frequent non-corrected entries to encourage fluency, risk-taking, reflection and searching for meaning • Topics: Assigned and/or free choice • Possible formats: free form, dialogue, poetry, drawing • Free writing/brainstorming • Clustering • Mapping	• Journals: Frequent non-corrected entries to encourage fluency, risk-taking, reflection and searching for meaning • Topics: Assigned and/or free choice • Possible formats: free form, dialogue, poetry, drawing, DIALECTIC • Free writing/brainstorming • Clustering • Mapping

Style/Language Structure/Usage

FIFTH GRADE	SIXTH GRADE	SEVENTH GRADE	EIGHTH GRADE	NINTH GRADE	AMERICAN LITERATURE/WESTERN LITERATURE
• DICTION: EFFECTIVE, PRECISE WORD CHOICE • SENTENCE VARIETY (LENGTH, TYPE) • SUBJECT–VERB AGREEMENT • PRONOUN USAGE • CORRECT PUNCTUATION TO CLARIFY IDEAS	• Diction: Effective, precise word choice • Sentence variety (length, type) • Subject–verb agreement • Pronoun usage • Correct punctuation to clarify ideas	• Diction: Effective, precise word choice • INCREASING SENTENCE VARIETY THROUGH USE OF PREPOSITIONAL PHRASES • Subject–verb agreement • Pronoun usage • Correct punctuation to clarify ideas	• Diction: Effective, precise word choice • Increasing sentence variety through use of prepositional phrases AND CLAUSES • Subject–verb agreement • Pronoun usage • Correct punctuation to clarify ideas	• Diction: Effective, precise word choice • Increasing sentence variety through use of prepositional phrases, clauses, VERBALS AND APPOSITIVES • Subject–verb agreement • Pronoun usage • Correct punctuation to clarify ideas • TRANSITIONAL WORDS, PHRASES AND SENTENCES • CONSISTENCY OF VERB TENSE AND POINT OF VIEW	• Diction: Effective, precise word choice • Increasing sentence variety through SENTENCE COMBINING • Subject–verb agreement • Pronoun usage • Correct punctuation to clarify ideas • Transitional words, phrases, and sentences • Consistency of verb tense and point of view • PARALLEL STRUCTURE • STYLE: SYNTAX, CLARITY, VOICE

Continued

FIGURE 8.1 Tredyffrin/Easttown Curriculum

Reprinted by permission of Tredyffrin/Easttown School District.

FIFTH GRADE	SIXTH GRADE	SEVENTH GRADE	EIGHTH GRADE	NINTH GRADE	AMERICAN LITERATURE/ WESTERN LITERATURE
		Expository Paragraph/Essay			
• PARAGRAPH: BASIC STRUCTURE (TOPIC SENTENCE AND SUPPORTING DETAILS) • LETTER WRITING (PERSONAL)	• Paragraph: Basic structure (topic sentence and supporting details) • Letter writing (personal)	• PARAGRAPH: POLISHING STRUCTURE, EXPANDING, REPERTOIRE (PERSUASIVE, HOW-TO, COMPARISON/CONTRAST ANALYSIS, CRITIQUE) • Letter-writing (personal AND BUSINESS)	• BASIC ESSAY STRUC-TURE: THESIS STATE-MENT AND SUPPORT • Letter writing (personal and business)	• POLISHING ESSAY STRUCTURE (AUDIENCE, ESSAY MAP, SUBTHESIS, INTRODUCTION, CONCLUSION) • Letter writing (personal and business) • EDITORIALS/LETTERS TO THE EDITOR	• Polishing essay structure (audience, essay map, sub-thesis, introduction, conclusion) • Letter writing (personal and business) • Editorials/letters to the editor EXPLORING TOPICS, NARROWING FOCUS • EXPANDING ESSAY VARIETY THROUGH BOTH LITERARY AND GENERIC WRITING OPPORTUNITIES • LITERARY (ANALYSIS/ CRITIQUE/INTERPRETATION OF CHARACTER, THEME, LANGUAGE, HISTORICAL CONTEXT, TONE/MOOD) • GENERIC (PERSUASION, COMPARISON/CONTRAST, MOVIE REVIEWS AND SO ON)
		Imaginative Writing			
• DESCRIPTION: CHARACTER/PLACE • NARRATION: SHORT STORY/DIALOGUE/SKIT • POETRY (ALL FORMS)	• Description: Character/ place • Narration: Short story/dialogue/skit • Poetry (all forms)	• Description: Character/place/ MOOD • Narration: Short Story/dialogue/ skit/PLAY • Poetry (all forms)	• Description: Character/place/ mood • Narration: Short story/dialogue/skit/ play/PARODY • Poetry (all forms)	• Description: Character/place/mood • Narration: Short story/dialogue/skit/ play/parody • Poetry (all forms)	• Description: Character/ place/mood • Narration: Short story/ dialogue/skit/play/parody • Poetry (all forms) • INTERNAL MONOLOGUE • DRAMATIC MONOLOGUE • NEWSLETTERS • ADDITIONAL SCENES/ "GHOST CHAPTERS" • ALTERNATE VERSIONS • BROCHURES • INTERVIEWS (BETWEEN AUTHOR AND CHARACTER, BETWEEN CHARACTER AND CHARACTER) • SATIRE: EDITORIAL CARTOONS WITH CAPTIONS

FIGURE 8.1 *Continued*

My discussion of each approach includes a section on assumptions about learning embedded in the approach. For example, the correctness approach assumes that students learn deductively, from lecture and from models. The personal growth approach relies more heavily on process-oriented writing instruction, which assumes that students learn best when they learn inductively, with less emphasis on analyzing models and more emphasis on writing. The rhetorical and sociocultural approaches integrate both kinds of learning.

Because writing assignments play a major role in defining the purpose of writing in the curriculum, they will be a large part of this discussion. By writing assignments, I mean any request for writing by the teacher, whether it will be graded or ungraded. It can be a short assignment in class or a long research paper. It can be a journal entry or an essay exam. The main criterion for distinguishing it from other kinds of writing is that the teacher will read it eventually as a finished product of its kind. Therefore, I am omitting prewriting and revising assignments from this category, though both kinds of assignments may precede a final paper, but I am including sentence-level and paragraph exercises.

We will examine how each approach addresses these questions:

1. What is the main purpose for teaching writing?
2. What are the most important writing skills?
3. How do students learn best how to write?
4. What kinds of writing assignments are compatible with this approach?

The Correctness Approach

This is the approach that will sound the most familiar to you. Its goal is to teach correctness in written expression, specifically correctness in the handling of grammar, punctuation, and spelling. Many instructors have supported this goal in the past as the major purpose for teaching writing, and some still do. The philosophy behind it (Anne Gere calls this approach the language as artifact approach) is that the "learner should manipulate each of these writing units separately in a situation, controlling for one problem at a time. He works his way from little particles to big particles until he arrives at whole compositions resembling those done in the outside world. Whatever the topic or kind of writing students do [in a curriculum based on this approach] the ultimate goal is likely to be to produce as polished, correct, and 'professional' a product as possible" (Gere 96). A traditional high school curriculum, based on this approach, divides instruction into units on the sentence, the paragraph, and then, finally, the whole essay. As we discussed in

Chapter 1, the language arts rebellion in the sixties and seventies was a reaction to the correctness approach.

The correctness approach, which relies heavily on models and drills, is tied to the research of behavioral theorists like B. F. Skinner, who view language as "one of many pieces of human behavior, all capable of analysis as a sequence of stimulus-response reinforcement without consideration of intention or meaning" (Meyers 5). In this conception of learning, language behavior is reinforced by the language of others. It assumes that students will model certain language behaviors if their efforts are rewarded. Students imitate what they hear or see by developing a bond of association between visual and auditory stimuli.

The sequence of assignments in the correctness approach begins with exercises for learning the parts of speech and identifying sentence patterns, followed by paragraph exercises. Students are given models of correct sentences and paragraphs, followed by exercises that require them to either imitate correct samples or rewrite correct ones. Numerous handbooks and textbooks have been designed for these purposes. *Composition: Models and Exercises* (Fleming, Glatthorn, and McFarland), for example, is a series of texts that focuses on the paragraph. There is one book for each grade level. Models and exercises for learning general characteristics of paragraphs, such as unity, how to write a topic sentence, how to develop and arrange the details of paragraphs, are followed by models of descriptive, narrative, and expository paragraphs. The last section gives instruction and models for writing different kinds of essays. In the introduction to this section, the authors say, "Your earlier experience in building good expository paragraphs will help you develop compositions several paragraphs long, for a well organized expository composition has the characteristics of an effective expository paragraph" (Fleming, Glatthorn, and McFarland 133). The same sequence is repeated in each text, with some variations and more sophisticated examples.

This approach has come under heavy fire during the last twenty-five years, as we discussed in Chapter 2. James Moffett, one of the earliest critics of this sequence, says,

> *The folklorish part [of this approach] is represented in the old saw about having to crawl before you can walk. But crawling is an authentic part of locomotion in its own right, not merely a sub-skill of walking. For the learner, basics are not the small focus, technical things, but broad things, like meaning and motivation, purpose and point, which are precisely what is missing from the exercise. ("Rationale for a New Curriculum in English" 152)*

Moffett goes on to say that when students write sentences or paragraphs in isolation, they are not learning what teachers think they are learning, but rather that "discourse need not be motivated or directed at anyone, that it is good to write, even if you have nothing to say, that there are such things as sentences and paragraphs for their own sake" ("Rationale for a New Curriculum in English" 152).

Although the skills identified in the correctness approach are important to know, and, indeed, must be a part of any composition program, teachers familiar with recent theory and research in composition are likely to integrate these skills with the acquisition of skills related to the thinking processes involved in composition, such as generating ideas, integrating them, and, eventually, modifying them. All students must learn how to write correct and varied sentences as well as paragraphs, which develop the content of their essays, but not necessarily in isolation. At times it is appropriate to focus on a particular element of writing, such as the sentence, because it is one way of preventing cognitive overload when teaching writing. In your own curriculum, you will most likely include some drills and exercises related to reinforcing certain skills, as we discussed in Chapter 4 on teaching sentence skills.

The Personal Growth Approach

There are those who would argue that the main reason for teaching writing is to encourage personal growth. For example, Allan Glatthorn says, "Too many competencies are derived from what an adult needs to survive rather than instead from an analysis of what an adult needs to grow" (29). In the tradition of diary writing, writing can help students to understand themselves, a prerequisite for personal development. Erika Lindemann says that writing can encourage students "to explore experiences and locate themselves in relation to a complex society" (7).

Writing programs that have "personal growth as their primary goal do not focus on form or correctness as the major structuring principal, but place at their core a set of experiences designed to motivate students to write about their concerns, their interests, their questions" (Foster 130). In one study where students were allowed to choose their own topics and write in whatever way they chose, and were not required to produce drafts, they wrote more fluent, error-free prose than those following prescribed modes and following steps of planning and revision (Foster 130).

The personal growth approach has received considerable attention during the last thirty years, in part because as a curriculum structure, it is the one

most closely related to interest in teaching the writing process and in keeping with the movement toward student-centered learning. For example, as
we have seen, many prewriting strategies help writers to explore their own
memories and interpret them. Donald Murray, a major proponent of the idea
that writers should write for personal development, says, "Writers' ideas are
locked inside their heads, unable to come out; the teacher's task is to create an
environment in which the writing which already exists in the form of ideas
comes out and makes itself public" (*Write to Learn* xi).

Proponents of this perspective believe that achieving personal growth
and becoming a better writer go hand in hand. Because the subject itself, the
writer's personal life, is so interesting to the writer, as he explores his own
ideas, he is motivated to become a better writer. This approach is based on the
idea that language is learned best when students are pursuing their own
interests. Lev Vygotsky, in his groundbreaking study on how school-based
learning is connected to learning outside of school, reminds us that language
development depends on a felt need to use language. Vygotsky says that
children will not grapple with the difficulties of writing until they have a
need to write.

The personal growth model supports individualized learning. Cleary, a
high school instructor and researcher says, "I mostly teach individuals, pursuing personal goals. Because kids are writing on topics they've chosen and
reading books they have selected, my teaching and their learning are about as
individualized as they can get . . .". The writers in her study reported more
intrinsic motivation when their tasks allowed them to make sense of their
own experience, to have some influence on their world, to have some choice
in what and how they were writing, to follow their own curiosity, and to answer real questions for real audiences and real purposes (Cleary 504). Tchudi
and Mitchell add that "If teachers give [students] confidence in their skills,
and a feeling of security about exploring new territory they will in the end, at
their own and natural pace, come toward the language behaviors identified
by the 'adult standards' model. . . . If teachers will approach language from
this student centered perspective, the adult standards will be acquired in a
much more solid fashion" (52).

Although student-centered writing in diaries, essays, and autobiographies was always seen as being appropriate for the elementary school, many
instructors at all grade levels, including the college level, have endorsed its
effectiveness. Because the writing that emerges naturally in settings where
students follow their own interests is personal in nature, various composition
specialists believe that personal writing is developmentally appropriate in
elementary school (Calkins), middle school (Atwell), high school (Tchudi and
Mitchell), and college (Murray). For example, the Tredyffrin/Easttown School

District language arts curriculum calls for journal writing in all middle school and high school grades to encourage "risk taking, reflection, and searching for meaning" (see Figure 8.1).

Nancy Atwell makes a strong case for personal writing to be assigned at the junior high stage. She says,

> *All the strong feelings and raging enthusiasms of adolescence get directed towards ends that are meaningful because students chose them. Whenever they can choose, junior high school students will write for all the reasons literate people everywhere engage as writers: to recreate happy times, work through a subject and learn more, convey and request information. . . . (42).*

Curricula that emphasize the personal growth model, like the one described in Nancy Atwell's text *In the Middle: Reading, Writing, and Learning with Adolescents,* invite students to write personal narratives about topics of interest to them (45). Another text, *Inside Out: Developmental Strategies for Teaching Writing* by Kirby, Liner, and Vinz, includes many activities for personal writing on the high school level. Suggested assignments include journals, personal responses to literature, and creative writing based on personal experiences (58). Atwell and Kirby, Liner, and Vinz draw on the work of a long list of composition scholars who have championed personal writing, including James Britton, Donald Graves, James Moffett, and Stephen Tchudi.

In the personal growth model, students write in many genres on a variety of issues. For example, students may write a research paper if they use the "I Search" process recommended by Ken Macrorie. The major distinction between this approach and the other three is that most assignments grow out of the students' interests, and most of them contain more information about the writer than about the content of the experience revealed by the writer. In *A Writer Teaches Writing* Donald Murray says, "When a student needs an assignment, the teacher should say, 'What do you want to say? What are you interested in writing about?'" (32). The student might choose, for example, the history of the ballet as a topic, and write a standard research paper, but if the student focused her essay on her own interest in the ballet and how writing the paper had enriched her enjoyment of the ballet, the paper would fit the personal growth model.

Macrorie's texts are ideal for building a writing program based on the personal growth model. He says, "This program gives the student first the freedom to find his voice and let his subjects find him, and second, to learn more professional craft and supplement his already considerable language skills" (*Telling Writing* viii). Figure 8.2 outlines the contents of this book.

CONTENTS

FIGURE 8.2   Telling Writing Contents

FIGURE 8.2 *Continued*

Reprinted by permission of Ken Macrorie, *Telling Writing*, Fourth Edition (Boynton/Cook Publishers. A subsidiary of Reed Elsevier, Inc., Portsmouth, NH, 1985).

The Rhetorical Approach

The rationale for a writing program based on the rhetorical approach is effectively summarized by James Kinneavy in the introduction to his textbook, *Writing in the Liberal Arts Tradition:*

> *Experience tells us that the result of a liberal education is a well rounded person, one who has useful knowledge and basic skills in a number of fields. One mark of the well-rounded person is to be able to communicate for different*

purposes and to different audiences. The goal of learning to write "in the lib-eral arts tradition" is the well-rounded writer—a person with training and experience in a range of writing tasks from term papers to poems and stories. We believe that well-rounded writing develops from knowledge and strate-gies which can be learned. (xiii)

The classical tradition, which is the foundation of the liberal arts tradi-tion, assumes that thinking and writing are related. Therefore, writing for dif-ferent purposes and audiences stimulates different kinds of thinking, such as logical thinking, exploratory thinking, aesthetic thinking, and expressive thinking. We need to master all of these to function as well-rounded persons in the liberal arts tradition.

Kinneavy points out that American education places a high premium on logic, the kind of thinking needed to prove a point, but has neglected other kinds of thinking that are equally important. He says,

It is not enough for us, if we wish to be critical thinkers, to be trained in sta-tistical methodology and axiomatic logic. We must also learn to think dialec-tically in exploring many topics and making political decisions. We must also learn to think aesthetically, both in making our own creations and in appreciating those of others . . . We must learn to think rhetorically, some-times to persuade others or allow ourselves to be persuaded by others. Finally—and this is the great contribution of the 19th century to the liberal arts tradition—each of us has to learn to think expressively; both as individ-uals and as members or groups we should be able to articulate our aspira-tions, values, and desires in emotional and intense credos and testimonials and be willing to listen and appreciate similar expressions from other indi-viduals and groups. (Kinneavy in Maimon, Nodine, and O'Connor 179).

The following exercise, from Kinneavy's textbook focuses on the variety of communication and thinking skills the average person uses during the average day:

Select what you would consider a typical day of the week for you, and keep a record of the different uses of language you engage in. Thus reading news sto-ries in the newspaper would be expository (informative), convincing a friend to let you use his car would be persuasive, watching a drama or comedy would be literary, and griping to your instructor would be expressive. (13)

Although these language activities involve reading and speaking, they require the same versatility of thought that writing for different aims demands. Experience in writing for different aims can improve our ability to think, read, and speak for different aims.

A curriculum based on the idea of writing for different aims requires descriptions of the kinds of writing used to accomplish these aims. Kinneavy as well as others have identified and described the major kinds of writing we use today. Kinneavy's categories have been used to structure curricula on both the secondary and college levels. In his classification system he separates "aim" from "mode." *Aim* refers to the purpose of the author, whereas *modes* are strategies that a writer or speaker uses to develop ideas for a particular aim. Kinneavy uses four categories to describe aims: *self-expression, literature, exposition,* and *persuasion.* Of course, at times, the aims overlap. For example, I might write a letter to a friend with several aims: to express my feelings of happiness or sadness, but also to persuade my friend to come for a visit, another aim. Kinneavy, following the classical tradition, believes that the thinking processes that are related to fulfilling each aim are different. Strategies for different kinds of proofs and explanations are rooted in thinking patterns. For example, persuasion requires the skills of logical argument, such as refuting your opponent's argument before offering your argument. (See Figure 8.3 for a summary of aims.)

The modes describe the way a writer "looks at a subject under discussion," the perspective the writer uses to consider his or her subject. The modes are categorized and defined in different ways by different rhetoriticians. Kinneavy's definitions are useful for explaining the modes and distinguishing

FIGURE 8.3 Aims of Discourse

Some Common Examples of Different Aims of Language

Self-Expression	Literature	Exposition	Persuasion
Of individuals	Short stories	Information	Advertising
Conversation	Jokes	News articles	Political speeches
Journals	Ballads	Lab reports	Religious sermons
Diaries	Folk Songs	Textbooks	Legal oratory
Gripe sessions	TV plays	Summaries	Editorials
Prayer	Drama	Encyclopedia articles	
Of groups	Movies	Exploration	
Protests	Novels	Dialogues	
Myths	Poems	Seminars	
Contracts	Epics	Discussions	
Religious credos		Proposed solutions	
Declarations		to problems	
Manifestos		Diagnoses	
Utopia plans		Explaining and proving	
Laws		Scientific reports	
		Research studies	
		Legal briefs	
		Mathematical theorems	
		Term papers	

Source: From *Writing in the Liberal Arts Tradition,* 2nd ed., by James L. Kinneavy, William J. McCleary, and Neil Nakadate. Copyright © 1990 by Harper & Row, Publishers, Inc. Reprinted by permission of Addison Wesley Educational Publishers, Inc.

them from aims: "*Narratives* report changes in objects, *classification* groups objects having some characteristics in common, *description* details the individual characteristics of an object, and *evaluation* rates the performance of an object in light of some goal" (*Writing in the Liberal Art Tradition* 247). See Figure 8.4 for a summary of modes.

Like the aims, the modes overlap. For example, I might narrate, that is, tell a story about my day at the beach, and then evaluate that day by comparing it to other days spent at the beach. The overall aim of my writing might be expressive, to understand better how I felt about the beach on that particular day, which might be related, for example, to a more complex question: What is the meaning of vacation for me?

FIGURE 8.4   Modes of Discourse

Examples of Each Mode	
Narration	*Description*
Biography	The makeup of a cell
History	A town or country
News stories	Geological formations in a canyon
Novels	Organization of books, plays
Short stories	Plot structure of a novel
Dramas	People
Case histories in psychology or medicine	Structure of a population
Sports reporting	Structure of a government, an industry
Accounts of process	
Classification	*Evaluation*
Definitions of democracy, novel, obscenity, freedom, change	Political systems
	Religious systems
Classifications of diseases, skiers, fish, governments, languages	Technique of producing something
	Farming methods
Comparisons and/or contrasts of religions, governments, dramas, dialects, writers	Football teams
	Actors
	Politicians
	Clothing
	Toothpastes
	Actions of individuals or groups
	Books
	Heroes
	Cements
	Buildings

Source: From *Writing in the Liberal Arts Tradition*, 2nd Ed., by James L. Kinneavy, William J. McCleary, and Neil Nakadate. Copyright © 1990 by Harper & Row, Publishers, Inc. Reprinted by permission of Addison Wesley Educational Publishers, Inc.

Writing programs were generally structured according to the modes until the revival of classical rhetoric in the 1960s, which stressed the importance of the aims of writing. One of the earliest essays proposing that high school programs be structured around the aims of writing rather than the modes is "Teaching Rhetoric in High School: Some Proposals" by Richard Larson. Larson advises teachers to abandon the traditional method for organizing instruction according to modes and to use aims instead. He says:

> *What I am suggesting is that teachers of expository writing in high school look at expository writing from the perspective employed by most classical and many modern writers on rhetoric and to encourage students to adopt the same perspective. I am urging teachers of composition to view writing not as a process of observing the rules of grammar, or of engaging in creativity as an end in itself, or of negotiating expository methods, that are regularly described in standard texts on composition, but rather as an art by which the writer tries to assure that his readers understand what he has to say, respects his opinions, and, if they reasonably can, come to agree with them. (122)*

In contrast to the traditional approach to teaching composition, in which the instructor assigns a comparison-contrast paper as an end in itself, instructors teaching from a rhetorical perspective will ask students to use comparison-contrast "as a way of organizing information to achieve a purpose" (Larson 125). For example, if you want to motivate students to come to your school (argumentative aim), comparing it to another school will emphasize particular features of your school. Comparison is a useful mode to use for the purpose of argument. If you want to persuade your parents to loan you the car, you might say "Mary's parents allow her to use their car."

Many schools have adopted a writing curriculum based on the rhetorical approach and follow the guidelines similar to those listed here, which I have excerpted from Richard Larson's essay:

> 1. *First, in many if not most of his writing assignments, the teacher can stipulate the audience to whom the students should address their papers. He can also suggest the purpose that students should try to achieve, in their writing, and he can specify an imagined or actual case for writing. If the designated audience is live and present (school administrators, officers of student government, members of the class just behind or ahead of those writing), so much the better. If the papers cannot reasonably be addressed to an audience outside the classroom,*

> *other members of the class can furnish a live audience for the students to envisage.*
>
> 2. *Second, whatever the audience or purpose for the theme, the teacher can encourage students to approach it with these questions in mind: what procedures ought I to follow in selecting and arranging my material so as to assure that I communicate completely with my reader? Given what I know of my audience and given my purpose, what strategies are available to me and which one will work best? Answers to these questions may suggest the amount and kinds of information the student will need to include in his theme and the pattern of organization best suited to bringing this information together.*
>
> 3. *Third, the teacher can invite students to make rhetorical analyses of contemporary writings and speeches. Students can decide for themselves what selected editorial writers, essayists, political orators, and advertising copy writers are trying to accomplish in their pieces, and can discuss why particular combinations of data, plans of organization, patterns of sentences, levels of language, and figures of speech appear in the pieces under discussion. (127)*

The rhetorical approach is based on a more traditional idea about how students learn best than is the personal growth approach. Teachers using a rhetorical approach believe that students learn best when knowledge is broken down into chunks that can be mastered individually. As Kinneavy says in his textbook:

> *The concept of skill separation is an important one for understanding the strategy of this text. The concept has been an important one since Isocrates, an educator in ancient Greece, compared the processes of learning to write to those of becoming an athlete. For example, the novice wrestler learned various holds and positions before he could engage in competition with a variety of opponents. Today, learning to be a tennis player involves the same basic strategy. The beginner might practice serving for a while, then work on her backhand, then try to improve her ground strokes, then serve and volley, and so on. In a match—and certainly in a series of them with different opponents, and on different courts, all of these skills would eventually be called upon: but the player must first have developed the individual basic skills.*
>
> *In composition too, a person needs certain basic skills. Fundamental grammar and vocabulary skills, for example, are obviously necessary for effective writing. But there are also skills that have to do with different kinds of papers, with collecting information, with strategies for different proofs and explanations, with techniques of adapting to different kinds of audi-*

ences, and so on. Student writers usually find it useful to single out these skills for special attention. (15)

As we noted in Richard Larson's guidelines, teachers are urged to use traditional methods, such as the analysis of models, to teach students the characteristics of different kinds of writing. However, the rhetorical approach also emphasizes techniques compatible with a process approach to writing, such as dividing the writing task into stages: prewriting, drafting, and revising, with special emphasis on the prewriting stage. Systematic questioning, related to different kinds of topics, discussed in Chapter 1, is an important device for inventing ideas in the rhetorical approach.

Sequence

In a curriculum based on the rhetorical approach, instructors teach students how to write for different aims and audiences, teaching them the organizational patterns for each form of writing, as well as the style. Kinneavy believes that students can benefit from practicing all kinds of writing at each grade level. Although no particular sequence has proven to be more effective than another, there is some agreement that expressive, or personal, writing should precede other kinds of writing.

Among others who have tried to develop some rationale for sequencing rhetorical writing instruction, James Moffett has developed the most extensive sequential scheme. Moffett, like Kinneavy and Larson, believes in the rhetorical approach to writing instruction, but he classifies writing in terms of a set of relations between the speaker, the listener or audience, and the subject matter. As the speaker moves further away from his or her subject and audience in space and time, more abstract thinking is required. Moffett's classification scheme is based on the psychologist Jean Piaget's theories about child development. Moffett says,

> *Piaget has formulated one of the most general laws of learning and one that bears profoundly on rhetoric: the cognitive perspective of the child expands gradually from himself outward so as to incorporate points of view foreign to his initially preferred egocentric outlook, to accommodate audiences remote from himself, and to encompass subjects broader and broader in time and space . . . The thought and speech of the child, says Piaget, gradually socialize, adapt to a listener. The speaker must embrace the other's world by incorporating his point of view and by speaking his language. Thus Piaget enables us to tie rhetoric to the cognitive processes and the basic biological fact of adaptation in general. ("Rationale for a New Curriculum in English" 153)*

Moffet's categories reflect an increasing psychological distance of the writer from his or her audience:

Reflection—intrapersonal communication between two parts of the nervous system.

Conversation—interpersonal communication between two people within vocal range.

Correspondence—interpersonal communication between remote individuals or small groups with some personal knowledge of each other.

Publication—impersonal communication to a large anonymous group extended over space and/or time.

Moffett suggests that the principle of psychological distancing can help us develop a sequence of assignments appropriate to the cognitive development of the writer, although he developed his theory to provide a basis for instruction in all the language arts, including speaking and reading. Moffett would say that writing to yourself (reflection) or a friend is easier than writing to a less familiar audience, such as the readership for a local newspaper: "Consider the shifts all down the line in all the substructures of the language that must take place each time the audience becomes more remote . . . allusion, diction, punctuation, style, sentence structure, paragraphing logic—all adjust to what the audience can understand, appreciate and respond to" (*Teaching the Universe of Discourse* 11).

Increasing the distance of the subject (things being written about) from the speaker or writer also increases the complexity of the writing task. Moffett categorizes this distance in these terms:

1. What is happening (recording)
2. What happened (reporting)
3. What happens (generalizing)
4. What may happen (theorizing)

This sequence requires that the students deal with progressively more abstract information. In the recording category students write about observations and firsthand experiences. In the reporting category students write about past experiences that have already been recorded. When they write about "what happens," they form conclusions about conclusions, and students writing about "what may happen" integrate an even larger number of generalizations to compose a theory that predicts the future. Moffett uses the following example to demonstrate this progression. He contrasts the police log of the events of a certain day (recording) to the police station's annual report summary (reporting), to the essay on crime that is based on many annual summary reports (generalizing), to the theoretical essay on trends in crime in the United States (theorizing).

With Betty Jane Wagner, Moffett has developed a curriculum sequence (K–12), which is based on both ideas: the distance of the writer or speaker from the audience, and the distance of the writer or speaker from the subject. In this sequence expressive writing, writing to oneself, and writing about immediate events are the kinds of assignments suggested early in the sequence. The rationale and assignments for this curriculum are presented in *Student Centered Language Arts and Reading, K–12* and *Active Voice, A Writing across the Curriculum Program*, which demonstrate how Moffett's assignments can be adapted to different disciplines.

The Sociocultural Approach

Similar to the personal growth approach, the sociocultural approach is more student centered than subject centered. In the sociocultural approach, the student's growth is linked to participation in the community, whether it be the classroom or the community at large. It is based on the social constructionist view of learning, which assumes that human development occurs through social interaction (see Chapter 1).

In Chapter 2 we saw how collaborative learning as a method of facilitating the composing process is a natural outgrowth of this perspective. When thinking about the goals of a curriculum based on this view of learning, scholars such as Kenneth Bruffee frame its goals in terms of students becoming participants in new communities because by definition that is what development means in this context. Proponents of this view believe that the transition from former communities to new communities cannot be achieved unless teachers and students become aware of the influence of community and family life on language patterns and customs. The more we understand about the language and culture that the students bring to the writing class, and the more *they* understand about academic language and academic culture, the easier it will be for the students to learn "new languages."

One of the reasons the sociocultural approach is appealing to educators is that it accounts for the differences in performance of various cultural groups. Some cultural groups, for example, children of college graduates, have a head start in joining the school community if the language students speak in communities outside of school is similar to the language spoken in school, as we discussed in Chapter 4, Teaching about Sentences. But in other communities such as those in North Carolina, where Shirley Brice-Heath has conducted research, there is an enormous gap between the way language is used in the school and the way it is used in the community.

Brice-Heath has completed several studies that offer dramatic illustrations of these differences and their implications for designing a curriculum. For example, in her study of language and literacy in Roadville, "a white working class community steeped for generations in the life of the textile mills" and Trackton, "a black working-class community whose older generations grew up farming the land, but whose current members work in the mills in the Piedmonts," she asked the question, "What were the effects of preschool and home and community environment on the language structures and uses which were needed in classrooms and job settings?" She hoped that by engaging students, teachers, and townspeople in this research, she could help develop effective curricula in reading and writing in these communities (1–14).

Brice-Heath spent several years recording the language learning habits of the children of these two communities, visiting the factories in these towns, the families, and the classroom. She says, "Together we took field notes, identified patterns of communicative interactions, and delineated what the school and mill defined as communication problems. We searched for solutions, wrote curricula and tried new methods, materials, and motivations to help working class black and white children learn more effectively than they had in the past" (355). Brice-Heath reports,

> *A crucial step in this approach was to involve the students as fellow researchers. Junior high and high school students kept journals, recording personal experiences as well as family and community experiences with language. By developing a curriculum which involved the students performing research on how language is used in and out of school, students began to accept the possibility of reacting according to the rules of either of these systems. Also, facility in articulating the ways their own home communities used language and comparing these ways with the ways of the school, weakened the boundary between the two systems. Students became engaged individually and as a group in translating and organizing community knowledge into the classroom and classroom knowledge into the community. (356)*

For example, in Roadville telling stories of actual as opposed to made-up events was rewarded, whereas in Trackton, students at home were encouraged to fantasize. This information explained why some students performed better on one kind of writing assignment rather than on another, and helped both instructors and students as they attempted the less familiar language activity.

Shirley Brice-Heath's work is an example of designing a writing curriculum for two towns in the rural South. Mary Mercer Krogness's work in the Shaker Heights Middle School demonstrates how one teacher adapted a traditional language arts curriculum for the students in the lowest track in that school, students who are typical of urban student populations "outside the mainstream." Krogness permitted her students to write about their experiences in their neighborhoods and families in the language they spoke outside the school. She used unconventional teaching methods to communicate with "unconventional" students. One of her former students told her,

> *Learning was easy in our class maybe because we didn't have to read those textbooks and because you wrote long notes on our papers. I liked those notes because they answered questions for me like what was good about my writing and what wasn't so good . . . I remember the time we made dictionaries of black slang. That project kinda just popped up out of nowhere after class and you talked about words. Me and all the black kids taught you what all the slang (black expressions like dissin and def and straight meant. Teachers should be students; they should hear what students say, instead of doing all the talking. (ix)*

A curriculum such as Krogness's curriculum will include methods and assignments that capitalize on the strengths of the linguistic background and culture that students bring with them to school.

Krogness and Brice-Heath challenge the idea that students must change to become members of our academic community. Both focus on students adapting their abilities and natural motivations to their work in school, but they never urge their students to abandon them. Composition experts, concerned about these issues, have argued that efforts to teach students the conventions of academic English are synonomous with social control and repression. I disagree and would favor the approach to composition instruction that validates the students' language and culture, while introducing the student to new discourse communities. An interesting text to read, which illustrates this kind of progression, is Mike Rose's *Lives on the Boundary.*

Perhaps the most dramatic cases of cultural and linguistic differences occur in classrooms in which students are not native speakers of English. When we teach writing in these classes, issues of language must go beyond the sentence level, such as the difficulties these students have using prepositions and articles. Issues of rhetoric are equally important, especially at the secondary level. For example, the rules of argument may be different. We ask such questions as, "What are the typical guidelines for using logical, ethical, and pathetic appeals appropriately?" In Arabic repetition with variation is a common form of developing ideas. An argument is strongly based on repeating some truth that the writer or speaker shares with his or her audience. Also, native speakers of Arabic provide more background information at a more abstract level than English speakers. For example, one student whose native language is Arabic began his essay with the sentence, "All over the world and in many places, we find families." To an American this would seem like an unnecessary statement (Moss and Walters 359). An instructor who is aware that choice of content, organization, and development of an essay for a non-English speaker may be determined by rhetorical practices of the native language will acknowledge their validity in that language when discussing the different conventions for argument in English.

Another important concept linked with the sociocultural approach is that students should learn the kinds of writing that will empower them in both their own communities and the communities they will enter. For example, in the Webster Groves School District Action Research project, students wrote about community problems in their journals:

> *I think the biggest problem in the world today is drugs. Drugs are everywhere. I see it everyday guys standing on the corner in cold are hot weather. You know that they have to be sailing something standing out in the cold when the temp is something like 5 or 10 outside . . . One time I even saw a man take some rocked cocaine, put it in a bag, and hide it by rubbing it in some leaves. So when the cops come by the can't get busted. . . . (Krater 296)*

A curriculum based on writing related to communities will not limit writing experiences to academic writing but will include writing that students need to function as citizens or as employees. Assignments might include reviewing and revising real documents, such as a telephone bill insert, a promotional letter for a credit card, or a local hospital's newsletter on patient information. Or students might draft a manual for high school students on getting a summer job, or prepare a pamphlet on the health concerns of teenagers (*Workplace Writing*). They may also write letters of request or complaint similar to the kind of letters we all write in our daily lives, and letters of introduction, which they will need for job or college applications. Figure 8.5 shows two assignments from a unit on workplace writing.

Teaching students to write in preparation for college belongs in this curriculum, especially when college is viewed as a stepping-stone to professional and public life. However, writing for the workplace will occupy an important place in this curriculum, because not all students go to college, and some may need to be able to use the kinds of writing needed in the workplace during their careers as high school students.

Consider Your Reader

Jarrell works as an assistant to the manager of a bus company that rents buses to organizations for day and overnight trips. Because of a very successful season last year, the company has expanded its tours, changed many of its schedules, and added several brand-new vehicles to its bus fleet. Jarrell's boss wants his regular customers—a large and loyal group of senior citizens—to know all this information. He has asked Jarrell to look over a letter he has drafted and to make suggestions for revision. The draft Jarrell was asked to review is shown in the next column.

Jarrell tried to remember what she learned in the business writing course she had taken in school. When she got home, she reviewed her notes. Her instructor had stressed putting the main idea first. The textbook she used stated:

1. Present important information early in the document.
2. Take a positive approach.
3. Explain exactly what you mean. Don't assume the reader knows.
4. Present information from the reader's point of view.

```
Dear Bus Patrons:

Enclosed please find reservation
forms and a complete schedule of
trips for our 19xx season. Our
bus fleet has expanded and we
changed many of our schedules.
We have new places to go, some
new overnight trips, and a chance
to see an excellent musical in
Central City. We expect to have an
even bigger and better season than
last year.

XYZ Tours is planning an exciting
spring, summer, and fall season.
We plan to visit the Berson
Gardens, the new Design Museum
in Pepperton, and the historic
Kellogg House. Our most popular
trip---fall foliage in the Endless
Mountains---is usually reserved
well in advance. If you would like
to schedule a day or overnight
trip for your club or organization,
or for yourself, you MUST make a
reservation. It is not possible to
hold a particular date without the
required paper work.

Also, we had to replace two
malfunctioning vehicles this
year with brand-new comfortable
buses. You're going to love them.
They have wider seats, softer
cushions, and more leg room.

We expect a great season this year
and hope you'll join us. If you
have questions, please call me.

Sincerely,
```

Jarrell decided that the purpose of the letter was to give information, but she wasn't sure what was most important. As she reread the letter, she decided it was the expanded bus fleet. Then she switched to the fact that new trips were being offered. Then she thought it was the procedures for reserving a trip. Finally, she found the main idea hiding in the middle of the letter. She copied it onto a clean sheet of paper and got to work.

Continued

FIGURE 8.5 "Consider Your Reader" (a revision exercise) and "Letter of Introduction"

Speaking, writing, doing

▶ **Letter of introduction.** Write a letter introducing yourself to someone at school or work. Possible readers: one of your classroom teachers, a former or current coach, or your new boss. Write about your career goals and the steps you are taking to prepare for that career. Also, include personal strengths and limitations that may affect your ability to get the job you seek.

Write your letter from a third person's point of view. For example, begin by introducing yourself as "This letter introduces (*your name*), a student in your fifth period class, or a candidate for the position of night manager." Throughout the letter, refer to yourself as he or she or as Ms. or Mr.

This letter draft can be helpful in seeing yourself as others do. Share your draft with class members and get their reactions. Ask them specifically to identify your main points. You may wish to actually send this letter to the intended reader or to revise it for your own file.

FIGURE 8.5   *Continued*

Reproduced from School-to-Work Series Newsletter Bulletin, Career Solutions Training Group, with the Permission of South-Western Educational Publishing, a division of International Thomson Publishing, Inc. Copyright 1995 by South-Western Educational Publishing. All rights reserved.

District Curriculum Guides and Classroom Writing Programs

The Tredyffrin/Easttown School District Curriculum Guide for Writing is typical of many high school curriculum guides. It includes material that reflects all four approaches to teaching writing: the correctness approach, the personal growth approach, the rhetorical approach, and the sociocultural approach. The first module, Responsive/Exploratory/Strategic, emphasizes the use of journals at all levels "to encourage risk-taking, reflection, and searching for meaning." Some topics are assigned, but free choice is encouraged. That no sequence is recommended suggests that this part of the curriculum is very student centered. Because frequent noncorrected entries are favored, correctness is clearly not a goal in this part of the curriculum but instead is stressed in another module, Style/Language Structure/Usage.

The Style/Language Structure/Usage module offers guidelines for sentence-level instruction in sequence. Correct grammar (e.g., subject–verb agreement) and correct punctuation are stressed in addition to stylistic diversity and effective word choice. The curriculum modules that deal with "kinds of writing" include elements of the rhetorical approach and the sociocultural approach, although the main emphasis of the Expository/Paragraph/Essay module is not on writing for different purposes and audiences but on learning how to write the expository essay. The emphasis on letter writing gives students some experience in writing for different aims and audiences and could be used to connect the writing program to the community. Writing for imaginative purposes occupies an important place in the curriculum because it has its own module, which emphasizes many forms of imaginative writing, for example, poetry, short stories, monologues, and plays.

Writing instruction is integrated with literature instruction as students apply the skills they learn in each category to writing about literature. They write journals, essays, and fiction related to the required reading in the curriculum.

Designing Writing Units

The Tredyffrin/Easttown School District curriculum, like many others, gives teachers freedom to develop their own writing assignments to carry out the curriculum's goals. Louise Jones, who teaches eighth and ninth grades in this district, has developed a series of writing assignments on the theme of literature and world cultures. Students wrote in a variety of genres such as essays, poems, letters, and monologues. Often they had a choice of topics and choice of genres. They had the opportunity to write drafts and to revise them. Most of the writing was integrated with reading assignments. Elements from all four modules of the Tredyffrin/Easttown School District guidelines can be identified in her writing program. Her assignments are prompts for practicing a rich array of writing skills.

To set the stage for the course, Jones had students read an essay entitled "What's American about America" by Ishmael Reed, and write a short response paper on the same topic (see Figure 8.6). They integrate their own ideas with ideas in the essay, but there are no formal requirements to include a thesis statement. This was a good "warm-up" assignment, which provided a transition from the Responsive/Exploratory/Strategic strand to the Expository Paragraph/Essay strand of the curriculum.

Jones comments about another essay assigned early in the semester:

> *In the assignment for the "Doum Tree of Wad Hamida" a short story by Tayeb Salih, the students had to—probably for the first time—develop their own thesis statement and clear essay map or sub-thesis for an expository paper. They were told to focus on connections to the material in their world cultures class and on fundamental Islamic beliefs. They could focus on an analysis of a character, or the role of a stranger in the story; they could also focus on the fear of change. I was looking for the ability to use the lines from the text as well as events to substantiate their thesis.*

See Figure 8.7 on page 223 for the student essay, "The Isolation of the Village of Wad Hamid."

FIGURE 8.6   Student Response to Ishmael Reed's Essay, "What's American about America?"

Megan Rogers
1994, 9th Grade

What's American about America?

In answering the question, "What's American about America?," people should think of what is unAmerican first. America is known as a place where people of different cultures have a chance to unite into one country. It is known as being "the land of the free," but there are many things which take away the freedom that people are looking for. America is believed to be a place where peoples' differences are respected and sometimes even admired. However, in the land of freedom and choices, some rights are forgotten as Americans claim to be proud of being free.

The United States has repeatedly been called a "melting pot." It is populated with people from every continent in the world. These people come to America seeking many things---money, freedom, or fame to name a few. As people from different places move to the US, they are often faced with racism and bigotry. Groups like the United Skinheads of America and the Ku Klux Klan are growing in members and threatening the freedom that immigrants are searching for. Racism is something that isn't American, but despite years of trying to eliminate it, is still happening.

Americans are guaranteed the right of freedom of speech by the First Amendment of the Constitution. Freedom of speech is American, whether it is in art, music, or writing. What is unAmerican is censorship, another thing that happens in the US that shouldn't. The thoughts and feelings of an artist are often labeled vulgar or obscene by another person, sometimes prohibiting the art from being published. The privilege of freedom of expression has been granted to Americans and shouldn't be taken away.

America is a great country to live in. It is a country with plenty of American opportunities that everybody should have, but some are denied. People should stop trying to build up America's image of freedom until they get rid of the unAmerican things which take away that same freedom.

Reprinted by permission of Megan Rogers.

FIGURE 8.7   Student Response to Tayeb Salih's Story, "Doum Tree of Wad Hamida"

"The Isolation of the Village of Wad Hamid"

The village of Wad Hamid is a town that is distinct from all other villages. The townspeople think and act differently just because they are exposed to the "Wad Hamid" way of life. "It is as though the village, with its inhabitants, its water wheels and buildings, had become split off from the rest of the earth." "No one has disturbed our tranquil existence." The village is not open to strangers because it is intentionally isolated and guarded from the outside world. Together with the help of the flies, the river, the Doum Tree, and the townspeople, this isolation is accomplished.

The flies can be thought of as the militia of the village. They are an army that swarms in a "dark cloud" through the hot, humid air. Playing the role of an army, the flies act as a protective gate into the city. "No one who isn't well accustomed to them and has become as thick-skinned as we are can bear their stings." The strangers are the people without thick skin. With that in mind, they are the ones who are most affected by their vicious bites. "It would be a swarm of those sand-flies which obstruct all paths to those who wish to enter our village." The people who actually are able to enter the town are driven away by fevers, running noses, swollen faces, malaria, and dysentery. All of these irritating symptoms are caused by the stings. The flies fulfill their niche in Wad Hamid by keeping the village free from strangers.

The river also keeps outsiders away. It symbolizes the village's security because "the river twists and turns below it (the Doum Tree) like a sacred snake, one of the ancient gods of the Egyptians." This line is of significance because the Egyptians "believed that the different gods controlled the forces of nature" (W. C. text 73). This knowledge establishes a link between the river and it controlling the forces of nature. In ancient Egypt, the Nile flooded every once in a while, and while it was flooded, it acted as a natural barrier. Salih, the author, may have been trying to link the Nile with the river in the story by describing it as an ancient god of Egypt. The fact that the river twists and turns also can suggest that the river acts almost like a moat around the city. In ancient castles, the moat kept the unwanted people out. The river keeps out the strangers, unwelcome people in Wad Hamid. In this way the river also isolates the village of Wad Hamid from the outside people.

The Doum tree acts as a guard over the village and the surrounding lands. "The shadow of the tree stretches across the cultivated land and houses right up to the cemetery. Don't you think it is like some mythical eagle spreading its wings over the village and everyone in it?" When the shadow is described as an eagle spreading it wings over the village and people, it puts the tree in the place of a guard. This is because its "wings" cover and keep the village safe. The tree also acts as the guard of the river (moat), "standing above it (the river) like a sentinel." During the creation of the tree, one woman described it as "leafless trees with thorns, the tips of which were like hawks." The thorns indicate a kind of protection that the tree gives. The relation with the hawks is important because hawks, in nature, are birds very similar to the mythical eagle. This further states the point relating to the protection the birds give. The Doum Tree, along with its shadow, is the watcher and guard of the village.

Continued

FIGURE 8.7 *Continued*

The townspeople themselves also keep strangers away. By repeating such lines as, "Were you to come to our village as a tourist . . . you would not stay long," to strangers, they are not exactly enticing outsiders to stay. The narrator, who can act as the representative of the townspeople, constantly repeats that line to the stranger. Is he trying to repeat it so many times to the stranger to drive the thought into his head or make him feel unwelcome? That may be his tactic. The townspeople also refused to have a stopping place for the steamer put in at the site of the Doum Tree. By keeping outside transportation from stopping in their village, the townspeople are isolating themselves by choice. Important also is the fact that when the narrator's son runs away from his home in Wad Hamid, the father feels, "It wasn't I who put him there; he ran away and went there on his own, and it is my hope that he will stay where he is and not return." An important point to make is that a person as close to a father as a son is not even welcome back after he becomes an outsider in Wad Hamid. This shows how important it is to the townspeople that strangers are not welcome into their private village. They are kept out through words and actions by the townspeople.

The cooperation of the flies, the river, the Doum Tree, and the townspeople together acts as a strong force that keeps strangers away. The villagers know that when "the number of young men with souls foreign to our own increases . . . maybe then the steamer will stop at our village—under the Doum Tree of Wad Hamid." By keeping out the strangers, they are trying to delay the time when that will eventually occur. This explains why the village is not open to strangers, but guarded and intentionally isolated.

Adapted and reprinted by permission of Michael Sha.

Throughout the year, Louise Jones alternates between imaginative and expository writing, sometimes requiring both, as in this assignment:

Read *The Chosen* by Chaim Potok. Type and submit two pieces of writing—one a creative piece in your choice of genre: short story, or poem(s) focusing perhaps on being chosen or not choosing that which has been chosen for you . . . and two, an analytical piece built on a clear thesis statement. Some suggestions for an analytical piece are below . . . but any topic if approved can be used.

Sample topics:

1. Compare and contrast father–son relationships in the novel.
2. Select a line that captures the heart of the novel and develop an essay around that line.

3. Put yourself in the "skin" of Reb Saunders and speak as you think he would on the issues of raising a son in silence.

4. Take your knowledge of the Jewish faith and traditions and apply it to the development of a thesis that shows how perhaps accurate or inaccurate the information and choices in this novel are. (You might want to focus on Chapter 6.)

5. Wrestle with the topic of the Zionist movement and the dilemma it presents to strict orthodox Jews like an Hasidic sect ... and the answer that evoked such a passionate response in Mr. Maltier.

6. Wrestle with the soul and the tragedy of having a brilliant child without a soul. Is the price Reb Saunders paid worth the end result?

7. Does history repeat itself? Is that the source of Reb Saunders's decisions in parenting and in being the leader of his people?

8. Use any of the opening quotes that we discussed and now you understand more fully as the springboard for your paper. Put your quote at the top and in the first paragraph. Of course have a thesis statement that either comes from the quote or is the result of the quote.*

Notice that Jones gives many topic choices to motivate her students. For this paper she requires a peer review, now that students are becoming familiar with the concept of the thesis statement. She adds to the assignment: "All papers must by reviewed by a peer before showing them to me and also highlighted and glossed as necessary." (See Figure 8.9 for her peer review sheet and Figure 8.8 for the essay entitled "Roles of the Talmud and Torah.")

To fulfill the requirements of the Imaginative Writing module, Jones often permits students to write letters, monologues, or poems to respond to readings. This type of assignment offers several alternatives. She provides students with examples for how to accomplish the assignment as well. (See Figure 8.10, "Four Women of Forty" assignment.)

Throughout her writing program, Jones places great emphasis on language. For example, she reminds students that during their oral presentations they must defend the metaphors they use to describe a character. To prepare for these assignments her students write journal entries, talk extensively about their ideas, write drafts, and with her assistance, improve sentences and correct errors in mechanics. In sum, her writing program conforms to the Tredyffrin/Easttown District Guidelines but reflects her interests and personal approach to teaching writing.

---

*Reprinted by permission of Louise Jones, Conestoga High School, Berwyn, PA.

FIGURE 8.8   Student Response to Chaim Potok's Book, *The Chosen*

"Roles of the Talmud and Torah"

Who is the tzaddik in *The Chosen?* That question is easily answered, for it is Reb Saunders. But where does Reb Saunders find guidance? For Reb as well as members of the Jewish nation, the Torah and Talmud work together and act as a code of law and ideas. They act as two writings which advise the tzaddik. The tzaddik, in turn, takes the information and applies it to the lives of his followers. In *The Chosen*, the Torah and Talmud form a link between Reb Saunders and his son, Danny. They also act as a bridge between both Reuven's sect and Danny's God. Finally, they give tips about living a healthy Jewish life. These two writings are the basis on which Reb Saunders, the tzaddik, gets his direction.

The Talmud seems to be the only link between Reb and Danny. The father–son duo has aged through the book without speaking to each other, except through Talmudic disputations. "Silence is good everywhere except in connection with the Torah." The Talmud breaks the silence between Reb and Danny. "We don't talk anymore, except when we study Talmud." "Silence was ugly, it was black, it leered, it was cancerous, it was death." Through debate of the Talmud, the suffering of Danny, caused by Reb's silence, is absorbed. Danny's frustration is let out during the discussions, and he actually enjoys it because he can speak and show his wealth of knowledge. "It's a kind of game almost." Danny is not the only one who gets satisfaction out of the discussions. Reb also enjoys the conversations and testing Danny's intelligence. "This time Reb Saunders agreed, his face glowing, that his son was correct. . . . Reb Saunders was far happier when he lost to Danny than when he won." Without the Talmud, how could Danny and Reb have communicated? This is how the Talmud and Torah unite Reb and Danny, two members of the Jewish race.

The Torah also links Danny's sect with Reuven's sect. Both sects are not very common in their practices, but they both study Torah. In this way, Reuven slowly learned to join in the discussions. "I realized that though they knew much more material than I did, once a passage was quoted and briefly explained, I was on almost equal footing with them . . . though I was unequal to Danny in breadth, I was easily equal to him in depth." This shows that though Reuven and Danny are different, they are still linked by the Torah and Talmud. Through these central writings, all Jews become closer to God and also each other. "If one man studies Torah, the Presence is with him . . . We are commanded to study His Torah! We are commanded to sit in the light of His Presence! . . . The people of Israel must study His Torah!" The "people of Israel" refers to the Jews. This means that all Jews must study the Torah. Therefore, all Jews are linked at least through the knowledge of what is contained in the Torah. In this way, knowledge or understanding the Torah linked Reuven and Danny even though they are from different sects.

The Talmud gives tips for living a good Jewish life. Jews then take that information and apply it to their own lives. Danny did this with a quote from the Talmud. "The Talmud says that a person should do two things for himself. One is to acquire a teacher. Do you remember the other? . . . Choose a friend." Danny found a teacher at Hirsch College, Rav Gershenson. More importantly, he found a friend, Reuven Malter. Reuven also listened to the Talmud. When Danny first came to apologize at the hospital, Reuven said to him, "You can go to hell, and take your whole snooty bunch of Hasidim along with you." Later he was lectured by his father for treating Danny so harshly. "You did a foolish thing, Reuven. You remember what the Talmud says. If a person comes to apologize for having hurt you, you must listen and forgive him." Reuven

FIGURE 8.8 *Continued*

took his father's advice and listened to the Talmud. If he had not made up with Danny, and they had not become friends, there would have been no story. By listening to the wisdom of the Talmud, the one-time enemies became lifelong friends. Talmud gave guidance to both Danny and Reuven.

Did the Torah and Talmud play a crucial part in the book? Yes, definitely so. It gave leadership, friendship, love, and links between the characters of the book. They helped unite the characters to create a closely knit web. This is how the Torah and Talmud helped in advising the tzaddik and his people. Through its information, it guided not only Reb, but also the Malters. In the end, a lifelong friendship resulted between Danny and Reuven.

Adapted and reprinted by permission of Michael Sha.

Peer Partner's Name _____

Reviewing Student's Name _____

Title of piece _____

Focus/Theme of creative piece(s) _____

_____

_____

Thesis Statement of analytical paper _____

_____

_____

Comments: (Be sure to tell your peer whether the thesis is proven with a clear essay map or subthesis and be sure to *highlight and gloss this first draft*.)

(For creative pieces—be sure they show an understanding of the novel, the characters, or the political issuers at work during this time period.)

_____

_____

_____

_____

FIGURE 8.9 Peer Review Sheet

Reprinted by permission of Louise Jones, Conestoga High School, Berwyn, PA.

FIGURE 8.10   "Four Women of Forty" Assignment

After reading the short story "Four Women of Forty," select one of the four women so that in your groups of four all four women of forty are represented.

After deciding on the woman of your choice, your job is to be as deeply involved in that character's motivations, frustrations, joys, and snares as possible. Knowing that these women are now living after the Cultural Revolution, your World Cultures knowledge will be helpful to you. At the heart of this story is the irony of which of the four is really happy and fulfilled.

Then . . . if you want to speak in the first person or if your preference (especially as a male . . .) is the third person, she, please write your "self"-analysis on your analysis of the person's entire life. You want to "paint" the woman's life . . . carefully selecting the pieces to lead up to where she is at forty.

You might want to use a metaphor to help present your understanding.

For example, in the movie *The Color Purple* one of the main characters is Celie . . . homely, abused, but not broken. She might . . . use . . . a metaphor comparing herself to a hard black floor . . .

In your oral presentations in front of the class, the metaphor, or the poem you write to illustrate the metaphor, would have to be discussed in true "Jonesian" back-and-forth dialogue as to why the metaphor is appropriate and which events in the story support this "picture" of Celie.

Adapted and reprinted by permission of Louise Jones, Conestoga High School, Berwyn, PA.

Conclusion

During the past fifteen years, many school districts have adopted some version of the rhetorical approach to structure their writing curricula. State guidelines, such as the Pennsylvania Framework for Reading, Writing, and Talking Across the Curriculum, have supported this trend. At least on paper there has been strong commitment to the idea of teaching students how to write for diverse purposes and audiences, from elementary school through high school. If the rhetorical approach is fully implemented, it includes the goals of the other three approaches: writing for personal growth, writing to achieve social literacy, and writing to develop sentence-level, paragraph, and essay skills.

We teach in a "rhetoric friendly" environment. However, even if your school or school district has adopted a rhetorically based program, you still may face several obstacles. First, the "correctness police" are always lurking nearby. Some parents, school board members, and even colleagues remain forever locked in the correctness paradigm. Nothing will suit them as a measure of writing ability but a grammatically correct sentence. Second, your school may lack materials designed to carry out the rhetorical approach. New textbooks are expensive; your students may be issued a traditional handbook as their only writing text despite the adoption of a new curriculum. And, finally, your students may be unfamiliar with the rhetorical approach, or for that matter, any approach, if they have not received much writing instruction in previous grades. You can implement a rhetorical approach without published materials (develop your own) and demonstrate that you can teach students how to write competent sentences while teaching them other equally important writing skills. As for your students, you will win them over with a writing program that teaches them how to write for greater self-understanding, for personal pleasure, and for the purpose of communicating with success both in school and in the world outside of school.

Questions for Discussion and Writing

1. Write an analysis of the Lower Merion School District Writing Curriculum (Appendix 8: Figures 8.11, 8.12, and 8.13) using the four categories: correctness approach, personal growth approach, rhetorical approach, and sociocultural approach. Identify the main emphasis of the curriculum in your analysis.

2. Identify a volunteer organization (i.e., Home and School Association) in your community and find out how writing is used in this organization. What kinds of writing are used to conduct the business of the organization? Who does the writing?

3. Decide whether the following statements found in *Workplace Writing* (3) are true or false. Give reasons for your answers.

   a. Good writing usually has big words and long sentences.   **T**   **F**

   b. Experienced writers always make an outline before they begin to write.   **T**   **F**

   c. Revising a document primarily means checking for spelling and punctuation errors.   **T**   **F**

   d. Experienced writers rarely revise; inexperienced writers revise a lot.   **T**   **F**

   e. Writing is usually easy for experienced writers.   **T**   **F**

   f. Learning the rules of grammar is the best way to improve your writing.   **T**   **F**

   g. It's important to get most all of your thoughts down on paper before you start reading and revising.   **T**   **F**

   h. Unclear wording and poor organization are two common problems in workplace writing.   **T**   **F**

i. Errors in spelling, punctuation, and grammatical usage can distract the reader from reading a document.   T   F

j. In planning a document, what the writer wants to say is more important than what the reader needs to know.   T   F

4. Develop a writing unit that includes four writing assignments, which have personal growth as their main purpose.

5. Develop four writing assignments based on James Moffett's theory of sequencing assignments.

6. Develop the instructions for writing a job application letter.

7. Write a letter to the editor of your community newspaper expressing your views about a community problem.

References

Atwell, Nancy. *In the Middle: Reading and Writing and Learning with Adolescents.* Portsmouth, NH: Heinemann-Boynton/Cook, 1990.

Brice-Heath, Shirley. *Way with Words.* New York: Cambridge University Press, 1983.

Calkins, Lucy. *The Art of Teaching Writing.* Portsmouth, NH: Heinemann-Boynton/Cook, 1994.

Career Solutions Training Group. School-to-Work Series: Newsletter Bulletin. Cincinnati, OH: South-Western Educational Publishing, 1995.

Cleary, Elizabeth. *From the Other Side of the Desk: Students Speak Out about Writing.* Portsmouth, NH: Heinemann-Boynton/Cook, 1991.

Fleming, Harold, Allan Glatthorn, and Philip McFarland. *Compositions: Models and Exercises.* New York: Harcourt Brace Jovanovich, 1971.

Foster, David. *A Primer for Writing Teachers.* 2nd ed. Portsmouth, NH: Heinemann-Boynton/Cook, 1992.

Gere, Anne Ruggles et al. *Language and Reflection: An Integrated Approach to Teaching English.* New York: Macmillan Co., 1992.

Glatthorn, Allan. "The Teaching of Writing: A Review of Research, Theory, and Practice." Philadelphia: University of Pennsylvania, 1983.

Jones, Louise. Teaching materials (unpublished). Conestoga High School, Berwyn, PA, 1995.

Kinneavy, James. *Writing in the Liberal Arts Tradition.* Eds., L. William, J. McCleary, and Neil Nakadate. 2nd ed. New York: Harper, 1990.

———. "Thinkings and Writings: The Classical Tradition." *Thinking, Reasoning, and Writing.* Eds. Elaine Maimon, Barbara Nodine, and Finbarr O'Connor. New York: Longman, 1989.

Kirby, Dan, Tom Liner, and Ruth Vinz, eds. *Inside Out: Developmental Strategies for Teaching Writing.* 2nd ed. Portsmouth, NH: Heinemann-Boynton/Cook, 1988.

Krater, Jone, Jane Zeni, and Nancy Carson. *Mirror Images: Teaching Writing in Black and White.* Portsmouth, NH: Heinemann-Boynton/Cook, 1994.

Language Arts Goals (Draft). Lower Merion School District. Ardmore, PA: Summer 1997.

Larson, Richard. "Teaching Rhetoric in High School." *Rhetoric and Composition.* Ed. Richard Graves. Montclair, NJ: Boynton Cook, 1966: 121–127.

Lindemann, Erika. *A Rhetoric for Writing Teachers.* 2nd ed. New York: Oxford University Press, 1987.

Macrorie, Ken. *Telling Writing.* Portsmouth, NH: Heinemann-Boynton/Cook, 1970.

———. *The I-Search Paper. Revised Edition of Searching Writing.* Portsmouth, NH: Heinemann-Boynton/Cook, 1988.

Meyers, Miles. "The All City High Project." *Theory and Practice in Teaching Composition.* Eds. Miles Meyers and James Gray. Urbana, IL: NCTE, 1983.

Moffett, James. *Active Voice: A Writing Program Across the Curriculum.* Portsmouth, NH: Heinemann-Boynton/Cook, 1981.

———. "Rationale for a New Curriculum in English." *Theory and Practice in Teaching Composition.* Eds. Miles Meyers and James Gray. Urbana, IL: NCTE, 1983: 150–159.

———. *Teaching the Universe of Discourse.* New York: Houghton Mifflin, 1968.

Moffett, James, and Betty Wagner. *Student-Centered Language Arts and Reading, K–12.* 4th ed. Portsmouth, NH: Heinemann-Boynton/Cook, 1991.

Moss, Beverly, and Keith Walters. "Rethinking Diversity: Axes of Difference in the Writing Classroom." *The St. Martins Guide to Teaching Writing.* 3rd ed., Eds. Robert Connors and Cheryl Glenn. New York: St. Martins Press, 1995: 347–370.

Murray, Donald. *A Writer Teaches Writing.* Boston: Houghton, Mifflin, 1968.

———. *Write to Learn.* New York: Holt, Rhinehart, and Winston, 1984.

Rose, Mike. *Lives on the Boundary. Struggles and Achievements of America's Underprepared.* Englewood Cliffs, NJ: Simon and Schuster, 1989.

Shaughnessy, Mina. *Errors and Expectations.* New York: Oxford University Press, 1977.

Tchudi, Stephen, and Diana Mitchell. *Explorations in the Teaching of English.* Reading, PA: Addison and Wesley Educational Publishers, 1989.

Tredyffrin/Easttown Language Arts Curriculum, 1995.

Vygotsky, Lev. *Thought and Language.* Cambridge, MA: M.I.T. Press, 1978.

APPENDIX

- *Language Arts Goals (Draft), Lower Merion School District, Ardmore, PA: Summer 1997.*

Language Arts Goals (Draft), Lower Merion School District

Recommendations from Language Arts Framework Group

We believe the following are prerequisites which must characterize teaching and learning in Lower Merion if these curricular goals are to be reached. Teachers must . . .

- have time for reflection
- have time and structures for more interdisciplinary teamwork
- have opportunities and structures for collaboration within and between grade levels
- have administrative understanding of and support for curriculum development efforts
- have high expectations of all students
- encourage students to be aware of their learning styles
- teach students to use appropriate strategies to accommodate their learning styles
- provide materials and learning experiences which engage students actively in their own learning
- hold students accountable for applying correct language skills across the curriculum
- use "writing to learn" strategies throughout the curriculum
- allow students time for reflection
- incorporate opportunities for self and peer evaluation in courses
- expect and provide opportunities for students to take responsibility for their own learning
- provide opportunities for interdisciplinary work and encourage students in making interdisciplinary connections
- allow students to bring talents and interests to their work by providing alternative methods for students to demonstrate mastery
- provide collaborative and group opportunities for learning
- make students aware of expected learning and performance outcomes and hold students accountable for demonstrating learning
- design meaningful performance tasks by which to measure student achievement

The drawing (shown in Figure 8.11) builds on a platform of specific goals for the LMSD graduate. These six goals are the framework on which this work is based. The second platform serves to illustrate the key skill areas—Communication Skills, Information Processing Skills, and Intrainterpersonal Skills—that are necessary to achieve these goals (see also Figure 8.12). The center rings illustrate the four components of the Language Arts Curriculum: Reading, Writing, Speaking, and Listening. There is a symbiotic relationship between each of the four components as well as a relationship to all other areas of the LMSD Curriculum. (See Figure 8.13.)

Literature is the focal point of the drawing as Literature is the focal point of the LMSD Curriculum. Literature is defined as any written work that

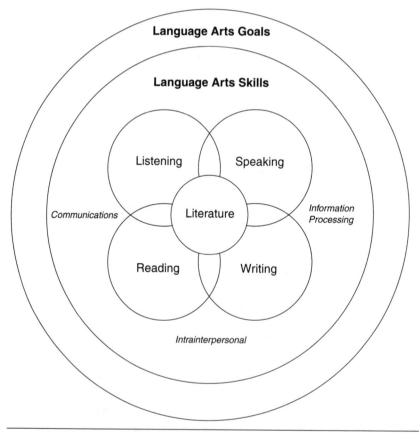

FIGURE 8.11   Language Arts Curriculum Framework

Language Arts

Skills:

Communications

Communicates with . . .

- clarity and precision

- commitment

- purpose and audience

- creativity

- fluency

- focus

- style

Information Processing

- Strategies and Processes

- Research

Intrainterpersonal

FIGURE 8.12   Key Skill Areas in Language Arts Curriculum Framework

Draft, Lower Merion School District's K–12 Language Arts Curriculum Framework.

instructs, informs, exposes, and enriches a student to a variety of perspectives. Literature is important as it allows one to examine, question, challenge, and affirm the values of the Human Condition as well as to recognize the perspectives of others.

> *"Reading and responding to literature expands the lives of students by broadening and enriching their experience, by enhancing their pleasure and appreciation of language and by acquainting them with the literary traditions of various periods and cultures."—PCRP II, p. 26*

FIGURE 8.13 Writing, Reading, and Speaking Components of Language Arts Curriculum Framework

Writing	by the end of 2nd Grade	by the end of 5th Grade	by the end of 8th Grade	by graduation
Uses effective intra/inter personal skills	• Is learning to develop effective intra/inter personal skills Intrapersonal traits: - writes about own experiences - shares writing with others - shows pride of ownership Interpersonal skills: - collaborates on projects - is developing cooperative skills - shares in tasks and assumes responsibility - is beginning to exhibit respect for others - shows commitment to group goal - takes pride in contributing to group projects	• Understands the need for effective intra/inter personal skills Intrapersonal traits: - reviews development as writer through use of portfolio - recognizes individual preferences in own work - reflects - recognizes individual preferences in one's own work - recognizes self improvement - sets short term goals - demonstrates pride of ownership Interpersonal skills: - collaborates - cooperates - shares tasks and assumes responsibilities - shows respect for others - has awareness of group goals - takes pride in contribution and product - responds to shared writing of peers - learns from others	• Is developing skill in using effective intra/inter personal skills Intrapersonal traits: - reviews development as a writer through use of a portfolio - is able to reflect on one's growth as a writer - recognizes individual strengths and weaknesses - recognizes growth and potential - sets goals - has pride in work Interpersonal skills: - collaborates - cooperates - shares tasks and assumes responsibilities - shows respect for others - has commitment to group goal - takes pride of contribution and product - responds to peer revision and editing - learns from others	• Uses effective intra/inter personal skills Intrapersonal traits: - is able to reflect on one's growth as a writer - recognizes individual strengths and weaknesses - recognizes growth and potential - sets goals - has pride in work Interpersonal skills: - collaborates - cooperates - shares tasks and assumes responsibilities - shows respect for others - has commitment to group goal - takes pride of contribution and product - response to peer revision and editing - learns from others

Writing

Information Processing	by the end of 2nd Grade	by the end of 5th Grade	by the end of 8th Grade	by graduation
	•Follows writing process with guidance Using varied techniques, process steps include: - pre-writing - drafting - revision (teacher) - editing (teacher) - rewriting (some) - publishing when appropriate	•Uses an identifiable writing process Using varied techniques, process steps include: - pre-writing - drafting - revision (includes self, peer, and/or teacher) - editing - rewriting - publishing when appropriate	•Continues to develop skill in using an identifiable writing process Using varied techniques, process steps include: - pre-writing - drafting - revision (includes self, peer, and/or teacher) - editing - rewriting - publishing when appropriate	•Uses identifiable writing processes Using varied techniques, process steps include: - pre-writing - drafting - revision (includes self, peer, and/or teacher) - editing - rewriting - publishing when appropriate
	•Uses varied forms - writes in a variety of forms with guidance	•Uses varied forms including: - narration - exposition (includes research) - persuasion - description	•Comprehends and utilizes the elements of varied forms including: - narration - exposition (includes formal research) - persuasion - description	•Demonstrates proficiency in varied forms including: - narration - exposition (includes formal research) - persuasion - description
	•Is beginning to use appropriate text and technology based tools - will have had experience with language-related activities involving technology for both language acquisition and production	•Is developing skill in using appropriate text and technology based tools to facilitate the following: - research (uses computerized library catalog, CD-ROM and is aware of on-line library resources) - composition (enters, stores, edits, and prints writing using age-appropriate software) - creativity and presentation (is aware of and uses technology to enhance presentations and projects)	•Is developing facility with and greater understanding of the appropriateness of text and technology based tools to facilitate the following: - research - composition - creativity and presentation	•Uses appropriate text and technology based tools skillfully to facilitate the following: - research - composition - creativity and presentation
	•Is beginning to select appropriate content/topic	•Is developing skill in selecting appropriate content/topic	•Selects appropriate content/topic	•Selects appropriate content/topic

Continued

FIGURE 8.13 Continued

Reading	by the end of 2nd Grade	by the end of 5th Grade	by the end of 8th Grade	by graduation
Fluency	• Is beginning to demonstrate understanding of basic language conventions (grammar, spelling, punctuation, phonics)	• Uses and demonstrates understanding of language systems and conventions (grammar, spelling, punctuation, phonics)	• Is developing fluency in the use of and demonstrates understanding of language systems and conventions (grammar, spelling, punctuation, phonics)	• Is fluent in the use of and demonstrates understanding of language systems and conventions (grammar, spelling, punctuation, phonics)
Manages Information	• Is beginning to understand and interpret information.	• Understands and interprets information.	• Understands and interprets increasingly complex information.	• Understands and interprets complex information.
	• Is beginning to think critically and evaluate information and opinions.	• Understands the need to think critically and evaluate information and opinions.	• Is developing skill in thinking critically and evaluating information and opinions.	• Thinks critically and evaluates information and opinions.
	• Is developing skill in applying reading skills across the curriculum.	• Is developing skill in applying reading skills across the curriculum.	• Applies reading skills across the curriculum.	• Reads skillfully in varied contexts.
	• Can see interdisciplinary connections of what is read with guidance.	• Sees interdisciplinary connections of what is read.	• Sees interdisciplinary connections of what is read.	• Sees interdisciplinary connections of what is read.
	• Works with teacher to monitor comprehension.	• Is beginning to use metacognitive skills to monitor understanding.	• Is developing skill in using metacognitive skills to monitor understanding.	• Uses metacognitive skills to monitor understanding.
	• Is learning to perform simple skills and functions such as reading instructions, correspondence, etc.	• Is developing skill in performing essential skills and functions such as reading manuals, instructions, correspondence, etc.	• Is able to perform essential skills and functions such as reading manuals, instructions, correspondence, etc.	• Performs essential skills and functions such as reading manuals, instructions, correspondence, etc.

Speaking

Information Processing	by the end of 2nd Grade	by the end of 5th Grade	by the end of 8th Grade	by graduation
	•**Has been exposed to and uses appropriate technology** - has been exposed to use of technology in language development	•**Understands the need for and uses appropriate technology** - for presentation - for interactive purposes with guidance - for documentation	•**Is developing skill in selecting and using appropriate technology** - for presentation - for interactive purposes - for documentation	•**Selects and skillfully uses appropriate technology** - for presentation - for interactive purposes - for documentation
	•**Is beginning to employ appropriate strategies** - preparation - rehearsal - performance/delivery - follow-up (gets feedback from others)	•**Is developing skill in employing appropriate strategies:** - preparation - rehearsal - use of prompts - use of appropriate gestures and expression - use of props and/or technology - performance/delivery - follow-up (feedback from others)	•**Is developing skill in employing appropriate strategies:** - preparation - rehearsal - use of prompts - use of appropriate gestures and expression - use of props and/or technology - performance/delivery - follow-up (feedback from others, self-reflection, conference, re-viewing)	•**Employs appropriate strategies for effective speaking:** - preparation - rehearsal - use of prompts - use of appropriate gestures and expression - use of props and/or technology - performance/delivery - follow-up (feedback from others, self-reflection, conference, re-viewing)
	•**Is beginning to select appropriate content/topic**	•**Selects appropriate content/topic**	•**Selects appropriate content/topic**	•**Selects appropriate content/topic**

Reference List

Boise Public Schools. *Language Arts English 10: Course Outline*. Boise, Idaho, 1990.

Department of Education, Office of Academic Programs. *English Language Arts Curriculum Guides Grades K–6*. (Bulletin 1588). Louisiana, 1986.

El Dorado County Office of Education. *Seeking Excellence in Education K–12: English/ Language Arts*.

Hill, C. *Incomplete Work of the Task Force of the Standards Project for Language Arts*. NCTE, Urbana, Illinois, 1994.

Hurst-Eules-Bedford Independent School District. *English Language Arts (Grades Pre-K–12) Curriculum Guide for Teachers*. 1993.

Lytle, S. L. and Botel, M. *The Pennsylvania Framework for Reading, Writing, and Talking Across the Curriculum*. Pennsylvania Department of Education, 1990.

New Hope-Solebury School District. *Writing Guide*. New Hope, Pennsylvania, 1991.

State Superintendent of Public Instruction. *English Language Arts (K–12) Curriculum Guides*. Olympia, Washington, 1993.

State Superintendent of Public Instruction. *Reading Curriculum Guidelines for Washington Schools*. Olympia, Washington, 1993.

Wilmette Public School District 39. *Literature Curriculum K–8*. Willmette, Illinois, 1989.

Wilmette Public School District 39. *Language Arts Curriculum*. Willmette, Illinois, 1988.

Wilmette Public School District 39. *Reading Curriculum K–8*. Willmette, Illinois, 1988.

also . . . Federal Way School District Outcomes. ????
    Scans Report
    Articles sent out to Framework groups

Reprinted by permission of Language Arts Coordinator, Dr. James A. Hay, and the Framework Committee.

9

Reflection, Research, and Teaching Writing

In an aptly titled article, "Surviving Your First October," Alan Teasley lists six basic needs of beginning teachers: a reasonable teaching assignment, an effective orientation, good mentors, help in developing professional expertise, time with other beginning teachers, and time to develop new skills. This list is followed by his strong recommendation for beginning teachers to use writing for the "habit of regular reflection." He states,

> *There's no way to escape experience; the trick is to learn from it. Growth comes when we think about the experience, examine our feelings, look for patterns, give the patterns meaning, adjust some aspect of our teaching, and note the effect of the adjustment on student learning. Reflection can come in conversation with a peer or a mentor, but as you learned in your language arts methods class, writing is also a powerful means of taking stock, generating insights, and making a record of your growth. So keep a regular journal of your teaching, or at least a log of activities used and annotations about what to do next time. . . . (94)*

Reflection and experimentation have become an integral part of many teacher preservice programs and peer tutoring programs. The purpose of this chapter is to encourage you to do both, to reflect and to experiment throughout your teaching career. If you are a student in a teacher education program, you have probably used teaching autobiographies, journals, or portfolios in one or more courses. If you are a "veteran" teacher but you never have used teaching journals or portfolios, I hope this chapter will motivate you to start.

In a course I teach for training peer tutors, Writing Instruction: Theory and Practice, in addition to reading about theories of peer tutoring, students write reports about their peer tutoring experiences and conduct research. They interview students and teachers to gain a better understanding of the tutoring context as they develop their skills as writing tutors. They are encouraged to modify their peer tutoring techniques as a result of reflecting and writing about their tutoring experiences and their research. At the end of the course, they say that they learn as much or more from these activities as they do from the assigned readings and class discussion.

Many a first-year instructor will probably feel, as I did when I started teaching, that being in charge of your own class is a giant leap from taking education courses. When you begin teaching, your students seem unique, even if the school in which you teach reminds you of the school you attended at that age. You will find yourself trying to implement your hard-won knowledge about teaching writing and literature to what appears to be a group of strangers. How rapidly we forget what it is like to be students!

Joe Ciepelinski, a former student in the English Education program at La Salle University, uses one of his journal entries, written while student teaching, to tackle this problem. As he tries to plan a unit on *Macbeth*, he writes,

> How do I want to go about teaching *Macbeth*? Sure, I can talk all day about wanting to do particular activities—I want them to write, I want to show part of the film. But . . . what happens from the twenty-seventh minute to the thirty-first minute of day three . . . I keep asking myself, "How do I plan this for the students?" How do I teach them? Would they like this activity? or that one? From all of this, I have discovered what my most pressing problem is at the moment: I don't know these kids. I know I have two classes juniors, track two. What the tracking system tells me about them I consider almost irrelevant. I never believed much in tracking, because it lumps kids into groups, rather than looking at them individually. I know that sophomores are reading American literature and juniors, British literature. I know that overall the behavior of classes is good, although there are certain children who will be problematic at times. I know that the seventh period juniors are "docile" because Laurie [the teacher] has told me they are. But what does it all mean? I really think that I'm going to have trouble writing lesson plans until I can picture the reaction of the girl in the fourth seat, third row to an activity.

Writing about how to teach *Macbeth* helps Joe to realize that his plans will be strongly influenced by the students in his class, and he needs to learn more about them before planning his lesson.

Whether you find yourself in familiar or foreign territory, writing about your fears and experiments will help you to think through teaching problems.

When I began teaching high school, I would never have thought of keeping a journal to begin to make sense of my first year of teaching in Chicago. I had grown up and gone to school in New York. My first teaching experience at the Laboratory School of the University of Chicago, where I was a long-term substitute, was little short of a disaster. What did I know about teaching in an experimental school where students were permitted to roam at will from class to class without the restriction of buzzers ending each period? My next job at a Hebrew day school with a population of students, many of whom were first-generation Americans who did not speak English at home, and who attended school from 8:00 in the morning until 5:30 in the afternoon, was equally perplexing. None of my courses in English Education had prepared me for either of these situations, nor had my experiences as a student in the New York City public schools. I had to learn to apply what I had learned about teaching English to unfamiliar contexts through trial and error, but mostly error!

Beginning teachers can use teaching journals to help them as they cross over to the other side of the desk. Experienced teachers, no longer concerned with surviving their first year of teaching, can also benefit from journal writing. Not only can they improve their own teaching by keeping a journal, but they can also benefit other teachers. The impetus for teacher reflection and research comes, in part, from new ways of thinking about the value of classroom-based research for other teachers, students, and the academic community.

This chapter discusses each of these ideas and suggests ways that you can use classroom-based observation and reflection to improve your teaching and to contribute to research in the field of teaching composition.

The Teacher as Researcher

The well-known adage "Those who can, do; those who can't, teach" implies that teachers know their subject well enough to teach their students. The teacher is seen as simply an instructor rather than "scholar." Such teachers dispense rather than create new knowledge: It is the relatively rare teacher who is a self-conscious researcher. The science teacher tends not to be a scientist, the English teacher tends not to be a writer, the math teacher tends not to be a mathematician.

In other words, English teachers teach students how to write and how to interpret literature but rarely write themselves or develop their own interpretations of literature, or new methods for teaching both subjects.

However, during the last fifteen years, the image of the teacher as lacking expertise has been seriously challenged. A teacher's main area of expertise is, in fact, teaching, and every lesson can be considered as research. This conception of teaching characterizes the teacher as scholar with a built-in laboratory—the classroom.

For teachers and others to view themselves in this way, teaching must be regarded "neither as a science—which means that we will probably never have scientific solutions to teaching problems, nor as an art which resigns [teaching] ability to intuition, magic and talent but as a reflective activity—one which encourages people to problematize teaching activities and raise to consciousness decisions, actions, and experiences" (Anson 191). Donald Schon, in *The Reflective Practitioner,* explains that many professions rely on the kind of thinking that enables the professional to frame new problems and explore possible solutions to them, without the hope of deriving definitive answers. His description of a "good practitioner" is suitable for defining the teacher as scholar. William Sullivan's summary is helpful for understanding Schon's main ideas. Sullivan says,

> . . . *A good practitioner is indeed a specialist who has learned the rules and basic techniques of a field. He or she develops a repertoire of expectations, images, and techniques as long as conditions of practice remain fairly routine; over time the practitioner's skills become habitual or tacit. [Shon calls this knowing-in-action.] However, the full dimensions of expertise are only revealed when a professional must respond to a new, less defined situation. Here the practitioner's habitualized techniques may be put into play, but now as facets of a holistic capacity to appreciate the novelty of the situation and to redefine it through experiment. For the expert practitioner, these experiments are not simply trial and error. Schon notes that in reflection in action, the practitioner does not keep the ends separate, but defines them interactively as he frames the problematic situation: "Neither does the practitioner separate thinking from doing, ratiocinating his way to a decision, he must later convert to action . . . implementation is built into his inquiry. The good practitioner, keeps redefining objectives, and, as he does, he tries to study a particular aspect of his job, and realizes that there is no way to review or revise objectives or practices by simply thinking about them. Reflective practice, conversation-with-a-situation, is a practical activity, once a learning and a doing."* (175)

Audre Allison, a participant in one of the National Writing Project Summer Institutes (see Chapter 10 for a description of the National Writing Project) is a good example of a reflective practitioner, a teacher who revises her plans interactively. Sondra Perl, the leader of the institute, describing Allison's teaching style, writes:

> *A teacher's ability to change plans from day to day—sometimes from moment to moment—is one of the main attractions of teaching for Audre. She wrote of the "sheer pleasure" of doing something which feels so right— being in a position to experiment when it begins to feel wrong—to change*

directions and to really find what one is looking for. . . . In class she fre-
quently makes new starts, changes direction, sometimes contradicts herself,
accepts her own contradictions. She relies on her reading of her students, her
strong sense of what matters to tell her where to go next. . . . In Audre's first
year as an eleventh grade teacher, the anchor of her curriculum was not so
much a sequence of lessons—those were constantly in flux, constantly
changing to meet the needs of the day—as her clear sense of what she wanted
to see happening in her classroom: students reading, writing, exploring
their own ideas, making their own discoveries, finding their own voices,
finding joy in writing and reading in themselves. When those things seemed
to be happening, Audre stayed with whatever she was doing; when they
didn't she tried something else. (Perl and Wilson 39)

As English teachers or students preparing for a career teaching English, you are now familiar with many of the teaching methods discussed in this text—how to teach students about the stages of the writing process, how to teach sentence-level skills, how to teach students to write about literature, how to evaluate and respond effectively to students' papers, and how to design assignments and curriculum units. As you gain experience teaching, like Audre Allison, these techniques will become automatic ("knowing-in-action"). However, for you to become a reflective practitioner, you need to employ these techniques in response to self-initiated questions and problems to what Schon calls "inquiry," because almost all situations will be novel situations. In other words, you need to do research, not the kind of research carried out by university faculty, but research nevertheless. For this reason *teacher-researcher* or *reflective practitioner* have to some extent become the common terms for defining the teacher's role.

Self-Initiated Questions

When we return to Joe Ciepelinski's student teaching journal, we notice that his underlying question is, "Which approach to Shakespeare will work best with these students?" He says,

We talked a lot about philosophies/views of language and education this week. I thought this was tremendously important. If I didn't have so many things on my mind right now, I'm sure I could come up with a very detailed belief system. But to be quite honest, I'm not sure how valid it would be. Part of me wants to say that these passing thoughts of approval or disapproval of different schools of thought need to be tested in practice. Perhaps, others observing me will be able to see that I'm a developmentalist, or an expressionist, or a social constructionist. Right now I feel as if I am all and none of these things. I fear that limiting myself to one mind frame will limit me to one methodology, and thus I'll never know if another path would have suited me better. So I'll try a lesson plan based on developmental theory. I'll try one which comes out of the "language as artifact" model. Whatever seems to work best, I'll stick with.

Joe's efforts will be somewhat futile until he can narrow the focus of his question. He wants his students to be interested in *Macbeth*. One possible way to motivate that interest might be to demonstrate the connections between Macbeth and today's political world. So, Joe's question might be, "How can I help my students to see the relationship of Macbeth to our own times? How is Macbeth, the man, similar to modern despots who try to overthrow governments, who attempt to gain power through force?"

In the literature courses I teach, I often assign reaction papers, ungraded writing that students do in response to each reading. This assignment is intended to increase students' abilities to interpret literature and to encourage them to be less dependent on me for the right answer. I posed the following research question to myself about this teaching method: "How can I use writing in the course, The Contemporary Novel, to encourage students to respond more independently to reading assignments, to take a more active role in small group discussion and in setting the agenda for class discussion?" Throughout the semester, students were writing reaction papers after each assigned novel. They were given several topics to choose from, such as: "What did you find puzzling in the novel?" and "Discuss the interplay of character, plot, imagery, or point of view with theme," and so on. They would discuss their reaction papers in small reading groups, consisting of four or five students, before I led the class discussion, which would then extend over a period of several days. Although I tried to structure class discussion around issues they had raised in their commentaries and small group discussions, I felt that I was not succeeding.

When we read *Howards End* by E. M. Forster, I changed the writing assignment:

> Each group will write both a general statement about its reaction to the text, which should include at least five questions about the text and a text commentary for a specific section of the book. Your reading group will become group leaders for that part of the text you have been assigned to write about.

As these comments suggest, student reactions to the assignment were mixed:

Student A: The only instance at which I did not think the class discussion worked smoothly was with *Howards End*. With individuals focusing on separate issues and parts of the novel, the entire theme did not seem to come together as a whole. The novel was not an extremely hard one, but simply lengthy. It did, however, have a large number of themes and presented ideas throughout its course. The conflicts of sex and class were dealt with. But with the organization of discussion, and the vast number of interpretations of the text, I never seemed to be able to truly grasp and understand a single idea. It may also be the absence of any guidelines from which to depart. Each person would have his own opinion of what was most important in his assigned segment of the novel, and simply discuss that aspect.

Student B: I thought the assignment for *Howards End* was good. Many people are afraid to speak in a public setting. It is necessary to learn how to speak in public. Also, the student exchange of ideas helps to get out new ideas and helps to develop new thoughts that you may not have thought of when you read the book. It was a good assignment.

Student C: The assignment for *Howards End* enabled me to see new perspectives in the novel from people in different groups, but it did not help me to gain a deeper insight into the novel. Instead of working on a concentrated subject within my group and being able to talk through it to its conclusion, the assignment only gave me a shallow look into the novel. It lacked the depth that I desire to look into the novel.

Student D: I really enjoy splitting into groups to discuss the novels. I think it's the best way to learn about them, and it gives people a chance to be creative without being intimidated by a large class. However, during the *Howards End* discussions, things were a little rocky. I think that adding new people to the groups upset the comfort level we had established with one another. Another difficulty was it seemed we wound up discussing the differences between the Schlegels and Wilcoxes an awful lot. When someone from another group came in with their passage, I found that our group had already discussed the passage previously. We managed to move forward, but there was some awkwardness.

Although the assignment encouraged more independent thinking, students were troubled by what they perceived as a lack of organization in the discussion. I learned that if I wanted to promote the idea that it was as important for them to exercise their own interpretive abilities as it was for us to discuss all aspects of the novel, then I had to try another approach. How to create more independence and greater involvement in my literature classes through writing and small group discussion continues to be a question for me.

My experiment in The Contemporary Novel course evolved into a teacher research project. Susan Lytle and Marilyn Cochran-Smith in *Inside/Outside: Teacher Research and Knowledge* describe teacher research as systematic, intentional inquiry by teachers about their own school and classroom work. By "systematic," they mean gathering and recording information, documenting experiences inside and outside of classrooms, and making it into some kind of written record. "Systematic" also refers to "ordered ways of recollecting, rethinking, and analyzing classroom events for which there may be only partial or unwritten records" (24). By "intentional," they mean that it is a planned rather than a spontaneous activity, although they do not mean that important insights about teaching are generated only in an organized setting. But research is not simply casual erratic observation, without any particular schedule, which may occasionally produce some new discoveries. Their emphasis on intention is related to the idea that "to learn deliberately, is to research" (Boomer 5) and to the belief that "every lesson should be for the teacher an inquiry, some further discovery, a quiet form of research" (Britton 915). Here inquiry refers to the motivation behind teacher research: the teacher's desire to remain open to new observations and understandings and to constantly interpret the classroom experience.

Glenda Bissex helps us to understand the role of the teacher-researcher by identifying some of the misconceptions about the requirements of research (Bissex and Bullock 4).*

The Teacher-Researcher

- A teacher-researcher is an observer. "Research means looking—and looking again," says Ann Berthoff. "This new kind of Research would not mean going after new 'data,' but rather REconsidering what is at hand . . . We do not need new information; we need to think about the information we have."
- A teacher-researcher is a questioner: Why is a certain student unwilling to read? How are poor writers related to good ones? Do they have different concepts of what writing and reading are all about?
- A teacher-researcher is a learner. In my ideal school, principals ask teachers "What did you learn today?" not "What did you teach?" Teacher-researchers will have much to say to this question. (School principals should be teacher-researchers too!)
- A teacher-researcher doesn't have to study hundreds of students, establish control groups, and perform complex statistical analyses. A teacher-researcher may not start out with a hypothesis to test, but a "wondering" to pursue. For example, "I wonder how much my students think about their writing outside of class. Vicky mentioned today that she mentally

*Adapted by permission from Glenda A. Bissex and Richard H. Bullock, "What Is a Teacher-Researcher?" *Seeing for Ourselves: Case Study Research by Teachers of Writing* (Heinemann, a division of Reed Elsevier, Inc., Portsmouth, NH, 1987).

revises compositions on the bus coming to school. What about the others who are not writing on their own topics?"

- A teacher-researcher does not have to be antiseptically detached. He knows that knowledge comes through closeness as well as through distance, through intuition as well as through logic.
- A teacher-researcher writes about what she's discovered; she need not make herself sound like a psychology textbook. Her audience is herself, other teachers, her students, their parents, her principal, maybe even the school board—none of whom is likely to be upset by plain English and a personal style. [I would add that her audience can also be the teaching community at large, if she chooses to write for one of the journals in the field that traditionally feature teacher research, such as the *English Journal* or *In the Middle.*]
- A teacher-researcher is not a split personality with a poem in one hand and a microscope in the other.

Bissex and Bullock enumerate many of the characteristics associated with *action research*, a term used in the literature on research in education to describe research often accomplished while the teacher is in the act of teaching and that has the greatest consequences for those involved—the teachers and students in their classrooms. We will look at those consequences in the next two sections of this chapter and examine some of the methods used in teacher research.

The Teacher as Writer

Most teachers write less often than their students. As Durst points out, "for most elementary, secondary, and community college teachers . . . writing is not a necessary part of the job. On the contrary, the responsibilities of their jobs generally work against finding the time and energy for writing. And of course, there are few job related rewards for being a teacher who writes" (262). Redefining the role of teacher as researcher requires us to also think of the teacher as writer. The two go hand-in-hand. Just as our students take notes to remember what happens in class, we need to take notes to keep track of our observations and reflect about them. Katherine Yancey, in "Portfolios as Genre, Rhetoric as Reflection: Situating Selves, Literacies, and Knowledge," says writing helps to carry out the reflection in action: "If I write something, it becomes real. I cannot take it back; I cannot forget it or deny it or pretend that it doesn't exist. I have to acknowledge it, engage it, account for it, challenge it: explore what it means to me, to others. That's reflection. And once a teacher realizes that writing enhances reflection, she will want to write more" (58).

Lynn Strieb, a former second grade teacher in the Philadelphia School District, comments on how writing stimulates more writing, and yet more observation:

> *The more I wrote, the more I observed in my classroom, and the more I wanted to write. As I reread my journal, I got more ideas for teaching. I expanded the journal to include other aspects of teaching-anecdotes, observations of children and their involvement in activities, interactions with parents, both in and out of my school, my plans, descriptions of the pressures on public school teachers. I also wrote about my continuing education through my own reflections and questions that emerged, through books, associations with colleagues in the Philadelphia Learning Cooperative, and the Prospect Summer Institutes. (3)*

Teaching Portfolios and Journals

Portfolios and journals are the most common forms of writing teachers use when they first begin to record classroom observations and their impressions about them. They are often used for the informal notes teachers frequently record before or after a lesson. The "teaching portfolio" is a more formal collection of materials. The teaching portfolio is often defined as "a collection of materials assembled by a faculty member that document and reflect teaching performance" (Anson 185). Anson says that some portfolio projects reflect the

> *communicative goals of portfolios as way of sharing one's teaching, others stress its role in assessment, still others its potential to encourage development. The portfolio can contain any combination of the following documents, depending on its purpose: syllabi, assignments of all kinds, study guides, student papers, perhaps with teacher comments, classroom materials, such as overheads or hand-outs, innovative classroom materials such as computer programs, logs from class visits [by someone other than the teacher], student evaluations, reflections on peer observations or videotapes, reflections on course evaluations, self-evaluations of all kinds, narrative accounts of problem solving responses to case studies and scenarios about teaching, journals documenting thoughtfulness about instructional issues, goal statements and philosophies and letters of assessment from others. (186)*

Portfolios for self-development and discussion with colleagues should include all of the primary documents, such as assignments and syllabi (most teachers keep these documents in some kind of folder already) and the notes and reflections from a teaching journal that you keep throughout the semester or year. If you are using the portfolio for a joint faculty project, then the group can decide what kinds of materials the portfolio will include. Your questions will guide the contents of the portfolio. For example, Anson lists several writing-related portfolio projects:

> *If participants in a writing across the curriculum program want to improve the way they read students' work, then the portfolio might contain examples of students' final and/or drafts of papers representing a range of quality, along with teacher's commentary and responses. Specific questions can be designed as prompts: Characterize their response style by examining a class-ful of your papers, and include a sample; what are your goals for student writing? How do your comments achieve these goals?*
>
> *If a department wants to work on improving writing assignments, the portfolio might include three sample assignments, with accompanying descriptions of their place in the scheme of the course and a rationale for their design. (192)*

The origins of my teaching portfolios are my teaching journals, which include notes and observations about my students' papers and class activities. For example, in The Contemporary Novel class, students wrote summary statements at the end of the semester commenting on the course's influence on their ability to understand novels and especially how their knowledge of techniques such as plot structure, style, point of view, and symbolism enhanced their understanding of the books we read. (See Appendix 9a for a sample Student Summary Statement.) My notes range from general observations to comments on specific students:

- Some students focus on the ability to notice point of view.
- Some focus on reading group discussion as important in challenging their first reading of the text.
- Some focus on the books themselves, raising evaluative questions (e.g., one student suggested that Ishiguro answers questions that Forster leaves unanswered).
- Bill contrasted this course with the history of the novels course.
- Mary, instead of answering the question, explained what she had learned about the novels.
- Dan said he learned to become speed reader.

I drew these conclusions: Students in The Contemporary Novel course enter the course at very different stages of development when it comes to reading and writing about literature and with very different goals for what they would like to get from the course. Although the questions they were to address in the Summary Statement reflected my goals for the course, students focused on aspects of the course that were most important to them, which perhaps made the deepest impression, or observations they were most proud of, such as the comment by Dan who said that he never thought he could read eight novels in one semester. Perhaps I can individualize instruction somewhat more than I do now by keeping these comments in mind.

Journal entries can be much less formal than mine, which came at the end of the semester. For example, Audre Allison, the eleventh grade teacher you met earlier in the chapter, writes in her journal,

- Wonderful day—all write.
- Lovely day listening to kids talking seriously about writing.
- Low point I'm working so hard to get seriousness . . . If only Dennis would care about his writing . . .
- Ed is not writing—keeps looking at what Tom has written . . . Some put pens down, fold arms, close up shop . . . Too many loll away a beautiful afternoon and I decide I'm not a teacher.
- If I could remember that it is not a continuous process, but occurs in spurts, it might be helpful . . .
- Some days bring malaise—it spreads like canned cake frosting—sickly over everything—The kids sink down into their chairs—ooze over their sides, smear across the table—and we get nothing done. Other days are crisp as fresh zucchini.

Sondra Perl, the editor of *Through Teacher's Eyes: Portraits of Teachers at Work*, writes,

> *Audre often stopped to observe her students and to change direction in response to what she observed. Although she had a rough idea in September of what she wanted during the year, her day-to-day plans changed frequently. ("I don't know what I'll be doing in January, . . . or sometimes tomorrow.") She often decided what to do next by writing in her journal about what was happening in her classroom. "Why does this group work better than that one?" she would ask herself. "Have we spent too much time on this piece of writing? Too little? Would a list of questions help Ed, who doesn't seem to know what to say about another student's writing?"(38)*

Allison's journal remains informal and chatty, as she responds to her classroom experiences. Her questions, however, continue to remain focused, concerned with specific strategies or specific students.

Beginning teachers tend to write about general issues, such as approaches to teaching, the content of courses, and fears about teaching, or sometimes about the value of journal keeping itself, such as this entry from La Salle student Joe Ciepelinski's journal:

> I've jotted down some ideas for activities which could be used for *Macbeth*, most of which come out of my education classes. I am trying to make use of my pedagogy; learning styles, developmental stages, Zones of Primal Development, and so on. It is always not easy, but it is helpful in creating effective lessons . . . It's amazing how much pedagogy you can keep inside your head while planning abstractly the events of the week. It's even more amazing that all of that can go out the window the second you begin to write things down. Things like time, the curriculum, and practicality take precedence.

Joe has recognized that one of the benefits of keeping a journal is that it reminds him of real-world constraints, such as the length of classes, the course requirements, and so on. The following guidelines enumerate the various purposes the teaching journal can serve:

1. Jot down reflections at least every few days about lessons that went particularly well and lessons that were disappointing, and write about how you might do things differently the next time around.
2. Keep a record of your observations, while grading a set of student papers. Note the characteristics of these papers.
3. Focus on one student. Use that student as a microcosm of a typical kind of student population you have in your class. Keep a record of that student's successes and problems.
4. Focus your journal on one kind of writing, writing about literature. Note how you prepare students for the assignments as well as their ability to write their papers.

The Mechanics of Journal Keeping

Given the best of intentions, the mechanics of journal keeping can sabotage your resolve. I prefer to keep mine on the computer. Some people prefer spiral notebooks, which are obviously more portable. I have become addicted to the word processor and find that I can no longer write by hand as quickly as I can type. However, whether you prefer to type or write, you can develop forms to organize your journal writing. For example, you can keep a list of questions to guide your writing, which can be used for examining issues related to writing courses. Your questions need not be aimed at a comprehensive review of your course. You may wish to focus on some issues rather than others during a particular semester or year. The following list of questions could be of use in evaluating writing assignments, the use of models, one-on-one conferences, and so on.

My Writing Program: Some Questions

1. Writing assignments:

   How do students react to my writing assignments? Do they seem motivated by them to write interesting papers?

   Are my assignments clear? Are most students' interpretations of my assignments similar to my own?

   Did my assignments help to accomplish the objectives for my course?

   Do students write better when they are writing for a grade?

2. Classroom instruction:

   Is peer review working in my class? Are students using their peer groups to give meaningful feedback to one another?

   Is the use of models having any effect? Do students seem more interested in models written by me, or are they more interested in papers written by students of previous semesters?

   Are nonexamples helpful? Do students seem to benefit from examining weak papers?

3. Conferences:

   Are students revising more frequently since I began holding one-on-one conferences in the classroom while the other students are writing?

   Are students comfortable conferencing while other students are writing?

Instructors can also use a form such as the one shown in Figure 9.1 for recording their observations about their writing classes.

Of course, if you find that your journal comments are more meaningful when you freewrite without structure, stick to your own technique. There is no right way to write journals. Leif Gustavson, who teaches eighth grade at Friends' Central School in Wynnewood, Pennsylvania, uses free association to write very rich, valuable journal entries. The entries at the end of the chapter illustrate how Leif uses his logs (sometimes he calls them "quickies" and "reflections") to plan the year, to clarify his ideas about the writing process, and to achieve a studio atmosphere in his classroom.

```
┌─────────────────────────────────────────────────────────────┐
│                                                               │
│      Writing Program Journal          Entry #_____          │
│                                                               │
│         Class _____     Date _____         │
│                                                               │
│   Writing Assignments                                         │
│   Notes:                                                      │
│                                                               │
│                                                               │
│   Commentary:                                                 │
│                                                               │
│                                                               │
│   Classroom Instruction                                       │
│   Notes:                                                      │
│                                                               │
│                                                               │
│   Commentary:                                                 │
│                                                               │
│                                                               │
│   Conferences:                                                │
│   Notes:                                                      │
│                                                               │
│                                                               │
│   Commentary:                                                 │
│                                                               │
└─────────────────────────────────────────────────────────────┘
```

FIGURE 9.1   Writing Program Journal

Writing by Teachers for Teachers

You may eventually write about your teaching for your colleagues and for publication. About ten years ago I heard a graduate student summarize her findings on teacher conversation in school settings such as the cafeteria and teacher's lounge. She found that teacher conversation is rarely about teaching. But this is changing. Not only are teachers conversing about teaching during the classroom day, but informal research groups in individual schools as well as on the regional level are becoming more common. (One such group has been formed at Elk Grove High School, where Susan Abbott teaches.) Two citywide groups, the Philadelphia Teachers Learning Cooperative and the Boston Women's Teacher's Group, which have been meeting for more than ten years, come together to share journals and portfolios with one another to reflect about their teaching.

Teachers use their journals and teaching portfolios as starting points when they start writing for publication. Journals such as the *English Journal, In the Middle,* and *Language Arts,* all published by the National Council of Teachers of English, routinely publish the work of elementary and secondary school teachers. A student in one of the graduate courses I taught several years ago was most surprised when I suggested that she revise a paper she wrote in my class for the *English Journal.* It was accepted and later translated into Chinese for a teaching journal in China!

Benefits: The Teacher-Researcher and the Teacher-Writer

The benefits of becoming a teacher-researcher can be dramatic. Susan Abbott writes that teacher research helped to restore her vitality in the classroom. She says,

> *I became a teacher researcher in 1987 when I was teaching my remedial (no heterogeneous grouping then!) sophomores basic English. It was really basic. I read aloud to them, tried to involve them in writing, and keep myself physically safe. My students were angry kids, kids with learning disabilities, kids on probation, and kids who just did not fit in anywhere else. It was my second year of teaching, and I was drowning in despair. . . . I felt like such a failure as a teacher that year; my kids scared me professionally, and I believed that they would never learn to read or write well enough to pass our proficiency test, and then I would be fired. I also feared for my sanity. My students' taunts and anger frightened me more than I would like to admit. (59)*

At this time Abbott took a workshop on classroom-based research at which the leader said, "nothing occurring in the classroom is a failure, only an interesting piece of data." Abbott says,

> *These were rules I could live with, so I began. The workshop participants were asked to take a second look at themselves and their students by asking the question "What would happen if . . ." I began to question my practice by asking "What would happen if I changed how I presented the material? If for example, I used a less auditory style and more kinesthetic, would my stu-*

dents do better? That year I recorded almost all my daily frustrations and
fears in my research log. Occasionally I would report on a lesson that seemed
to break through and bring some success. (59–60)

She explains that other teachers in her research group would "help me
pull out of my log successes, even when I could not see them" (59).

Having been won over by classroom-based research, Abbott conducts a
different project every year. One of her research projects was aimed at helping students improve their prewriting skills by having them discuss and tape
record their ideas during the prewriting stage.

Ernie Page, director of the Kern/Eastern Sierra Project, enumerates the
ways teachers change as a result of conducting teacher research:

1. They become reflective thinking teachers. They evolve into instructional
   leaders who are able to measure the results of their teaching in student
   learning.
2. Their teaching changes because they think about and learn through what
   they are doing in the classroom.
3. Teacher-researchers become more organized and structured as teachers
   because there is a purpose for teaching that transcends student learning.
   They are learning too.
4. Assessment of learners by teachers becomes more human and real. Students are not just numbers, but become a part of a shared, open process of
   evaluation, especially when student portfolios are used in the classroom.
5. There is a rekindling and rejuvenation of positive thoughts and feelings
   about teaching. The concept of "I can't wait to go back to the classroom"
   resurfaces.
6. Teacher-researchers feel that they belong to a community of writers
   because they experience what they ask of their students.
7. Finally, they understand that what is known about teaching comes not only
   from traditional research but from those who practice teacher research.

Writing about your research has many benefits. Whether you are writing
for yourself, for your research group, or for publication, you will experience the
same problems students confront when they write. Especially when writing for
publication, you will work through all of the stages of the writing process from
prewriting to drafting and revision—excellent preparation for teaching students the techniques for managing these processes. In "Strategies for Getting It
Down," Leif Gustavson demonstrates how he translates his experience as a
writer into advice to students (see Figure 9.2). The teacher who sees herself as a
writer will be a better writing teacher. The teacher-writer can also share her
writing with her students as a motivational tool, or as an example of the kind
of writing and thinking she expects, as we discussed in Chapter 3.

FIGURE 9.2   "Strategies for Getting It Down"

Mr. G.
10/5/95

I must confess that, as a writer, I seldom use any of those artsy, brainstormy strategies (you know: webs, outlines, bubbles, graphs and charts, etc.). More often than not, I begin thinking about a subject or a piece by writing at it. What I mean by that is that I just have to sit down and write. Give myself some time to actually find an idea by writing through all of the junk that comes beforehand. Some may consider this approach, slogging through the trash, as a waste of energy, but I think it is the only way to discover what it is you really want to write about. Here are a few alternative ways of getting going as a writer. Sometimes they work for me. Who knows, maybe they will work for you. Experiment with them. Tell me how they work in your Reflections and Inquiries.

- *Speculative pieces*—Asking yourself questions . . . considering what the piece would be about . . . What would be difficult to write about? Usually that is where you should be as a writer—right where the idea nags and irritates you. Let your questions find the piece.
- *Blast pieces*—Sheer Energy . . . Push through ideas. Go as far as you can go. Jolt Cola kind of stuff. Set time limits and goals. O.k, I am going to write for a half hour about the time I got stuck on the toilet. Find the FLOW . . . Let the piece energize you to write more and pursue the idea.
- *Spider pieces*—3-4-5-6 short pieces around the same general experiences. different angles. Looking for the hook. Looking for the anchor piece. Let the writings teach you things about yourself and your style of writing.
- *Opposition pieces*—Best of times/worst of times. Contrasts: then and now, Good and Bad. I used to think, but now I feel. Let the ideas rub together and irritate each other.
- *Talking pieces*—Voicing your ideas, notes to myself. Chat, chat, chat. Talk yourself into new understandings about your past.
- *Character throwing pieces*—Start with a person, gossip, describe, criticize, admire, ramble, talk to him/her. Let the character tell you what the piece is about.

Reprinted by permission of Leif Gustavson.

The Value of Teacher Research for Students

Students feel much more like stakeholders in research-based classrooms, and take more responsibility for the success of the class than they do in classes where research projects have no place in the course. At the beginning of each semester, I tell my students, "We are all in this together. If this class is boring, you are probably as much at fault as I am." I also let them know when I am trying something new, as the example from The Contemporary Novel class illustrates. In another course used for training peer tutors, I included considerably more collaborative work outside of class than I had in the past and informed the students that they would be asked to assess the success of these projects. Lori, who seemed most skeptical about the value of collaborative projects ("the low success rates of collaborative projects drives me insane") wrote,

> My group—Jenn, Nick, Tom, Jenn, and I collaborated on the third unit, "How Does Peer Tutoring Work?" Immediately we saw the need to divide the project into sections due to the variety of issues the unit addresses. This approach worked out well, especially in Nick and Tom's case. Their performance in role playing was really the only way to illustrate difficult tutoring situations. Jenn P, Jenn H, and I decided to split up the three remaining essays and prepare separate presentations. I worked with the Brooks essay on minimalist tutoring. Jenn P's presentation on the stages of the tutoring process and the various paradigms served as the structure for my essay and Jenn H's on collaboration and ethics. We presented on the same day, and all three essays synthesized nicely. In the sense that everything came together with our presentations, I think this group effort worked well. We each essentially worked alone and then combined our efforts; I see no way around this sort of division. The same problem applied to our inability to really work with Nick and Tom. While we all met once or twice to decide what we would do, it ended up being two smaller groups and then individuals working on their own. However, I think the project was a success in that we knew what everyone else in the group was working on and how it related to our topic. I think that's the only way collaborative projects can really work—by serving as a synthesis of a number of individual efforts.

Many of the students in this class learned how to participate more effectively in collaborative projects because they were asked to help me evaluate them. Classrooms in which students collaborate with teachers to question teaching methods illustrate the "student as active thinker model." In these classes teachers freely admit that they do not know everything, whether it be how to interpret literature or how to teach writing. Pamela Carroll says, "In a classroom in which the teacher does not pretend to know all the answers, students are free to ask questions, to voice confusions, to suggest interpretations, to construct meanings, students are more engaged in learning" (25). Although Carroll is speaking about interpreting literature, students will respond to their teaching environments with honesty and intensity if teachers admit they do not know all the answers.

Dixie Goswami believes that student involvement in teacher research also "helps learners achieve mature language skills" (quoted in Hoff 53). Because they are communicating with each other as well as the teacher about issues important to the success of the class, they are highly motivated to speak and write with clarity. Speaking and writing are not merely exercises in these exchanges between teachers and students.

Some action research advocates such as Garth Boomer say that you cannot become a teacher-researcher without involving students, who are an integral part of the "teacher as researcher" model of schooling. He argues that students and teachers should embark on a research approach in every course of study, proposing that "any learning sequence should begin with negotiation of intentions to the point that both teacher and student intend in the same direction and mutually own the curriculum as jointly planned. This model presupposes that the curriculum itself is a piece of action research into learning which can be evaluated by teacher and student... Intentions become shared, thinking power is increased and through reflection on learning teachers and students learn more about how to learn" (12).

The Value of Teacher Research to the Academic Community

As a teacher-researcher, you will not only contribute to your own and your students' development, but you will also be contributing to knowledge in the field. This may sound like a far-fetched idea, especially to new teachers, students preparing to be teachers, or teachers who never thought of themselves as teacher-researchers. However,

> [academic] research has moved from a craving for abstraction to an interest in understanding what happens in the minds of individual teachers who are interested in personal experiences, and act on their own experiences. Your professors are becoming more and more interested in what you have to say. You are on the front lines, and college professors are not. You are a part of the educational community they wish to study, and they are not. They need you. (Anson 192)

Marilyn Cochran-Smith and Susan Lytle offer an excellent summary of the value of teacher research to the academic community:

> Just as teachers read and use the research of university-based researchers, many academics committed to teacher education and/or the study of teaching and learning undoubtedly will find the research of teachers a rich and unique source of knowledge. We can imagine at least four important ways in which the academic community can benefit from teacher research. Teacher's journals, for example, provide rich data about classroom life that can be used by academics to construct and reconstruct theories of teaching and learning. In this capacity, teachers serve primarily as collectors of data, but their data are unlike other classroom descriptions that have been selected, filtered, and

composed in the language of researchers. If teachers observe that pre-writing instruction with seventh graders doesn't seem to work unless they talk frequently during the pre-writing stage, then a university researcher may choose to formulate a hypothesis to be tested based on this information.

Second, because teacher research emanates from the teacher's own questions and frameworks, it reveals the seminal issues about learning and the cultures of teaching. Classroom teachers may be better judges of what constitutes an important question for their class. For example, if motivation to write is seen as the key problem in teaching writing by classroom teachers, then it should be studied by college researchers.

Third, as Shulman (1986a) argues, both "scientific knowledge of rules and principles" and richly described and critically analyzed cases need to constitute the knowledge base of teaching. Teacher research provides these rich classroom cases. Because cases are often more powerful and memorable influences on decision making than are conventional research findings in the form of rules and generalizations. (Nisbett, Ross, 1980; Shulman, 1986a), teacher education can use teachers' studies to study how practitioners learn from the documented experiences of each other. A "case" is a richly textured description of a teaching event, with all of its contextual variables included. Janet Emig used the case study approach when she attempted to discover how high school students write, The Composing Process of Twelfth Graders, NCTE. In addition to summing up her research through generalizations about the composing processes she included the "cases" of several students who participated in the project. Including a report about the "trials and tribulations" of these students strengthened her study considerably.

Finally, through their research, teachers can contribute to the critique and revision of existing theory by describing discrepant and paradigmatic cases, as well as providing the data that ground or move toward alternative theories . . . What teachers bring will alter not just add to what is known about teaching. As the body of teacher research accumulates, it will undoubtedly prompt reexamination of many current assumptions about children, learning, and classroom practices. (20)

Shirley Brice-Heath's research with classroom teachers is a good example of teacher research (discussed in Chapter 8) that had considerable impact on the field. Her work forced theorists to place greater emphasis on the role played by the social context in the teaching of writing. The teachers who worked with Brice-Heath demonstrated that children from poor rural areas become very interested in writing through literacy research projects in their own community. Traditional forms of writing instruction were far less effective with such students.

It seems somewhat cliché to say that a good teacher never stops learning, but it is true! In the past, that often meant that a good English teacher kept up with new research performed by university professors trained in the methods of research in their fields. English teachers felt that they had to keep up with new trends in literary criticism, with modern fiction, poetry and drama, and with scholarship about the techniques of teaching literature and writing. But today, when we say that a teacher is always learning, we mean much more than that. We mean that as teachers we are constantly learning how to teach better or revise our teaching practices to meet the needs of different sets of student populations in schools, perhaps unlike those we attended, by systematically recording and interpreting our observations in our own classes, in other words, through our own research in our own teaching situation.

Conclusion

An excerpt from a report by a student in our peer tutoring training program seems to be a fitting close to this chapter. The new peer tutors were asked to review their first round of peer tutoring conferences and think about ways to improve them in view of the future. Lori not only tests her conference method against the class readings, but also takes into account the needs of the students. She questions the validity of her fears, the effectiveness of her conference techniques, and then comments about her successes as well as her disappointments. Would that all of us would continue to question our teaching practices with the same intense concern and thoughtfulness as students like Lori!

> The conferences were, to my surprise, sort of fun. I got to meet the students, get an idea about who they were, and what kind of attitudes they were harboring about school and this class. Generally, I just got to know them a little more and learned a lot. Granted I was a nervous wreck. First, I was convinced that they would forget or show up at the wrong time because of some failed communication. Then, I thought they just wouldn't like me or take the situation seriously. I was expecting disastrous two-minute conferences in which they would grab their papers and go.
>
> Thankfully just the opposite happened. Each student arrived on time . . . Right away I tried to employ one of the techniques we talked about in class. I asked the first student how the class was going, how he was in general; this really eased the tension, I think. I tried to use similar devices throughout the conference. I would ask what they thought of an assignment and if they understood it. One question I eventually asked, but now regret not asking first, was if they had any questions about the paper or the assignment. This might have helped gear the conference in a direction that would most benefit the student.

Each student was very responsive and welcoming of my comments; none seemed annoyed or resentful about being there. They asked many questions and wanted to know what I "thought" of the paper. This is a strange question now that I think about it. It seems they were fishing for a more subjective observation of their work, as if they wanted me to give a grade for the paper. I'm not sure if that's the way they are thinking, but it seems like many students want that from a writing fellow . . . They asked some questions really I couldn't answer, about the relevance of their topic to mineralogy. Here I could only encourage them to see Dr. Smith to double check their ideas and make sure they were going in the right direction.

Student C admitted to me that he was having a very hard time putting the words of his sources into words. I tried to remember how I learned to paraphrase, and winged an explanation. . . .

In my conferences, I found that I agree with David Taylor's approach, that the tutor/student relationship is a "helping relationship" (26) in which effective listening and questioning go hand in hand. I tried to ask leading questions, but sometimes failed. I tried to listen to their fears about writing their papers, which a couple of them openly talked about. This helped me to hone in on problems specific to that student, rather than just assuming from their papers what they have trouble with. While I see why Joann Johnson believes that questions can inhibit the students' thinking, I think it is just a matter of the type of question you ask and how you ask it.

Goals for the Next Round:

Next time around, my primary goal is to be more organized. I would like to speak more with Dr. Smith about the nature of the assignment, problems I came across and the progress he thinks he made with students . . . I want to be more prepared the day I pick up papers. . . . I would have liked more time between conference sessions: two were within an hour, and it was a little too much. I could have used more time to mentally prepare for the second conference. . . . The worst thing I did was something we learned from the first week of class not to do. I sat across from them in the conference. I could kick myself now. The only excuse I have is that I conferenced so long after we discussed the basics of the session. Since them I have re-read my notes, and made a reminder sheet for myself for the next round of papers.*

Much to her disappointment, Lori never got to conduct that second round of conferences. But, as her journal entries indicate, by observing, reflecting, and writing, Lori learned a great deal about peer tutoring that will be most helpful to her in future tutoring assignments.

*Reprinted by permission of Lori Hill.

Questions for Discussion and Writing

1. If you are presently teaching, try keeping a daily teaching journal for one week. Use a freewriting approach. Write about whatever topic seems to be of interest to you (one to two pages). At the end of the week, write a one page summary describing issues, problems, and successes you noted in your journal.

2. List five questions you would like to ask about your classroom writing program. If you are not teaching, list five questions about the teaching of writing and interview five teachers in the English department.

3. After reading Leif Gustavson's journal entries (see Appendix 9b), summarize his major concerns and his approach to teaching writing.

4. Interview your classmates and/or your colleagues about the importance of knowing Grammar III in order to write well. Write a brief report on your findings (two to three pages).

5. Compare your methods of teaching to the methods of your high school instructors. Have you modeled your approach to teaching writing on their practices? Please explain.

References

Abbott, Susan. "What Would Happen if . . . ? A Teacher's Journey with Teacher Research." *English Journal* 83 Oct. 1994: 59–62.

Anson, Chris. "The Teaching Portfolio: Writing on the Way to Reflective Researchers." *New Directions in Portfolio Assessment*. Eds. Laurel Black, Donald Daiker, Jeffrey Sommers, and Gail Stygall. Portsmouth, NH: Heinemann-Boynton/Cook, 1994, 185–200.

Bissex, Glenda, and Richard Bullock. "What Is a Teacher Researcher?" *Seeing for Ourselves: Case Study Research by Teachers of Writing*. Portsmouth, NH: Heinemann-Boynton/Cook, 1987.

Boomer, Garth. "Addressing the Problem of Elsewhereness: A Case for Action Research in Schools." *Reclaiming the Classroom: Teacher Research as an Agency for Change*. Eds. Dixie Goswami and Peter Stillman. Portsmouth, NH: Heinemann-Boynton/Cook, 1987.

Britton, James. "A Quiet Form of Research." *Reclaiming the Classroom: Teacher Research as an Agency for Change*. Eds. Dixie Goswami and Peter Stillman. Portsmouth, NH: Heinemann-Boynton/Cook, 1987.

Carroll, Pamela S. "Metamorphosis: One Teacher's Change/One Class' Reaction." *English Journal* 83 Oct. 1994: 22–29.

Durst, Russell K. "Portfolios and Writing Teachers." *New Directions in Portfolio Assessment*. Eds. Laurel Black, Donald Daiker, Jeffrey Sommers, and Gail Stygall. Portsmouth, NH: Heinemann-Boynton/Cook, 1994.

Emig, Janet. *The Composing Process of Twelfth Graders*, NCTE Research Report No. 13. Urbana, IL: NCTE, 1971.

Foster, E. M. *Howards End*. New York: Vintage Books, 1989.

Hoff, Laurie. "From Omnipotent Teacher-in-Charge to Coconspirator in the Classroom: Developing Lifelong Readers and Writers." *English Journal* 83 Oct. 1994: 42–51.

Lytle, Susan, and Marilyn Cochran-Smith, eds. *Inside/Outside: Teacher Research and Knowledge*. New York: Teachers College Press, 1993.

Page, Ernie. "Does Real Research Mean Teacher Research?" *English Journal* 83 Oct. 1994: 51–55.

Perl, Sondra, and Nancy Wilson. *Through Teacher's Eyes. Portraits of Writing Teachers at Work*. Portsmouth, NH: Heinemann, 1986.

Schon, Donald. *Educating the Reflective Practitioner: Toward a New Design for Teaching and Learning in the Professions*. San Francisco: Jossey-Bass, 1987.

Shakespeare, William. *Macbeth*. New York: Signet, 1963.

Strieb, Lynn Yermanock. "Visiting and Revisiting the Trees." *Inside/Outside: Teacher Research and Knowledge*. Eds. Susan Lytle and Marilyn Cochran-Smith. New York: Teachers College Press, 1993.

Sullivan, William M. *Work and Integrity: The Crisis and Promise of Professionalism in America*. New York: Harper Business, 1995.

Taylor, David. "A Counseling Approach to Writing Conferences." *Dynamics of the Writing Conference*. Eds. Thomas Flynn and Mary King. Urbana, IL: NCTE, 1993.

Teasley, Alan B. "Surviving Your First October," *English Journal* 83 Oct. 1994: 92–94.

Yancey, Katherine Blake. "Portfolios as Genre, Rhetoric and Reflection: Situating Selves, Literacies, and Knowledge." *Portfolios in the Writing Classroom*. Ed. Katherine B. Yancey. Urbana, IL: NCTE, 1992.

APPENDIX

Appendix 9a: Summary Statement

Natalia Beylis
Contemporary British and American Novel
Professor Soven

                    Portfolio Summary

I would like to begin my commentary on my reading of
contemporary novels by expressing the enjoyment which I
received from the class. Reading is one of my favorite
activities and I was delighted to encounter so many new
authors and novels through the class. I had never before
read anything by the authors who we studied this
semester but now that I have been introduced to them, I
am planning on reading more novels by them this summer.
This was the first English class I have had at La Salle
in which I have been required to read this amount of
literature and I was very happy to find that I was able
to read eight novels in one semester. Thank you for
introducing me to so much good fiction!

I would like to begin my portfolio commentary by
summarizing what I wrote about throughout the semester.
For my initial portfolio entry on *To the Lighthouse,*
I was struck by the importance of developing an
opening paragraph which immediately grabs the reader's
attention. By beginning the novel with Mrs. Ramsey
providing an answer to a question which the reader has
not had the privilege of knowing, Woolf draws the reader
into the novel with full attention focused on the plot.
In this portfolio, I commented on the author's style of
writing and how difficult it was to understand at times
due mainly to unusual punctuation. Finally I wrote about
Woolf's description of character.

The second portfolio entry was about the essay written by Woolf. I found this particular entry to be extremely interesting. I am rarely given the opportunity in a literature class to read essays written by the authors whose novels the class is studying. By reading Woolf's essay in conjunction with her novel, I was able to understand her viewpoint on characters and writing in general. This helped me a great deal since *To the Lighthouse* was a difficult novel to understand from my first reading and reading Woolf's views on character helped me take a step back from the action of the novel and see what Woolf was trying to do in her writing. For the portfolio entry, I summarized the essay and wrote about the duty which the author has to allow her characters to live. I believe that the essay on "Mr. Bennett and Mrs. Brown" influenced me through the remainder of my portfolio writings since I have noticed that often in my portfolios I comment on the establishment of character in the novel.

For the entry on *Howard's End,* I commented on the author's use of setting in the opening paragraph of the novel. I also wrote about the importance which houses have in the text and some of the meanings which houses had attached to them in the novel. I also commented on the author's style of writing and how the text establishes Helen's character.

Forster's essay "Aspects of a Good Novel" offered me the opportunity to view Forster when he took on the role of critic. I briefly summarized and explained the essay and tried to deduce whether Forster as a writer follows the rules that he sets up as a critic. I was again excited at the opportunity to examine an essay by an author whose novel I was concurrently reading. Reading both texts helped me understand what Forster was trying to do in *Howard's End*.

My portfolio entry for *The Heart of the Matter* focused mainly on Greene's use of setting to introduce the novel and the characters. I also commented on the description of character. When I examined a passage from the novel, I wrote some about the language which Greene uses in the passage and on his description of character.

The essay written about *The Heart of the Matter* gave me a perspective on Greene which was different than my own. Often when I read a novel, the only opinion I have about the writing is my own. By reading this essay, I was able to see another person's response to the novel. In the portfolio, I gave examples to illustrate the way that Greene uses setting to describe character. The assignment for this entry was made a great deal easier since I had an essay which answered a similar question and helped me see how Greene uses setting description to help the reader understand his characters.

For my entry on *Remains of the Day*, I discussed the clues a reader must pick up while reading the novel to understand the character. I also pointed out that Stevens was on the verge of a journey and that the beginning pages of the novel where actually a summary of the events which would occur throughout the remainder of the text. For my commentary on the passage, I wrote about how unusual the perspective of the main character was for me to understand. Since Stevens was writing from the view of a British butler, his views on the world, and more specifically on banter, were alien to me. I was amused at how much time Stevens devoted to agonizing over the issue of bantering.

In *The Heart Is a Lonely Hunter,* I focused on relationships in the book. I wrote about the relationship which Anatonapolus and Singer have and the way that Singer forms relationships with the other characters in the novel. I also addressed the issue of what the relationships which we encounter in the novel between the characters might tell us about McCullers. At the conclusion of my commentary, I ventured a guess as to what the novel would be about.

The next portfolio entry was on the essay "Nihilism in Black America" and how the essay helps us to better understand the characters in the novel. I thought that the essay was brilliantly written and the views expressed by West were extremely enlightening. The essay exposed me to a texture of our culture which I had never before seen. For the portfolio entry, I briefly summarized West's essay and commented on how West's concepts of nihilism were affecting the characters in the novel *Jazz.* The essay enriched my reading experience with the novel because I was able to view the characters in a different light.

Writing the plot summaries for *Jazz* helped me to organize the novel in my mind. I was better able to focus on the plot after writing out the lives of the characters in a linear summary. Morrison's style of writing in *Jazz* makes it difficult, at times, to understand what was going on with the characters. Through the plot summaries I was able to envision what happened to whom, how, and when.

The final portfolio entry which I have is on the novel *Crossing to Safety.* I commented on the way that the initial paragraph provides the reader with an abstract view of what the premise of the novel will be.

The first passage allows the reader to understand that the novel will be a flashback. In the second part of my portfolio entry, I commented on the beauty of Stegner's style of writing. I was impressed with Stegner's control over language in the novel.

When I take a look back at all the entries which I wrote, I realize that I often focus on character in my portfolios. I think that this occurred because the first essay which the class read discussed the use of character in modern novels and from then on I was very alert to the authors' use of characters. I also notice the settings of the novels and the way that the setting might contribute to the events of the novels and how setting might predict tone and affect the outcome of the story. The final thing which I noticed about the novels was the writing style of the authors. The authors we read all write in such distinct ways that it was exciting to move from one novel to the other.

Keeping a portfolio on my progress as a reader of the contemporary novel has benefited my reading skills. The assignments in which we had to write out a passage which struck us from the first section of the novel helped me focus on the language of the novel and on the writing devices that the author was using. Reading the essays in conjunction with the literature was also beneficial. I was able to learn much more about each of the novels we were studying by either reading another work by the same author or an essay which commented on some aspect of the literature. The class has helped me better connect with the contemporary novel. I now know many devices which help the reader probe more deeply into the literature and see the concepts and ideas which underlie the basic elements of the novel. I feel that I now have a better connection with contemporary literature. Since the class read many contemporary novels in such a short time, I was constantly bombarded with elements of the contemporary novel. I now understand many of the themes and similarities which exist in contemporary literature and the major influences which contemporary authors have. I have enjoyed my experience with the contemporary novel over this semester and plan to continue reading more contemporary British and American novels in the summer and for years to come.

Adapted and reprinted by permission of Natalia Beylis.

Appendix 9b: Notes from a Teacher's Journal

Leif Gustavson
Reflection #15
10/25/95

I was thinking about what we are doing today, and this came to me. Maybe it can help us use the time even more effectively.

Using a Model to Gain Understanding

In the artist's studio, the artist studies the model in front of him or her. The artist takes notes on the model. Maybe the artist makes a sketch of the figure so that he or she has something with which to work. The artist examines every curve of the bowl of fruit, looks for shadows and different tones and colors of the flowers that are in the vase. The artist searches for details of the model that will give him or her a way in to creating the sculpture or painting.

In the writer's studio we must do the same thing. The model--our group of four--is in front of us. What do they tell us about the way that we work? What can we use from their example to help us be more effective with our groups of four? What kind of advice can we give them to help them improve as a group whose primary goal is to help each other with his and her writing?

Another way of looking at it:

We are scientists in the lab. We're examining a specimen, watching its patterns of movement, looking for unusual behavior. We're taking notes to be able to look back and make some kind of hypothesis about the specimen, to gain a better understanding of the specimen.

We do the same thing in the writer's studio. Today, the specimen is the group of four. Let's look at them under the microscope. Examine how they work. Use their patterns of behavior as evidence to come up with a hypothesis at the end of the time. Jot down lab notes that will help generate discussion as you study the model.

Reflection on Studio
8/24/95

I need to find a way to incorporate writing, reading and the concept of the studio all into one in the beginning of the year. I think that they should all be linked in some way. In other words, maybe the writing should be self-exploratory--looking at how they work, what kind of people they are, the kinds of expectations they have of themselves, teachers, and classes. Maybe the reading can wait for a few weeks until we get into a regular routine with the writing. I need to get them into the writing habit. I need to get them used to the idea of sharing their work on a regular basis. We need to create an accepting atmosphere in the class. We need to get used to each other. The waiting should help strengthen all of these areas. From this exploratory writing in the first two weeks or so, they can pick one of the pieces to elaborate later. This will be our first publishing project. Before we do that, however, we will use the journal drafts to initiate discussions about writing, reading, and the studio as classroom. I will give them opportunities to read in small groups, getting feedback from their peers, and we will read in front of the entire class. I need to remember to model everything that I expect from them. For example, I should bring in a reading response from the portfolio about a book that

I am reading at the time. I guess I could have them read a book of their choice during the first two weeks or so and have them respond to it in their portfolio.

The free-writing will be an opportunity for them to tell me who they are and the experiences that they have had with writing, reading, and Language Arts in the past. I will respond to this writing personally. The next piece will be more geared toward the class and what they expect. Although, maybe we should spend some time in writing getting to know each other. Maybe they could tell the funniest family story that they have. After telling the story in a small group, we could write them down exactly the way they told them. Maybe they could describe someone in their family or a close friend, choosing any form that they want to describe him or her. We could write about something that we really love or hate. We could write about their favorite hobby from the perspective of the object. We could write about a time when we were punished from the perspective of the punisher or punishee. We could tell a very complex yet believable lie or truth about ourselves and have each other guess whether it is true. So, through these quickies, we will get used to writing every day, we will get used to working in small and large groups, we will get comfortable with one another, we will learn about each other, we will be introduced to the studio, and we will get used to class discussions. After this introduction, I will hit them with the expectations for the class, involving the portfolio, the amount of writing, the responses, etc.

8/25/95

The natural progression of writing, if I want to nail it down to some form of a time line, may be starting with the personal--writing about themselves, their families, their personal experiences. Once they are comfortable with writing about themselves, we can move to expressing their feelings about stories, poems, novels, essays that they read by others, starting first with the gut instinct, writing about exactly how they feel. These quickies can get us discussing issues in the writing. We can discuss author's intention. What is he or she trying to say? We can talk about point of view. We can write two more pages of the story. We can focus on the minor characters. We can look at tense and how that affects the piece. We can look at metaphor, simile, and symbolism. We can imitate the author's style. We can write letters to the author. Once they are comfortable attacking literature from all different sides, we can delve into expository writing, making sure that they do not lose the rich, personal voice that they are discovering through the other two stages of the process. It will be important for me to bring in examples of rich, poetic expository writing that we can discuss. We can explore expository writing through comparison and contrast, debates, editorials, business letters, speeches. I must remember to publish these and give the students ample opportunity to present these to the class. There is plenty of time for drafts and discussion about the form, remembering to let the students make the decisions. Let them use themselves to gather information and direction. I can always say, "go back to your group and get their opinion."

Here is the reading list for this year:

<u>7th</u>
The Good Earth--Pearl S. Buck
Animal Farm--George Orwell

A *Midsummer Night's Dream*--William Shakespeare

A *Christmas Carol*--Charles Dickens

I *Heard the Owl Call My Name*--Margret Craven

Poetry

Short Stories

8th

This Boy's Life--Tobias Wolff

I *Know Why the Caged Bird Sings*--Maya Angelou

To Kill a Mockingbird--Harper Lee

Night--Elie Weisel

Lord of the Flies--William Golding

Romeo and Juliet--William Shakespeare

Poetry

Short Stories

I should look into peppering the novels with poetry
and short stories. It may give my students new insight
into the novels. It will also expose them to all
different kinds of voices. It will reinforce the
multiculturalism of the class. I am going to need to
make sure that I do not bring home a lot of writing work
because I am going to need the evenings to read and
write on my own. I need the time to research and bring
in examples and pieces that will light my students on
fire. I can see starting the seventh grade with short
stories after we have grown accustomed to writing and
responding. I think I should stick with short shorts
that we can read and respond to in a period. Two to
three pages allows my students to explore the form. It
also lends itself to imitation. I think I will try to
implement some theatrics into this unit. It works well
when the students act out a short short. Through this we

can explore voice, meaning, and structure of a short story. Through writing several quickies based on ideas that we get out of our reading, they will choose one that they would like to elaborate and then I will publish a book of their writing at the end.

While it may be difficult to start the eighth grade with *This Boy's Life,* it may be easier after we have explored the form loosely through personal writing about themselves and their families. Since I feel so excited about the art of memoir, I think it would be a strong way to begin the year. I just need to make sure that they do not get sick and tired of writing about themselves. A way to get jazzed about the whole idea is to barrage them with great examples of memoir from published writers. I need to find racy, challenging pieces that will jog their minds. We will go through a similar process that we went through with Kirby this summer--Name, Snapshot, Family Artifact, Neighborhood, Favorite Kid Hangout, etc. As we move through, I will bring in examples of these techniques from other writers, and I will have my students bring in examples from *This Boy's Life.* They can even bring in examples of other techniques that we have not tried yet. They can use these themselves and present them to the class. They need to feel comfortable with their small groups so that they can share personal things. I would also like the groups to present a dramatic reading of their work toward the end. They will collect each piece in their portfolio, working on the ones that particularly interest them. Then I will have them combine them in some way, using their group for insight and direction. I must not forget to have them audit their work every week and free write at the end, assessing their work through the entire unit.

Just read the chapter on publishing, and I have a bunch of ideas. The first thing I am going to definitely do is have a space on the wall for possibilities to publish outside of the school, though I do not think I should put that up until later in the year when we are comfortable enough with our writing to take the plunge. I must start looking for magazines where I can try to publish my work. The great thing about this is that through my students, I will be forced to publish, something that I have been wanting to do for years. I will publish their work in in-class books often. And I can use the boards outside my room to publish work. I like the idea of bringing in particularly colorful paragraphs and sentences every Monday. Have that be a handout even before we get into the daily writing. We can read it and I can talk briefly about why I have selected what I have selected, making sure to publish all students.

I am also going to implement the student editorial board. Once we have started working and have a working vocabulary for writing that we think is going places, I will turn the job of publishing over to the editing boards, which will be comprised of the reading groups of four or five. Each week they will look at the work handed in in the previous week and choose what should be published. They can work on the computer in my room and hand me the disk at the end of the week and I will print it out and copy it over the weekend. This means that they will not be working on whatever technique we are exploring in the studio for that week. But I think that is ok. They will be developing in other ways through the publishing exercise. They will hone their proofreading eyes. They will be reading an incredible amount of work. They will be exercising their editing muscles. They will learn how hard it can be to accept or reject a colleague's work. This job will rotate every week. And if the students feel like they are missing out on something by doing this all important job, they can work on the exercises we are doing in class for homework. They can decide how the publication will look as long as they know that the deadline will be the following Friday. This work can be part of their audit for the week, where they will explain how they worked on publishing the writing for the previous week. I will need to make sure that I have thirty-second conferences with them often, keeping them on track and making sure that everyone in the group is working. I think groups of four are perfect for this.

We could even have a board for acceptances and rejections later on. I will make sure that my rejections go up on the board first. Maybe that will demystify the entire process and then we can turn the rejection into a joke, seeing who can get the worst or most bizarre response from some magazine. I just want to make sure that the importance of publishing is never diminished.

I guess I need to start thinking about the room and how it will look at the beginning of the year. I was excited about creating the cold, sterile room in the beginning to shock the students, but maybe I should get away from those shock values and rely on my content. I am slowly building some content and really feel like I can start arguing for why I want our class to go the way that I hope it will go. I should start working with that confidence. Always remembering that my primary reason for being in the class is to facilitate the work of my students and that I am there to work with them. What does a studio look like? Well, if I look at a painter's studio, his or her tools are everywhere, always at the ready for whenever he or she needs them. The room is in disarray to a person coming in off the street -and making a snap judgment, but everything is exactly where the artist wants it. This atmosphere cannot be built until after my students have begun working and working in the space. It will also be hard to do with four or maybe more classes in my room during the day.

So maybe we need to do what Duchamp and other artist did and still do. Make the studio portable. We can start with our portfolios. Our portfolios can contain everything that we need to work with for our time in the studio. That means everything from all of the writing that we have done, to the notes that we have taken on our writing, to the things that stimulate us to write-- that little gnome doll, or a postcard, or a song lyric or CD case--whatever is going to help us create. The desk can be moved to anywhere in the room, or the student can work on the floor. And it is here where the student can set up his or her studio. But that still does not answer the question of how the room should look to begin with. Obviously it needs to be accepting and open. No one should feel intimidated when they come into the room. Maybe I should start the class out with pictures of all different artists doing what they do. I can talk with Rhoni about any paintings that she may have that show the artist in his or her studio. I can cut out pictures from magazines of glass blowers and potters working at their craft. What about posters of work? Maybe I can find pictures and posters of coal miners, doctors and nurses, railroad workers, taxi

drivers, window washers, athletes, everybody working. I
can use these pictures to give my students ideas of what
work is all about. What kind of work do they want to do?
The pictures can emphasize the idea that to be
accomplished at whatever you do you must practice and
that to be a good writer you must be willing to
practice. Maybe these pictures will help facilitate some
of the opening writing and discussions about work and
the studio. Oh yeah, I need posters of writers working
at their craft as well.

9/10/95

It has been a few weeks since last I wrote, but I
have been thinking about the studio and classes every
single day. I must say that I am a bit worried about the
fact that I am not "ready" in the traditional sense. In
other words, I have not written all of my students'
names into a grade book. I do not even have a grade book
yet. My thinking here is that I am not going to grade
any of their work for the first few weeks anyway. We
must first explore the concept of the class and begin to
enjoy the work that we are going to do there. I have not
done the preliminary thinking that I usually do in terms
of giving information about the class, setting the right
stern tone, giving them everything that they need to
know. We may not even get to the syllabus the first day
of class, since I think that we are going to start off
with the roll, then see if every one knows each other's
name, then we are going to go right into a free writing
exercise where the students have an opportunity to tell
me anything that they want me to know about their
experiences with Language Arts or English. Let the idea

of the class set the tone. That may take the period. If it doesn't, I can always hand out the information on the studio.

I have been telling myself that I must be careful that I do not talk at my students about the studio. I must keep on reminding myself that the studio concept is an organic one that must grow on its own. It can grow into any form and none of those forms are predetermined or wrong. I cannot go in with preconceptions. I think that if we read through the syllabus and discuss what the quote means, the students will get a sense of what the class is all about. There may be a lot of I don't knows and we'll have to find outs and that is o.k.

I think that it is important for me to enter the school tomorrow with a completely open mind. I must keep my judgments to myself and, if I can, not make any judgments at all. I must look at my students as all new. People can grow an awful lot in a summer. I know that I have. There is no room for the benefit of the doubt, because that implies that there was doubt to begin with. All of my students have the power to succeed in this class and I will do everything in my power to facilitate the process to whatever the students decide is success. What this means is that I must be careful about what I say in homeroom. I must be careful about the jokes I make. I must be careful how I respond and react to all of the students. Be confident. I know what I am doing and I love what I do, so I must express that in every way that I can. The students will get a good vibe from that kind of attitude. Mike is right, there is very little room for sarcasm directed at the student in the classroom. I can make fun of myself, but never my students.

Just a quick look at tomorrow.

Homeroom: Moment of silence. Take roll. Play the name game (name your neighbors). Introduce myself. Emergency Cards. Any time? Harper's Index.

Classes: Moment of silence. Play the name game (first name, and kind of food you are). Free writing (write about your experiences with and feelings about Language Arts/English). Any time left, we'll introduce the studio.

Advisory: Moment of silence. Play the name game (lie game). Advisee Questionnaire. My purpose as advisor.

Adapted and reprinted by permission of Leif Gustavson.

10

Joining the Profession

English Teacher X teaches five classes of ninth grade English. She teaches literature, writing, and oral expression. Her writing program includes some instruction in the writing process but is primarily focused on the elimination of error and teaching the expository essay. Although she requires students to write drafts, she rarely reads them. On weekends she often takes home a stack of student papers and spends much of Saturday and Sunday grading them. The only time she discusses teaching with her colleagues is at the school in-service meetings, held twice a year. She likes to read fiction, but rarely writes for her own enjoyment. She feels somewhat isolated professionally but attending conferences and reading journals would force her to devote more time to a job that already consumes many hours.

English Teacher Y also teaches five classes of ninth grade English. Like Teacher X, she also teaches literature, writing, and oral expression, but unlike Teacher X she tries to integrate the teaching of these skills. Her writing program, based on Nancy Atwell's studio model, involves her students in planning the program. They often choose their own topics for assignments and receive feedback from each other and from Ms. Y. Teacher Y saves her weekends for errands, leisure activities, and reading the latest issue of the *English Journal*. One of her favorite NCTE books is Gene Stanford's *How to Handle the Paper Load*, a text filled with ideas for streamlining the process of evaluating student papers. Teacher Y is currently writing an essay on the studio approach for the *English Journal* with Teacher Z, whom she met last March at the NCTE national conference.

Which of these teachers will you become? Teaching can be a profession or a job. The choice is yours. You can be like Teacher X, who most likely will "burn out" if she spends every weekend grading papers, or like Teacher Y, who still finds teaching a challenging profession. Burnout is less apt to happen to Teacher Y. For Teacher Y, there are always new questions and new students and interested colleagues, who are tackling the same issues.

The National Council of Teachers of English

Chapter 9 discussed teacher research groups as one way of exchanging information about teaching writing. These groups are often school based or local. This chapter provides the information you need to participate in the national dialogue on teaching composition. It offers several suggestions for keeping abreast with new trends in the field. Joining the major professional organization for English educators, the National Council of Teachers of English (NCTE), is the first and most important step you can take in this direction.

What Is the NCTE?

NCTE, the world's largest subject-matter educational association, is devoted to improving the teaching of English at all levels of education. NCTE has 100,000 members and subscribers in the United States and other countries. Individual members are teachers, supervisors of English programs in elementary and secondary schools, faculty in college and university English departments, teacher educators, local and English specialists, and professionals in related fields. Since 1911, NCTE provides a forum for the profession, an array of opportunities for teachers to continue their professional growth throughout their careers, and a framework for cooperation to deal with issues that affect the teaching of English.

(From "About this Forum" on the NCTE web site: <www.ncte.org>. See Appendices 10a and 10b for more information.)

Box 10.1 lists contact information for NCTE and other important professional organizations.

Professional Journals

As a member of NCTE, you join the elementary, secondary, or college section and receive that section's journal. *English Journal,* the secondary section journal, includes articles on all aspects of teaching English on the secondary level. It keeps you up-to-date on the latest pedagogical research and practice in the teaching of literature as well as the teaching of writing. *Language Arts* is the journal of the elementary school section and *College English,* the journal of the college section. NCTE publishes several other journals to address the special interests of its members. Box 10.2 lists several journals of interest to secondary school instructors.

BOX 10.1   Professional Organizations

NCTE address, phone numbers, and World Wide Web address:

National Council of Teachers
  of English
1111 W. Kenyon Rd.
Urbana, IL 61801-1096
Phone: 1-800-369-6283 or
          (217) 328-3870
World Wide Web:
http//www.ncte.org

National Writing Centers Association
c/o Michael Pemberton
University of Illinois
Department of English
608 Wright Street
Urbana, IL 61801
Phone: (217) 333–7014

Teachers and Writers Collaborative
5 Union Square
New York, NY 10003-3306
Phone: (212) 691-6590

Teachers of English to Speakers
  of Other Languages
1600 Cameron Street
Alexandria, VA 22314-2751
Phone: (703) 836-0774

International Reading Association
800 Barksdale Road
P.O. Box 8139
Newark, DE 19714-8139
Phone: (302) 731-1600

BOX 10.2   Journals of Interest to Secondary Teachers of Writing

College Composition and Communication (quarterly) Urbana, Illinois, NCTE

Computers and Composition (three times a year) Houghton, Michigan, Michigan Technological University

English Journal (eight times a year) Urbana, Illinois, NCTE

Journal of Teaching Writing (twice a year) Indianapolis, Indiana, Purdue University at Indianapolis

Research in the Teaching of English (three times a year) Urbana, Illinois, NCTE

Voices in the Middle (for middle school teachers) (quarterly) Urbana, Illinois, NCTE

Written Communication (Research reports on social and cognitive factors in discourse production for young and adult writers) (quarterly) Beverly Hills, CA: Sage Publications

---

For example, Research in the Teaching of English (RTE) focuses exclusively on research. It publishes lengthy reports on cognitive development and language skills, the composing process, and studies on the effectiveness of teaching practices. The October 1988 volume, for example, includes three essays on research in composition: "Some Characteristics of Memorable Expository Writing: Effects of Revision by Writers with Different Backgrounds" (Graves et al.),

"Text Revisions by Basic Writers: From Impromptu First Draft to Take-Home Revision" (Bernhardt), and "Children, Stories, and Narrative Transformations" (Hade). Occasionally the *English Journal* will devote an entire issue to teacher research, such as the October 1994 issue, which includes several essays referred to in previous chapters of this book, for example, "Metamorphosis: One Teacher's Change/One Class' Reaction" by Pamela S. Carroll and "Real Research into Real Problems of Grammar and Usage Instruction" by Mitzi Renwick. However, you need to read RTE if you are interested in reading about large scale or in-depth studies.

As a member of NCTE, you also receive *Notes Plus*, a quarterly of practical teaching ideas, and *Ideas Plus*, an annual collection of teaching strategies. The short articles (500 words is the limit) in these two publications are written by middle school, junior high, and high school teachers. The "Idea from the Classroom" column from the March 1996 issue, reprinted in Figure 10.1, is a good example of the practical emphasis of *Notes Plus*.

In addition to its journals, NCTE publishes affordable texts on all aspects of teaching English, adding approximately fifteen to twenty new titles a year. The popular TRIP series (*Theory and Research Into Practice*) includes several monographs on teaching composition: for example, *Creative Approaches to Sentence Combining* (Strong), *Designing and Sequencing Prewriting Activities* (Johannessen, Kahn, and Walter), *Observing and Writing* (Hillocks), and *Writing About Ourselves and Others* (Beach). New as well as experienced teachers, find these short texts very useful. They more than live up to the TRIP description in the NCTE catalog of publications to "provide teachers with a review of the best educational theory and research on a limited topic, followed by descriptions of classroom activities that will assist teachers in putting that theory into practice."

There is no shortage of materials on composition teaching. Most of the NCTE state affiliates publish their own journals, such as *The Journal of Teaching Writing*, published at Indiana University-Purdue, Indianapolis, Indiana. In addition, many other teaching journals include articles about composition of interest to junior high and high school instructors. (See Box 10.2 for a selected list of journals.)

Policy and Curriculum Issues

Becoming a professional means more than just keeping up with new research. Demonstrating concern about school-related issues such as the budget, the curriculum, enrollment, and assessment is almost just as important. For example, some schools have adopted "intensive scheduling," which permits a school to offer fewer subjects each semester, thereby lengthening class periods, a major benefit for writing classes. Keith Gustavson and Debbie Fedder, the two teachers from Friends' Central School in Wynnewood, Pennsylvania,

FIGURE 10.1

Ideas from the Classroom

All about Writing
With a few exceptions, the teaching strategies in this issue of *Notes Plus* are all about writing—writing to explore, writing to communicate, writing to respond, writing to learn. In "A Writing Topic on Which Everyone Is an Expert," students write about what they know—themselves and their families. In "Year-End Writing Reflection," students reflect on their best writings from the previous year and on areas they still need work on. In "Turning Childhood Keepsakes into Polished Stories," students follow Antiguan author Jamaica Kincaid's example and explore the stories surrounding their own childhood keepsakes. And in "Comparing Books and Movies," students predict and then evaluate how the film version of a literary work stacks up against the original. These and other strategies will involve your students in writing for a variety of purposes both in and out of the classroom.

Linking Writing Journals and Reading
I start out the school year committed to having the students write regularly in their writing journals. It seems we soon run out of ideas. In an attempt to keep students gathering ideas and becoming aware of ways to link their reading with their writing, I occasionally use this technique. (My students keep reading logs, but this goes in their writing journal.)

Modeling
From your own reading, model a few quotes that seem to express timeless thoughts, challenge thinking, and/or spark a memory of an event or happening. This is one I used when I was reading *East of Eden* by John Steinbeck.

> [He] got into a book, crawled and groveled between the covers, tunneled like a mole among the thoughts, and came up with the book all over his face and hands.

Gathering
Ask students to be watching for timeless quotes while they read. Students may take their quotations either from a book of fiction or nonfiction they are currently reading or from a book they read recently, but not from a book of quotes. Distribute 3" × 5" or 4" × 6" note cards the day before the quotations are due. On the card, students write only the quote, the page reference, and the title of the book—no editorial comments or reader responses are requested yet.

Dispersing
Prepare to present selected quotations to the class for response. (You will probably find that not all of the quotations students have turned in will work equally well for this purpose.) Possible options are to prepare a handout sheet that lists selected quotes, to write one quotation a day on the chalkboard, or to prepare a transparency of selected quotes. I prepare a handout sheet, omitting the titles of the works because I don't want the students' responses to be colored by their knowledge.

Here is an example of a quote submitted by one of my eighth-grade students:

> The questions seemed to chase each other endlessly through the mind . . .
> *The Homing* by John Saul

Continued

FIGURE 10.1   *Continued*

Response
Have the students freewrite for seven to ten minutes in their journals. This technique enhances students' writing fluency while making them aware of connecting writing with the printed word. (One source of information about freewriting is *Nothing Begins with N. New Investigations of Freewriting*, edited by Peter Elbow, Pat Belanoff, and Sheryl I. Fontaine. Southern Illinois University Press, 1990.)

After writing responses, we discuss individual quotations and how they link the plot and characters of the work from which they are taken. In this way we achieve a many-faceted purpose, one goal of which is to introduce students to more selections they might consider reading.

Marianne Darr-Norman, Thorncreek Center School, Columbia City, Indiana

---

you met in previous chapters, support intensive scheduling. They agree that the thirty-five-minute period (the length of a period before intensive scheduling) is not ideal for writing instruction. But, as with any new idea, intensive scheduling is controversial. Teachers and administrators who believe in its value will need to speak out. You may be called upon to defend innovations such as intensive scheduling or the use of portfolios for evaluating writing.

To play an important role in decision making on issues such as these, you need to be aware of public as well as professional opinion. Whether you teach in a public or private school, the parents, the general public, and the legislators are watching. Education is expensive, and those who are footing the bill, through tuition or through taxes, want more than ever to make sure that their dollar is well spent. The public is especially concerned about the "basics," reading, writing, and mathematical skills. However, the criticisms of schools by parent groups and elected officials are often ill informed. Joining with your colleagues to oppose the implementation of policies leading to unsound teaching practices, such as more grammar instruction, is just as important as collaborating with them to support sound innovations.

The *English Journal* covers a variety of subjects outside the field that influence the teaching of English in its monthly columns "From the Secondary Section" and "The World of English." For example, the October 1994 issue dealt with public criticism of the English Standards Project, a national project designed to answer the question, "What is the subject of English?" In the first column, Helen Poole, a member of the NCTE Steering Committee at that time, summarizes how she would explain to the public what is happening in English classes today: "As an English teacher, supervisor of the language arts, and a member of the NCTE Steering Committee, I have been asked to respond on several occasions and to defend the need for English at all." After addressing several old-fashioned assumptions about what gets taught as the subject of English, she says that literacy is the real subject of English classes today. In response to the critics of the English curriculum who claim that "English classes have been teaching subject-less reading and writing," she says, "I suspect they are referring to workbooks and test preparation materials which are, in fact, 'subject-less.' It is one of the reasons that NCTE and other professional organizations have continually objected to reductionist testing and test preparation materials which do nothing to teach students about effective language use" (15). Poole's article can help us respond to criticisms of the English curriculum.

For longer articles on policy issues, read *SLATE* (*Support for Learning and Teaching of English*), the newsletter which reports on activities of the NCTE Steering Committee on Social and Political Concerns. The charge of this committee is "to influence public attitudes and policy decisions that affect the teaching of the English language arts, at local and state levels." *SLATE* routinely covers topics as the back-to-basics movement, the national standards movement, efforts at censorship, and so on. *SLATE* newsletter chair, Judy Duprez, explains *SLATE*'s ongoing activities:

> We track political developments which have a significant impact on the teaching of English and endeavor to help individual teachers cope with community pressures. We work to create an environment for free and responsible teaching and learning. To this end, we listen and respond to concerns of affiliates who are struggling with censorship of printed materials, with large class sizes, with violence in the classroom, and with public distress over controversial teaching methods such as journal writing, whole language instruction ... We can support embattled teachers with professional research and expert opinions, but our best help can come before they are placed in a defensive position. (3)

In the same issue, *SLATE* announces a new NCTE committee charged with investigating school uses of on-line communication. Duprez says, "Questions of access and censorship in schools will be examined with attention to distinctions between access in school settings and access by publics outside of school" (3). All teachers will be faced with access issues as computers become more widely used in schools. Many English teachers already encourage their students to use the Internet for research. There is always the danger of the "thought police," those people interested in censorship, becoming, as the *SLATE* editor says, too heavy-handed when it comes to the Internet. We may find ourselves having to defend our own assignments, when they require students to "go surfing."

You too can write for *SLATE*. In addition to publishing committee reports, *SLATE* accepts short (500-word) articles on any sociopolitical issues that relate to teaching and learning from NCTE members.

Professional Conferences

Journals are a great way to keep in touch with new research, new teaching methods, and contemporary issues related to teaching composition, but nothing replaces attending a national conference for making you feel a part of the profession and for sheer inspiration. NCTE holds two national conferences a year and several regional conferences. The largest of the two, the NCTE Annual Conference, includes teachers from kindergarten though college. The other one, the Conference on College Composition and Communication (4Cs), held in March, is primarily for college instructors, but secondary school teachers will find much on the conference program to interest them.

I attended my first national NCTE conference in Denver in 1975 and have not missed attending either the NCTE Annual Conference or the Conference on College Composition and Communication every year since then. It is hard to describe the excitement of a national conference. When I return from an NCTE conference, I try to share some of that excitement with my students. I pass around the thick program booklet filled with inviting titles of panels and workshops and ads for new books. But there is no way I can duplicate the experience of being among 6,000 interested teachers hurrying into the hotel's main ballroom for the opening session, wearing their name badges, programs and pads in hand, greeting the friends they made at last year's conference. No signs of burnout here! For three or four days teachers rush to panel discussions and workshops, trying to get the most out of the conference. They browse the book exhibit, which includes representatives of all the major publishers of secondary-level textbooks, leaving the exhibit hall with stacks of books and posters. Everywhere you look, you see teachers engrossed in lively conversation about teaching, trading ideas, and in some cases, planning projects together. Most of us go home feeling refreshed and eager to launch several new projects in our classrooms.

Submitting Proposals

When you receive the "Call for Proposals" for next year's NCTE conference, consider submitting a proposal for an individual presentation or collaborating with several colleagues to form a panel or conduct a workshop. First-time presenters are given preference during proposal reviews, and you may find yourself on the program sooner than you would have thought possible.

The following proposal was written for the annual meeting of the 1997 Conference on College Composition and Communication. It grew from a teaching experiment—my revised course for training peer tutors, discussed in Chapter 9.

"Sharing Authority with Students in a Peer Tutor Training Program"

Training peer tutors is a complex task. To master peer tutoring skills, students must not only learn methods of evaluating and responding to student papers, but they must develop an understanding of the process of collaboration critical to the success of a good peer tutor. The peer tutor training program should become a model for the collaborative approach to learning which peer tutors will practice as they work with their peers to help them improve their writing.

The focus of my remarks will be the revisions in the course I teach as part of La Salle University's curriculum-based peer tutoring program. Last year I revamped this course to shift the authority for learning to the "other side of the desk." The course was conducted as a seminar in which the students participated in the designing of each unit in the course and conducted individual research projects related to these units: "The Basics of Peer Tutoring," "How Does Peer Tutoring Work with Different Students," and "College Writing Assignments." The course progresses from reviewing basic peer tutoring techniques to learning how to apply them in different contexts, contexts defined by different academic disciplines and the diverse student populations at La Salle University.

Students met with me in small groups to structure classroom discussions and activities around these topics. They designed instructional materials and in some cases invited students and faculty from various departments and programs to participate in class discussion. In addition, the peer tutors conducted three research projects, one related to their peer tutoring experiences, the other two focused on the perceptions of students and faculty about peer tutoring and academic writing. They compiled materials from both their collaborative work and individual projects in a portfolio in which they summarized their development as peer tutors.

As part of my presentation, I will include descriptions of the assignments and excerpts from the peer tutor research reports and their evaluation of the course.

Notice that the proposal has three sections: The first paragraph explains the objectives of the course, the second and third paragraphs describe how the course was conducted, and the fourth paragraph describes materials I will use to document the changes in the course and students' attitudes to the course revisions. Most speakers write a seven- to eight-page paper, and either read their paper or speak more informally from an outline based on it. NCTE strongly advises the latter.

If you are somewhat hesitant about giving your first presentation at a national conference, then submit a proposal for a regional or state conference. Audiences at local and regional conferences are especially enthusiastic and appreciative. I gave my first presentation in the seventies at the Delaware Valley Writing Council conference, a local consortium of English teachers (unfortunately defunct) interested in the teaching of writing at all levels.

Writing a paper for a talk, like other forms of writing, is a wonderful opportunity to clarify your ideas on a teaching issue. If you have been keeping a teaching journal and a portfolio, you will have ample material for such presentations. If you do not keep a teaching journal, then review your writing assignments from the past year and discuss their strengths and weaknesses. Other teachers will be interested in the imaginative projects you have developed to encourage good writing.

In conclusion, I urge you to get into the "conference habit" immediately, if you have not already done so. Students are welcome and are charged a reduced registration fee. Meeting with other teachers as interested in the teaching of composition as we are often inspires us to do our best work. My professional life has been transformed by my colleagues and friends from all over the country, who attend NCTE. Perhaps yours will be as well.

Support for Your Research

NCTE funds research on teaching composition and literature in addition to serving as forum for disseminating research. The NCTE Research Foundation was created "to encourage research, experimentation, and investigation in the teaching of English." The research foundation awards grants-in-aid for research that "has significance for the teaching and learning of the language arts or closely related fields." Four types of grants are available. Secondary school teachers are eligible for the teacher research grants, which are awarded to Pre-K–14 teachers for classroom-based research on the teaching of English and language arts. The "Call for Proposals" says, "These grants, which have a limit of $2,500, are intended to support investigation of research questions which grow out of teachers' classroom experiences and concerns and that are directly relevant to the work of the applicant. . . ." (NCTE Research Foundation RFP, 1994).

If you are a new teacher, who has begun a research project in your college methods course or during your student teaching, which you would like to continue, why not apply to NCTE for the Research Foundation for funding?

If you are an experienced teacher, writing a research proposal may be just the thing to do to motivate you to begin your teacher-researcher career!

The National Writing Project

The National Writing Project (NWP), a teacher development program begun in the mid-1970s, offers summer workshops for experienced teachers interested in improving their skills as teachers of writing. NWP programs are organized by state. You can find out about the project in your state and request a copy of *The Quarterly*, the NWP newsletter by writing to this address: National Writing Project, School of Education, University of California, Berkeley, CA 94720.

Once you have begun teaching, you will be eligible to be nominated to become an NWP Fellow. The Project's Teaching Institutes are usually held during the summer, though in some states, such as Pennsylvania, follow-up sessions are held throughout the academic year. NWP Institutes focus on a variety of topics such as "Teaching the Writing Process" and "Evaluation." But regardless of the topic, most of the projects require teachers to do a great deal of their own writing. In "What Makes a Summer Institute Different from Taking a Course," an article which appeared in the Invitation to Apply to the Pennsylvania Writing Project, the leaders of the Project stress the emphasis on experiential, practical learning, which characterizes all of their Institutes. They point out that very little lecturing occurs, group work is the most common mode of instruction, and the focus is on practical application. NWP Fellows return to their schools to conduct workshops on teaching writing in all disciplines.

Most NWP Institutes participants express enthusiasm about their programs. The following comments by former NWP participants are typical. Marybeth Mason, Willis Junior High School in Chandler, Arizona, says:

> As teachers of writing we were expected to write. For many of us this was the first time to exchange personal writing with our peers, and we heard ourselves spouting the same apologies we hear from our students before they allow someone to read their writing. I remember passing our duplicated copies of my first paper and prefacing it with "I didn't have much time to work on this, so it's not really polished," when, in fact, I had labored over it for hours and was sure it was a masterpiece. The group responded to the content, style, and form of my writing, offering constructive criticism and encouraging suggestions for future compositions. I found I was anxious to continue my writing for my receptive audience and took great pride in my contributions to the project's anthology published at the end of the five weeks. I vowed to use the peer editing and publishing process in my classroom. (4)

An anonymous participant offers this comment:

> One of the best things about our group was how much we enjoyed each other. We came from different teaching backgrounds—novice to experienced, kindergarten to high school, language to math and science—but we were all able to find some common ground in our writing. As we shared our thoughts and experiences, a group of strangers became like a family . . . We supported each other through the work load, through our presentations, and through a number of family crises which occurred during the five weeks . . . No one wanted what began at the Institute to end.

James Squire, former director, National Council of Teachers of English, says:

> I will take away so much from the Institute. First, I will take away tons of practical classroom writing ideas. That in itself is a very exciting thing to have gained. I have also gained a network of writing colleagues. I now have teachers from grade 1 to college on whom to call for materials, support, suggestions. (3)

In the National Writing Project Institutes, teachers model the practices they will introduce in their own classrooms, and, as these comments suggest, teachers emerge from the Institutes feeling that they have been rejuvenated.

Special-Interest Organizations

In addition to the National Council of Teachers of English and the National Writing Project there are other associations that should be of interest to English educators. For example, the National Writing Centers Association promotes communication among the staff of writing centers on the elementary, secondary, and college levels. It provides a forum for schools that already have a writing center or that have a plan to develop a writing center. The association meets semiannually and publishes *The Writing Center Journal*. Another organization, the Teachers and Writers Collaborative, includes teachers and writers who are interested in imaginative writing. The Collaborative is known for its visiting writers programs, which make it possible for students to meet and work with professional writers in their own schools. Teachers especially interested in teaching English as a second or foreign language can affiliate with Teachers of English to Speakers of Other Languages (TESOL). TESOL publishes several journals and holds an annual meeting in March. No list of associations of interest to English teachers would be complete without the International Reading Association (IRA). The purpose of IRA is to "improve the quality of reading instruction and promote literacy worldwide." (See Box 10.1 for more information about these associations.)

The Internet

E-mail and the Internet may be two of the most practical options for "joining the profession" for the busy high school English instructor. Your colleagues are only as far away as your computer when you become e-mail and Internet literate. You can continue the luncheon conversation you had the second day of the NCTE conference without the expense of a long-distance call or the inconvenience of a busy signal. As an Internet surfer, you can use the Internet to join your colleagues in cyberspace to trade ideas and learn about meetings and new publications.

You have several options, once you turn on your computer. You can click on to the NCTE homepage (http://www.ncte.org) to start (see Appendix 10a) and then click on to other web sites that include resources of interest to you. You can receive lesson plans and worksheets from instructors at other schools. Many schools have their own homepage. Several publications such as *The Internet Resource Directory for K–12 Teachers and Librarians*, 94/95 Edition, list the e-mail addresses of schools and other organizations that may have materials on the Internet of interest to you.

You can participate in relevant Internet conversations by posting your e-mail address on one of the international listservs, such as NCTE-talk, focused on teaching the English language arts. You can join NCTE-talk by calling or e-mailing NCTE headquarters. (The address is listed in Appendix 10b.) With my name on the listserv for writing program administrators, I have been joining in conversations on such topics as curriculum, the division of literature and composition in many universities, and how to train peer tutors. One of the advantages of electronic conversation is its immediacy. If I am frustrated about a particular teaching problem, I can receive comments about the problem within a day or two.

The case is still out on the value of the Internet for classroom instructors. But, as with the other suggestions for joining the profession, much depends on you . . . how much use you make of the Internet and how you contribute to it.

Conclusion

One of my instructors in graduate school pointed out that curriculum guides are often dust collectors. Unfortunately, often their main function is to keep the other texts on the shelf company. Don't permit this chapter to be a "dust collector." Use it to launch your participation in the professional community you have worked hard to join. We need you as much as you need us.

Questions for Discussion and Writing

1. Read three essays on a subject related to the teaching of writing (e.g., teaching prewriting skills, teaching revising strategies, using portfolios, etc.) in the *English Journal* or *Voices in the Middle*. Compare and contrast the three essays. How is their treatment of the subject similar? How is it different?

2. Summarize the contents of a recent issue of the *English Journal* or *Voices in the Middle*. Which article or section did you find the most helpful? Why?

3. Compare the contents of an issue of the 1960 volume of the *English Journal* to the contents of an issue of the 1997 *English Journal*. How are they similar? How are they different?

4. Choose a controversial topic, such as assessment or the teaching of grammar, and find two opposing essays on the subject. Write a brief response supporting one or the other point of view. Note: You can use general periodicals or newspapers in addition to teaching journals.

5. Read an article on writing instruction in *Research in the Teaching of English*. What are the implications of the study as reported in the article for teaching writing?

6. Request a "Call for Proposals" from NCTE. Write a proposal for the next NCTE conference. Propose a talk on a successful teaching strategy or assignment you have developed. Ask a fellow student or teacher to read a draft of your proposal.

References

"About this Forum." World Wide Web, http//www. ncte.org., Mon. June 21, 1996 Subject: about.html.

Beach, Richard. *Writing About Ourselves and Others.* Urbana, IL: NCTE, 1977.

Bernhardt, Stephen. "Text Revisions by Basic Writers: From Impromptu First Draft to Take Home Revision." *Research in Teaching English* 22 Oct. 1988: 266–281.

Duprez, Judy. "From the Chair," *SLATE,* 21 April 1996: 3.

Graves, Michael, et al. "Some Characteristics of Memorable Expository Writing: Effects of Revision by Writers with Different Backgrounds." *English Journal* 22 Oct. 1988: 242–266.

Hade, Daniel. "Children, Stories, and Narrative Transformations." *English Journal* 22 Oct. 1988: 310–326.

Hillocks, George. *Observing and Writing.* Urbana, IL: NCTE, 1975.

"Ideas from the Classroom." *Notes Plus: A Quarterly of Practical Teaching Ideas.* March 1996: 1.

Johannessen, Larry, Elizabeth Kahn, and Carolyn Calhoun Walter. *Designing and Sequencing Prewriting Activities.* Urbana, IL: NCTE, 1982.

Mason, Marybeth. "A Vacation That Sustained Me for Three Years." *Pennsylvania Writing Project Newsletter* (Summer, 1997), 4–5.

Miller, Elizabeth. *The Internet: Resource Directory for K–12 Teachers and Librarians,* 94/95 Edition. Englewood, CO: Libraries Unlimited, 1994.

NCTE Catalog, 1996–1997. *Publications for Elementary, Middle, Secondary & College Teachers.* Urbana, IL: NCTE, 1996.

"NCTE Research Foundation Teacher-Researcher Program," revised. Urbana, IL: NCTE, 1994. (The NCTE Research Foundation Program is advertised in most issues of the *English Journal.*)

Poole, Helen. "What Is English?" *English Journal* 83 Oct. 1994: 15–16.

Squire, James. "A Vacation That Sustained Me for Three Years." Invitation to the Pennsylvania Writing Project: Summer Institute for the Teaching of Writing, West Chester, PA: West Chester University, 1997.

Stanford, Gene, ed. *How to Handle the Paper Load: Classroom Practices in English.* Urbana, IL: NCTE, 1979.

APPENDIX

Appendix 10a: NCTE Homepage

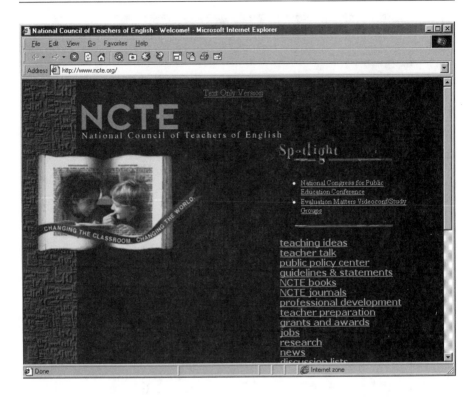

Appendix 10b: NCTE-Talk: A Listserv

(a)

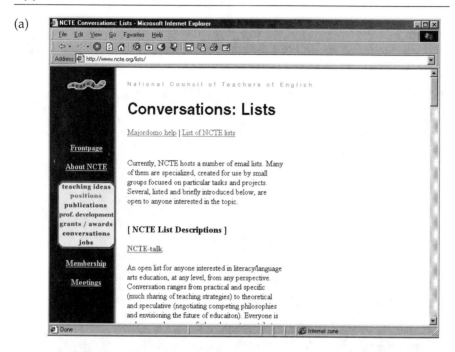

(b)

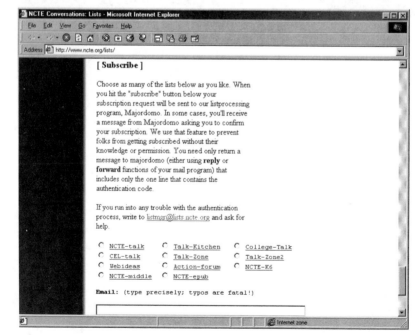

Index

DATE DUE

12/1/05			